The Rise of
the Corporate Economy

ລ

The Rise of
the Corporate Economy

SECOND EDITION

ᘉᘉ

LESLIE HANNAH

ᘉᘉ

Methuen
London and New York

First published 1976 by
Methuen & Co. Ltd
11 New Fetter Lane, London EC4P 4EE
First published as a University
Paperback 1979
Second edition, completely revised
and reset, 1983
Published in the USA by
Methuen & Co.
in association with Methuen, Inc.
733 Third Avenue, New York, NY 10017
© 1976 and 1983 Leslie Hannah
Printed in Great Britain by
Richard Clay (The Chaucer Press) Ltd,
Bungay, Suffolk

British Library
Cataloguing in Publication Data
Hannah, Leslie
The rise of the corporate economy. – 2nd ed.
1. Corporations – Great Britain – History
2. Big business – Great Britain – History
I. Title
338.7'4'0941   HD2847
ISBN 0–416–34850–5
ISBN 0–416–34860–2 Pbk

To my mother
and to the memory of
my father

ನಲ

Contents

ౠ

The fundamental problem . . . of the social science, is to find the laws according to which any state of society produces the state which succeeds it and takes its place. This opens the great and vexed question of the progressiveness of man and society; an idea involved in every just conception of social phenomena as the subject of science.

J. S. MILL, *System of Logic* (1852 edition), p. 503

Preface to the first edition

౨౦౨

I have been fortunate in accumulating a large overdraft of intellectual debts to tolerant fellow economists and historians, particularly to past and present colleagues at Nuffield College and St John's College, Oxford, and at the University of Essex. Max Hartwell, William Reader, George Richardson, Aubrey Silberston and John Wright have at various times stimulated my interest in the subject, and their critical reading of earlier drafts of some chapters led to improvements. Many others have helped with specific problems, including Sam Aaronovitch, G. C. Allen, Alfred Chandler, Denys Gribbin, Peter Hammond, Lutz Haber, Peter Hart, William Kennedy, Jeremy Lever, David Lethbridge, Peter Mathias, John Naylor, Ralph Nelson, Peter Payne, Sigbert Prais, Hilary Rubinstein, Clive Trebilcock and Philip Williams. My especial thanks are due to John Kay, who read and helpfully criticized earlier drafts and also permitted the use of previously unpublished results from our joint work on mergers and industrial concentration. Many industrialists and politicians who have taken part in the events analysed have also given me their time and advice, and I am particularly grateful to Arthur Knight, the late Lord Swinton, Lyndall Urwick, Harry Ward, the late Sir Horace Wilson and Arthur Young, and to the companies and individuals who gave me access to private collections of papers not normally available for public perusal. Much of the statistical work incorporated in the appendices was financed by the Nuffield Foundation and the Social Science Research Council, and skilfully executed by Margaret Ackrill and Patricia Wright, who also provided constructive suggestions. The editors of *Business History*, the *Economic History Review* and *Oxford Economic Papers* kindly permitted me to reprint passages from articles originally published in their journals. A difficult manuscript became a readable typescript through the capable ministrations of Alison Hunt, Beryce Vincenzi and Sue Dawson.

I am grateful to them all, but these acknowledgements do not, of course, implicate them in any errors or omissions which remain. The omissions, at least, may be cheerfully admitted, for our knowledge of many aspects of the rise of the corporate economy will surely be further enlightened, not least by the ongoing work of those acknowledged here.

Wivenhoe Park   December 1973
Colchester

Preface to the second edition

ಬಬ

In the decade since the first edition was written a great deal of work has been published on the corporate economy, by the hands mentioned above, and by others. In addition, colleagues who have adopted this book as a text for their course on twentieth-century business history have made many suggestions for improvement, and a project by J. A. Kay and the author, financed by the Social Science Research Council, has provided more solid statistical information on the sources of changes in industrial concentration. It was essential in producing a second edition to take account of this new work. The basic structure of chapters has been maintained, but few pages remained unscathed by additions or emendations, and some chapters in the second half of the book have been completely rewritten to incorporate new evidence. I have also taken the opportunity to reproduce lists of the largest 50 firms at various dates in a new Appendix 3, in a response to recent requests for such lists to be more readily available. I am very grateful, especially to my colleagues in the Business History Unit, to the many who have made helpful suggestions for additions and improvements. Marjorie Huntley and Carol Wardle quickly and efficiently typed the final manuscript.

London School of Economics   January 1983

I

Business: history and economics

Just as microscopic work on cells may throw new light on
the human body, so detailed study of the growth of
particular business units may add to knowledge
of the industrial system.

T. S. ASHTON, *An Eighteenth Century Industrialist:
Peter Stubs of Warrington* (Manchester, 1939), p. ix.

౧౦ౖ౦

It is a commonplace that in the course of the present century British
industry has witnessed a transformation from a disaggregated
structure of predominantly small, competing firms to a concentrated
structure dominated by large, and often monopolistic, corporations.
The 100 corporations which now occupy the dominant position
account for around 40 per cent of total manufacturing output,[1] while
at the turn of the century the largest 100 firms probably accounted
for barely 15 per cent of output (see Appendix 2). The large
enterprises of today have achieved this increase in their relative
economic power partly by internal expansion and partly by the
absorption and competitive elimination of smaller rivals. The
number of small firms, employing 200 people or less, which was
already only 136,000 in 1935 had by 1963 declined to 60,000, and
their share in manufacturing output over the same period was
reduced from 35 to only 16 per cent.[2] In qualitative terms also the
firms of today, and particularly the larger ones, differ significantly
from their Victorian forebears: they are more diversified, they have
more complex organization structures, they spend more on research,
they are more likely to acquire control of rivals, and they are now
themselves more frequently the subject of takeover bids. Many of
their products are also very different from those of Victorian firms,
for the development of large corporations is closely bound up with
the 'second industrial revolution', with twentieth-century economic
growth based on electricity, the motor-car and chemicals, rather
than steam, railways and textiles. Precisely when, and in what
stages, such developments took place, and the underlying reasons

for the transformation in economic life which they implied, will be a major theme in the chapters that follow.

These developments were not, of course, confined to the United Kingdom; indeed, the tendency to increasing industrial concentration is one of the better attested facts of the recent economic history of most economically advanced Western countries. Moreover, in Britain as in America, the large corporations themselves have been no respecters of national boundaries, but have expanded overseas as well as in the domestic economy. By the 1970s the sales of the largest corporations in the United States and Europe exceeded the national income of many of the member states of the United Nations. The development of these corporations has, therefore, been a major preoccupation of economists, and the importance of an understanding of these changes can scarcely be exaggerated.

The significance of this organizational transformation extends beyond the economic sphere; there are profound political and sociological implications also. It has facilitated, and perhaps induced, substantial changes in the relationship between government and industry. It has brought an increasing number of workers into the employment of large organizations. It has extended to the wealthier middle class what the industrial revolution accomplished for the working class: breaking the links between family and work, which survived in the Victorian family business but are increasingly rare today. In making this break, it has divorced the role of saving and investing from that of managing and directing, yet it has none the less preserved substantial inequalities of wealth and power. Despite the persistence of such inequalities, the economic success of managerial capitalism appears to have reconciled significant numbers of the politically conscious electorates of industrialized nations to a programme of modifying capitalism by political agreement rather than by revolutionary change. The harshnesses of capitalism that remain may still bear down heavily on individuals, but they now do so less as a result of competitive market pressures on employment and wages, and more as a result of decisions which emanate from a managerial hierarchy which has supplemented the market as a means of co-ordinating economic activities. Authority structures and managerial prerogatives, as well as the market itself, are now commonly (and properly) the focus of moral and social criticism of the economic system.

The economic significance of the rise of the corporate economy is also rooted in the replacement of the 'invisible hand' of the market place by what Alfred Chandler has felicitously called the 'visible hand': that is by the more conscious integration and organization of economic activities within large firms. In the nineteenth century the flow of production, from the winning of raw materials to the final sale to the consumer, typically involved many middlemen, each with a specialized function; and resources for production were, broadly, allocated by a market mechanism mediating the relationships between many producers and consumers. Increasingly, now, however, resources and intermediate products are allocated not by dealings between firms in markets, but rather within firms – by an administrative mechanism rather than by a price mechanism. Indeed, the rationale of a firm is that there are costs to using the price mechanism – transactions costs – on which a firm can economize, and 'the distinguishing mark of the firm is the supersession of the price mechanism'.[3] The boundaries of a firm are determined by the relative costs of market and firm, as businessmen periodically seek to adjust the activity of their firms at the margin in response to these relative costs. Among the private costs faced by a businessman using the market, for example, might be listed uncertainty, contractual costs, advertising and other sales costs. In a broader perspective, a businessman might count among the costs of the market the fact that, by competing with other firms in a market, he has to forgo externalities, economies of scale or monopoly profits, which would be possible if he enlarged his firm. The increased role of large firms in economic activity does, then, suggest that the private benefits of planning and organizing production within the firm have been increasing relative to the advantages of dealing in markets. The head offices of the large corporations, which now rise on the banks of the Thames near the administrative and political heartland of London, perform much of the work of organization and co-ordination formerly achieved less conspicuously by market transactions. They thus fulfil as important a role in modern economic life as the commodity exchanges and other venues for market transactions of the nineteenth-century economy.

The precise implication of this change remains a matter of much dispute. It has, for example, been suggested that the managers who perform the organizational task – Professor Galbraith's 'technostructure'[4] – have objectives differing from those of the classical owner-entrepreneur, and that it is now they, rather than wealth owners, who determine major economic choices. On the other hand many markets still exist, and the competitive discipline on firms in the final product market, not to speak of the threat of takeover in the capital market, can still set limits to the freedom of action of managers even in the modern corporate economy. Moreover, there are, in fact, many ways in which modern corporations can, in their internal decision-making, mimic the rules of the price mechanism which they have replaced. Within a large corporation, for example, a number of managerially independent divisions normally compete with each other for resources from head office. In a way reminiscent of the allocation of resources by the capital market among firms, the head office will normally assess requests from divisions according to past performance and likely future profitability, so that the resulting economic decisions may not differ markedly from those in the capital market. Both systems may, in fact, be directed towards maximizing returns on investments and, if this is so, it is the means rather than the end that has changed. Such themes will naturally recur in the following historical analysis of the evolution of the corporate economy.

A crucial factor in determining the relative costs of market and firm is management itself. Fortunately, with the recent publication of a number of business histories, we can now make a clearer assessment of the significance of changes in management costs and practices. Although Professor Charles Wilson, in the preface to his pioneering *History of Unilever*, modestly averred that 'it is not necessary to claim that business history is history of the highest calibre',[5] his apology now seems unnecessary in view of his own contribution and a run of works of comparable quality such as Professor Coleman's *Courtaulds* and Dr Reader's *ICI*.[6] Given the distance in time from the decisions which such histories record, they are usually able to provide for the historian a franker analysis of events than is available to the student of contemporary business decisions, and they provide a detailed and suggestive treatment of the strategy and structure of major enterprises in the corporate economy. Yet business historians, who in general quite properly prize their allegiance to the facts of the individual case, have sometimes tended to see events in the history of the firm as unique, biographical events explicable in terms of particular or even accidental concatenations of historical forces. They rightly reject econometric reasoning as inappropriate to the single case, but the absence of generality has perhaps unnecessarily inhibited business historians in the rigorous development of causal interpretations.

In Britain,[7] then, it has fallen to an economist, Professor Edith Penrose, to exploit historical case study material and to develop a model of the growth of the firm. In her important contribution to the dynamic theory of the firm, however, she wisely warned her readers of the difficulty of developing effective generalizations from the biased sample of case histories which is available:

> Consistent examples are [she admitted] . . . no more a proof than are inconsistent examples a disproof of a general argument unless the examples are presented in sufficiently large numbers and selected in such a way that they constitute a representative sample . . . the examples presented in the following chapters are illustrative only. There is not sufficient systematic information available as yet to enable any comprehensive testing of the generality of the theory.[8]

This *caveat* also applies to many of the generalizations below. However, by focusing attention on mergers and industrial concentration, it has been possible to assemble fuller statistical data (which are presented in the Appendices) to strengthen the case-study analysis of the growth of firms. Moreover, with the release of much new archival material by both business and government,[9] the generalizations which have in the past been made about the forces making for increased industrial concentration are now more tractable to systematic analysis. Even so, there remain many dark areas where our knowledge is limited, and inferences drawn from contemporary views, or from incomplete or biased data, are still in some cases the only basis of interpretation which is available.

The focus of much of what follows differs somewhat from traditional studies in this area, which have been concerned not so much with the growth of the firm as with the implications of monopoly in individual markets. Of course, businessmen have in the past, as now, welcomed the opportunity of strengthening their market position and achieving monopoly powers. It is precisely because of this, however, that the desire for monopoly cannot provide the major explanation of change: the monopoly motive alone has no *diachronic* significance. Businessmen who now enjoy a monopoly no doubt like it, but so presumably would their nineteenth century forebears have liked it. The *historical* problem is to explain why changes in structure occurred when, in the event, they did. Other causal variables must therefore be introduced into the model to explain the changing configuration of firms over time. The technical and institutional background to entrepreneurial decisions is here very important. Government often sets the rules of the game in the market place, and it can be argued that official tolerance of restrictive practices in the past inhibited the natural tendency to merger and concentration.[10] Capital market imperfections, the managerial difficulties of running large organizations, consumer dislike of monopoly, the slow development of the takeover bid, and a widespread preference for small, family-controlled enterprises; all these might also act as a significant brake on mergers. When such institutional variables are introduced into the analysis, we will suggest, the steady growth of the large corporation with national market power becomes a more intelligible phenomenon. While the desire for monopoly must be an important element in any model of increasing concentration, then, it has little explanatory value by itself.

The analysis presented here attempts, using economic theory and historical evidence (where these are available in appropriate form), to explain the rise of the corporate economy, which has been such an important part of recent economic history. The aim is to identify systematic factors favouring or retarding the growth of large firms at successive periods in history, with emphasis on the interwar years in which so many of the significant developments occurred. Already, at that time, the possibility of increasing returns in industry leading to a high level of concentration was well understood. Alfred Marshall, for example, drew attention to the point that, with the potentially perpetual life of a joint stock company, and increasing returns to scale, there was almost 'nothing to prevent the concentration in the hands of a single firm of the whole production of the world'.[11] More recently, economists building on the earlier work of the French statistician Gibrat have shown that, even if there are no systematic tendencies to increasing returns to scale, concentration may still increase.[12] This possibility – now known as the 'Gibrat effect' – might be thought of as a process of natural selection, the result of a situation in which in any period some firms do well and some firms do badly. This dispersion in performance over successive periods can induce a steady increase in the dispersion of firm sizes, and as the successful firms increase their share at the expense of the unsuccessful ones concentration will increase. Thus even without any systematic tendency for large firms to experience more rapid growth than other firms, output will become increasingly concentrated in the hands of the successful firms.[13] Professor Prais, indeed, has suggested that this phenomenon, which he terms 'spontaneous drift', may have been the major cause of rising concentration in the first half of the twentieth century.[14] However, this judgement depends on rather generous assumptions, and a more plausibly constrained model of the Gibrat process indicates that, though its impact can in some periods be considerable, it cannot by itself account for more than a fifth of the concentration increase which has actually occurred.[15] The bulk of the historical change in concentration has been due to more systematic factors, and it is with these – and particularly with the growth of mass production and the impact of mergers – that we will principally be concerned.

The central thesis of this book is that these changes were slower in Britain than in America, but that when they came they had no less profound an effect. Chapter 2 presents evidence that Britain had fallen behind both Germany and America in the structure of her industry in the decades before the First World War. The following chapters review the institutional changes – in business opinion, the capital market, government policy and management practices – which helped to change matters in the interwar years. Chapters 7 and 8 present the qualitative and quantitative evidence for the central argument that these changes caused in the 1920s a merger wave and other developments in large corporations which marked the birth of the modern corporate economy in Britain. Chapter 9 reviews the settling down of this structure in the 1930s and 1940s and Chapter 10 examines the experience of the renewed merger wave of the 1950s and 1960s, followed by the post-1973 depression. Throughout there is an attempt to relate these changes to the trend improvement in Britain's economic performance (relative to her own past though not to the performance of her competitors) in the twentieth century. Chapter 11 examines more explicitly, but briefly, the arguments for the impact of the changes described on growth and welfare.

2

The industrial inheritance: the growth of firms to 1914

We have to reckon with the probability . . . one might without
exaggeration say the certainty . . . that we are in the early
stages of the evolution of the form which industry
will take in the future.

H. W. MACROSTY, *The Trust Movement in
British Industry* (1907), pp. 330–1.

ഇ൧

The growth of large-scale corporations of the modern type is
historically related to the process of industrialization, but the link
between the two is neither simple nor direct, for large companies
predate industrialization, and small companies remain common even
in mature industrial societies. Before the onset of the industrial
revolution in England, there were large joint stock overseas trading
companies,[1] and in 'pre-industrial' manufacturing industries also
there were large enterprises such as the naval arsenal at Chatham and
Whitbread's brewery in London. Although large-scale firms were
not, then, unknown before the onset of industrialization proper, it
was the introduction of new machine technologies and the application of steam power to manufacturing processes which, from the
later eighteenth century onwards, radically transformed the nature
of capitalist enterprise, and created an economy in which factory
concerns employing hundreds (and in some cases thousands) of
workers became the representative form of business unit.

This transformation in the structure of enterprise was first evident
and advanced most rapidly in the cotton textile industry, which
within several generations changed from a pre-industrial, home-
based, craft industry into a highly mechanized, capital-intensive
factory industry.[2] In the first half of the eighteenth century cotton
manufacture was typically organized and financed by merchant-
manufacturers who 'put out' the cotton 'wool' to be spun into yarn
and woven into cloth by workers in their own homes. The unit of

production was small and family-based. Typically the work on the hand-operated spinning wheels and looms would be carried out by husband, wife and children working in a domestic setting. Some of the merchants who organized the links between domestic workers, and dealt in the raw materials and final product markets, employed many thousands of individuals and many hundreds of looms; but their direct problems of supervision and management had little in common with those of the later factory masters, and fixed investment per operative was rarely more than a couple of pounds. However, after a series of mechanical innovations in the processing of cotton and with the subsequent application of steam power to these innovations, there was an enhanced need for close control over labour and for centralization of operations to gain full access to economies of scale in the operation of machinery and power equipment. The advantages of factory-based production thus increasingly made themselves felt, and the number of mills grew rapidly. Already in 1784, Sir Robert Peel's calico printing partnership in Bury employed about 7000, but mills more commonly numbered their employees in hundreds rather than thousands. By 1822 the representative Manchester cotton mill employed between 100 and 200 operatives, each backed by an average capital investment of between £50 and £90. By the 1830s, new mills containing 40,000 spindles and costing over £80,000 – an increase by a factor of ten on the scale of production familiar a decade earlier – were the order of the day.[3]

It might reasonably be expected that this development would lead to the concentration of production in fewer and larger plants in the hands of a small number of firms. Yet this was not the case, for although the size of firms was increasing rapidly, the growth of the market matched their rate of expansion and in some years even outstripped it. The quantity of raw material processed by the cotton industry, for example, rose by more than 200 times between 1750 and 1850[4] so that, despite a substantial rise in the average size of factories, the market was sufficiently large to accommodate many competing firms at the end of this period, as at the beginning. Many new sources of scale economies were opened up by this expansion of the market, but using Marshall's celebrated distinction between internal and external economies,[5] we can see that scale economies did not necessarily lead to larger firms. Many of the scale economies were external to the firm. The specialized cotton markets and services which grew up in Lancashire, for example, achieved economies by servicing many firms locally concentrated. Where the scale economies were internal to the firm, they appear to have been exhausted at a scale well below the full extent of the market, so that no firm had a dominant share of output. This pattern of development, favouring the multiplication of small firms rather than the dominance of large ones, continued for most of the nineteenth century. Between 1792 and 1850, for example, the number of factories increased from about 900 to over 1400, with their average throughput increasing by thirteen times over the same period.[6] The modern dilemma – that of enjoying the economies of large-scale production yet preserving the benefits of competition between firms – did not present problems for the nineteenth-century cotton industry.

This pattern of development in the textile industry during the industrial revolution was the harbinger of future developments rather than the typical form adopted by contemporary industry. There was a tendency to increasing scale over a wide range of industries,[7] but many others, like the Birmingham metal trades, typically retained a structure of small workshops and enterprises in which the master worked closely with only a few men, a structure both less concentrated and with less dramatic social consequences than the factory system. It was not until the later era of large machine tools, engineering standardization and the assembly line that they were to gain access to internal economies of scale comparable to (and indeed greater than) those in the cotton industry.[8] Other industries, such as pottery, brewing, chemicals and iron smelting (which even before the industrial revolution had not been organized on a domestic basis but rather in plants separate from the workers' homes), did show increasing returns to scale, as a result of technical changes and further divisions of labour during the industrial revolution. Again, however, rapidly expanding markets were sufficient to neutralize the effects of such new scale economies, so that competition between many firms was also preserved in these industries. By 1871, then, when over half of the working population were employed in factories (and considerably more than one half of output was produced in factories), it could be argued not only that the degree of competition was no less than it had been previously, but even (given larger markets and greater competition between larger numbers of firms) that it had become more intense.[9]

This is not to say that there were *no* imperfections of competition in the British economy during industrialization. Indeed it may legitimately be doubted whether the idealized state of 'perfect' competition (as conventionally defined in economic theory) existed at this (or indeed at any other) time. Certainly contemporary classical economists nurtured the deep-rooted belief that there were widespread restraints on competition in the nineteenth-century economy, with harmful effects on welfare. There is evidence of semi-monopolistic price agreements between manufacturers, particularly in the earlier years of the century,[10] and earlier still Adam Smith had provided a salutary warning about the prevalence of informal or secret arrangements:

> We rarely hear [he wrote] . . . of the combinations of masters, though frequently of those of workmen. But whoever imagines, upon this account, that masters rarely combine is as ignorant of the world as of the subject. Masters are [he concluded] always and everywhere in a sort of tacit, but constant and uniform combination.[11]

In the main, however, while employers did often discuss wages, prices and market conditions, their market power was severely limited by the competitive forces inherent in the nineteenth-century industrial structure of many small firms operating in large markets. The efforts of trade associations to control prices were rarely attended with success, and one might almost conclude that the existence of such associations was a symptom of severe competition rather than a serious restraint on it. As the nineteenth century progressed, therefore, contemporary economists principally directed their criticisms not to the only weakly monopolistic arrangements in manufacturing industry, but rather to those like the chartered overseas trading companies which derived permanence and security from statutory sanction. The widespread dislike of such monopolies, which were less subject to competitive restraints than manufacturing firms, stimulated the withdrawal of statutory monopolistic privileges from these companies on a tide of legislation inspired by enthusiasm for free trade and *laissez-faire*.[12]

Yet at the same time as such well-established monopolies and restraints of trade were being broken down by legislative and economic forces, there were independent industrial developments which presented new monopolistic challenges and created even larger concentrations of economic power. The railways are the foremost example of this tendency. The railway companies operated on a scale far greater than that seen in the cotton industry or, indeed, in any nineteenth century manufacturing industry. Interestingly, it is possible to discern many of the characteristics of modern corporations in the large railway enterprises of the period.[13] In addition to displaying conventional economies of scale in operation, they were involved in amalgamations and takeovers to strengthen co-ordination and spread managerial overheads. The majority of railway companies were also quoted on the London and provincial stock exchanges and this promoted the divorce of ownership and control, with shareholders seeing their holding as a *rentier* investment, leaving the conduct of the business to professional managers who frequently held only a minority shareholding and pursued different goals. In other respects, however, the railways presented unique problems different in kind from those encountered in large manufacturing corporations. Their needs in management planning and marketing were rather different and, like similar enterprises in the gas, water and electricity industries (but unlike most manufacturing corporations), they were 'natural' monopolies in the sense that uncontrolled competition between many lines running between the same two points could be grossly wasteful of resources. Although a *modus vivendi* was devised which partially met these difficulties, the new problems of regulation which the railways posed fitted uncomfortably in the Victorian compromise of private enterprise, *laissez-faire* and regulation by competition rather than by the state.[14] Yet, while the railways posed a problem by themselves being potential monopolists, their main impact on manufacturing industry was in the contrary direction of weakening monopoly power. By cheapening transport they promoted the unification of local markets into a national one and, indirectly, by promoting urbanization, they encouraged the standardization of tastes and a trend towards mass production. Thus, whereas in the early stages of the industrial revolution a few manufacturers in a small town might have a local monopoly in their product, by the mid-Victorian period they were increasingly having to reckon with goods 'imported' from neighbouring regions on the expanding railway network.

In the 1870s and 1880s, then, after a century of rapid growth both for individual firms and for the economy as a whole, competition in the manufacturing sector was strong, indeed stronger, some would argue, than it has been in any subsequent decade. Most industries had a multiplicity of what, by modern standards, would be considered small firms, and most consumers faced an expanded choice between the goods of a larger number of sellers from a wider area. Product differentiation enabled a few manufacturers of specialized products to obtain a favoured market position[15] and other producers enjoyed a local market protected by local tastes or long distances from other potential competitors. In general, however, such factors mitigating the severity of competition were rare. In almost all industries demand was growing rapidly and, in many, more rapidly than the size of firms. Thus, despite their explosive nineteenth-century growth, it is unlikely that the largest 100 firms in 1880 accounted for even as much as 10 per cent of the market, compared with their 40 per cent share a hundred years later (see Appendix 2).

Yet these very conditions of competition and rapidly expanding markets contained within them the impetus to the division of labour which in the long run was to result in the greater concentration of output in the hands of large firms. Towards the end of the nineteenth century it became generally recognized that these tendencies to industrial concentration were becoming increasingly marked. This development was perhaps in part a natural result of the continued growth of firms, coupled with the slower expansion of the market as the pace of economic growth in Britain slowed down.[16] It was also the result of a process which had hitherto had little impact on competition but which had in fact been set in train at a very early stage of the industrial revolution. The essence of this process was sketched by Adam Smith in the early chapters of the *Wealth of Nations*, and encapsulated in the famous phrase: 'the division of labour is limited by the extent of the market'.[17] Sustained growth was possible in Smith's model of economic evolution because not only did expanding markets increase the opportunities for divisions of labour, but each division of labour in its turn raised productivity and thus made possible a further expansion of markets, bringing the process into a self-sustaining virtuous spiral of progress. Competition, in Smith's model, provides a spur to firms to achieve economies of scale and specialization. An increase in demand, he argues, 'encourages production, and thereby increases the competition of the producers, who, in order to undersell one another, have recourse to new divisions of labour and new improvements of art, which might never otherwise have been thought of'.[18] The contrast between this view and the concept of competition in the equilibrium models of later economic theory is noteworthy. In the modern formal models possible divisions of labour are assumed to be exhausted and the appearance of further economies of scale would be inconsistent with the continuance of competition. In Smith's dynamic model of economic evolution, also, the question arises of how competition will be maintained in the presence of increasing returns to scale, though Smith himself does not appear either to have been troubled by this problem or to have resolved it. There are a number of possible explanations of the failure of such long-run tendencies to materialize.[19] We have already noted one of these – the growth of the market itself. An increase in market demand must be met either by the further expansion of existing firms or by the entry of new ones. The precise balance between the contribution of the methods will depend on the degree to which the newly enlarged market induces new internal economies of scale. There can be no general presumption, at least from Smith's imprecise and intuitive model, that the magnitude of such internal economies will exceed the extent of market growth. Indeed, as we have seen in the cotton industry, the evidence suggests that technical progress and the division of labour proceeded rapidly but not as rapidly as the growth of the market. Hence the expansion of production was achieved by a combination of the growth of existing firms and the entry of new ones.

The maintenance and strengthening of competition by the new entrants in the cotton industry was greatly facilitated by the emergence of a specialized engineering industry, a further important 'division of labour and improvement of art' induced by market expansion. Specialist machinery builders would supply factory equipment incorporating the latest designs of, say, power looms and the steam boilers and engines to drive them, and this encouraged the entry of new firms on equal terms with existing ones. Since the machine building industry was itself competitive, such equipment was freely available on the open market. Yet there could be no presumption that this would continue indefinitely, and experience soon showed that control over machine technology could evolve differently. As competition among machine builders and users stimulated further inventions and division of labour, the inventors and machine builders perceived an alternative strategy which promised them higher financial returns. The essence of this was that a firm which could reserve the use of a new or significantly improved type of machine to itself could expect to use this monopoly to grow more rapidly than its competitors and gain a market share larger than would be necessary purely to achieve any economies of scale inherent in the equipment itself.

An example of such a change drawn from the tobacco industry will perhaps make the opportunities opened up by this alternative strategy clearer. Tobacco was traditionally sold in loose form, but by the mid-Victorian period rolled cigarettes were becoming increasingly esteemed and, in the manner of Smith's model, an expansion of the market for such cigarettes stimulated a search for machines which could roll them efficiently. An important element in the success of the firm of W. D. & H. O. Wills (whose branded cigarettes were market leaders) was that they acquired exclusive control of one such invention, the Bonsack cigarette machine, a US invention which could produce from 300 to 500 cigarettes a minute. For this machine, neither capital costs nor operating economies of scale were large in relation to the rapidly expanding market, but, by improving on the basic machine and by buying out the patents of its rivals, Wills were able to gain an important competitive advantage over other producers. Demand for their mass-produced penny cigarettes, such as Woodbine, increased dramatically, and by 1901 Wills's share of cigarette sales was as high as 55 per cent of the UK total. That this offered substantial scope for monopoly profit is confirmed by Wills's rate of return of 62 per cent on capital employed in that year, four times their rate of profit of two decades earlier.[20]

The advantages of such a near monopolistic position, conferred by an assured lead in a specialized machine technology, were perceived in other industries,[21] but there were also many markets in which dominance was achieved not by restricting the use of technology but simply because the technology developed was efficient only at such a large scale that a small number of plants could satisfy the whole of the market demand which could reasonably be anticipated. For this reason also, therefore, firms began to expand at a pace which outstripped the rate of growth of markets. This development was accelerated in the closing decades of the nineteenth century by significant changes in the nature of market demand for some consumer goods. As urbanization progressed, and urban incomes rose, consumer tastes for a range of common products became more standardized and the possibilities in large cities of scale economies in marketing were increased.[22] There were, for example, economies both in advertising branded goods, and in establishing sales forces to promote them through the multiplicity of highly competitive retail outlets. These marketing economies also had repercussions on production economies of scale. Where demand for a product could be standardized, and perhaps also widened, the short and specialized production runs which had been necessary to cater for more sharply differentiated local tastes could be replaced by longer runs and often by more economical and more capital-intensive processes. These tendencies were not by any means a new phenomenon, but they do appear to have intensified from the 1880s onwards. Significantly, it was in industries which experienced such a shift in the pattern of demand – cigarettes, wallpaper, flour, soap, sewing cotton and linoleum – that tendencies to higher concentration were most conspicuous.[23] Even in the brewing industry, where the emergence of a mass urban market had stimulated the growth of firms at a much earlier period, the tendencies to higher concentration were given a further impetus by new marketing developments, as local magistrates after 1869 attempted to limit the number of public houses by reintroducing a restrictive licensing system. This stimulated a scramble to acquire small breweries and groups of public houses as the big brewers sought to consolidate their hold on the mass urban markets.[24]

In a significant number of industries, then, firms in the closing decades of the nineteenth century were facing important shifts both in the technical basis of production and in the nature of market demand. In industries where this resulted in the emergence of economies of scale in production and marketing, there was (given that the majority of them contained a large number of vigorously competing firms) an inevitable tendency to overextension of capacity and price cutting.[25] If bankruptcy for all were to be avoided there were a number of possible responses to this situation. In some industries leading firms extended their plant to the new optimum efficient size, and by reducing prices to below the marginal cost of the earlier technology they eliminated many of their rivals. In others the majority of existing firms renewed their attempts at collective price and output control. Such combinations were, however, inherently unstable, for, although there was a general interest in the controls, individual members had a powerful incentive to maximize their revenue by expanding production secretly and selling below the agreed price. One possible response to this realization was a more permanent and watertight merger of interests. In contrast to a cartel, a merger of this kind had the advantage that the otherwise divergent interests of the contracting parties were closely and formally cemented together into a common cause, and the individual firm's incentive to renege on the agreement was eliminated.

Of course, the possibility of a full merger of interests had been appreciated in earlier decades of the nineteenth century. Indeed, merger, viewed simply as the combination of businesses, is at least as old as marriage, and alliances of family business interests cemented by marriage and kinship remained a major source of additional finance and business expansion throughout the nineteenth century. The division of firms between heirs on the death of the owner was also practised, underlining the essentially personal and familial nature of business alliances (a contingent result of such division was to check the tendency of marriages to increase the size of businesses). Despite the constraints of this familial framework, it was possible for a small number of outstanding businesses to grow to a considerable size. As early as 1795 the Peels (then the largest business in the cotton industry) owned twenty-three mills in Blackburn, Bury, Bolton, Burton-on-Trent and Tamworth; and many other entrepreneurs, in this and other industries, extended their control over many factories as they reinvested profits and gained competitive advantages over rivals which enabled them to buy them out.[26] Increasingly, capital needs for such expansion were also met by accepting money on loan from the general public and also by admitting partners – whether 'sleeping' or otherwise – to formal participation in the enterprise. In some industries where capital requirements were large, the partnership was the normal business form and British entrepreneurs had not in general been averse to diluting family ownership by merger in this way where it was economically advantageous to do so.[27]

However, it seems clear that before such *ad hoc* partnerships could develop further into a more modern form of corporate enterprise, institutional developments both in company law and in stock exchange practice were necessary. Formally, the required legal changes came in England and Wales between 1844 and 1856 when first joint stock companies and then limited liability companies received the general sanction of parliament.[28] These had already been available under separate legislation for public utilities or by private act of parliament, but by these new acts the way was opened for a relatively cheap company form for manufacturing industry also. The facility of joint stock was more convenient than either a full partnership or the deposit of money with a firm, since the shares were readily transferable and the rights of control which they carried strengthened the security of the investor. Finally, with the granting of limited liability, the joint stock investor was also relieved of the responsibility for the whole of the debts of the firms in which he held shares. In retrospect, the simple device of making him liable only up to the value of shares for which he undertook to subscribe seems to be both realistic and just. It was a natural extension of the similar rights which had beeen accorded to investors in, for example, railways, and reduced the risks of *rentier* investors in businesses which were in reality run not by them but by the directors.

Yet this favourable view of the new company form was by no means shared by all contemporaries. Indeed the balance of public opinion (as expressed to the numerous parliamentary committees which discussed the merits and demerits of the proposals) reacted unfavourably to the idea of allowing shareholders in a business to repudiate responsibility for its debts and foist part of their risks on to suppliers and customers. Even those who accepted the arguments in favour of limited liability – principally its favourable effects on investment – saw little future for the new companies, since, as they were forced to advertise their limited liability status by the tag 'Limited', suppliers and customers would, it was thought, be reluctant to deal with them. There were also serious doubts about whether the management of such companies would be efficient and reliable, and the view of Adam Smith was still commonly held:

> The directors of such companies [he wrote] . . . being the managers rather of other people's money than of their own, it cannot be well expected, that they should watch over it with the same anxious vigilance with which the partners in a private copartnery frequently watch over their own. . . . Negligence and profusion, therefore, must always prevail, more or less, in the management of the affairs of such a company.[29]

This view was rooted in the direct experience of businessmen as well as in inductive reasoning. The elder Sir Robert Peel, for example, thinking of the problems of large-scale management, felt that, 'It is impossible for a mill at any distance to be managed unless it is under the direction of a partner or superintendent who has an interest in the success of the business.'[30] Moreover, the early years of limited liability abundantly confirmed that these contemporary fears and prognostications were not entirely without foundation. Over 30 per cent of the public companies formed between the achievement of general limited liability in 1856, and 1883, ended in insolvency, many of them in the first five years of their existence. There was a strong suspicion that this rate of failure resulted from the activities of crooked promoters out for a quick speculative profit, a view lightheartedly reflected in W. S. Gilbert's *Utopia Limited*:

> Some seven men form an Association
>   (If possible all Peers and Baronets)[31]
> They start off with a public declaration
>   To what extent they mean to pay their debts
> That's called their Capital . . .[32]

The early failures deepened distrust among the public and doubts were strengthened also by the multiplication of unexpected calls on partly paid shares (a form of share which was then common, though it eroded the limitation of liability). As a result, by the 1880s perhaps only 5 to 10 per cent of those larger-scale businesses which might have been expected to benefit from outside investment had in fact adopted limited liability company status.

Already by that time, however, there were improvements in the practices of limited liability companies which were to give them wider popularity. Smaller uncalled liabilities and lower share denominations became more common and this, together with the development of underwriting, led to a wider market in industrial issues. Solicitors, stockbrokers, company agents, bankers and accountants acted as intermediaries with the investing public, with whom they were closely in touch; and large firms in industries such as iron and steel and shipbuilding began to see benefits in raising their additional capital needs through these channels. Public demand for issues of shares in manufacturing industries was also boosted by some popular and oversubscribed issues in the consumer goods field. In 1886, for example, Guinness was floated as a public company and in 1890 there followed the flotation of the sewing cotton combine J. & P. Coats. There was then a rapid and continuous increase in the paid-up capital of companies and many of these companies offered their shares to the public. Between 1885 and 1907 the number of firms in domestic manufacturing and distribution with quotations on the London stock exchange grew from only sixty to almost 600,[33] and the provincial stock exchanges 'were almost of greater importance in relation to home securities than London'.[34]

This development of the stock market not only facilitated the growth of firms facing the pressures for economies of scale in marketing and production, but also created new economies of scale in financing, and thus added to these pressures. Many of the companies which might have wished to seek capital on the provincial or metropolitan stock markets were too small to raise money economically themselves.[35] They could, however, join together with other firms and make a public flotation of the businesses as a merged company. Access to economies of scale in the capital market of this kind appears to have been the aim behind many of the mergers of these years. It has also been suggested[36] that these developments in company financing created a new financial impetus to the merger movement by encouraging speculative activity in the stock market. Investors were relatively inexperienced in assessing the shares of manufacturing firms and their profit expectations were rather insecurely based. It was a simple matter for an unscrupulous company promoter to inflate these expectations by issuing an optimistic prospectus, for neither the state nor the Stock Exchange Committee provided any real safeguards for the inexperienced investor. The potentially large benefits of economies of scale and monopoly profits which could be promised in a merger could be particularly appealing in the new issue market. First, however, the promoter had to convince the present owners of the companies (whose profit expectations would be tempered by experience and close personal acquaintance with the business) that the sale of their businesses to the public could be lucrative. To do this it was necessary to offer them a price which significantly exceeded the discounted present value of their own more securely based profit expectations. The evidence suggests that a number of promoters could successfully achieve this. Frank Harris, for example, was 'admirably received'[37] by the owners of the Bovril Company when it was known that he was acting for Ernest Terah Hooley, a promoter with a series of successful promotions to his credit. Harris claims that the owners wanted £1½ million for their business and that he offered £1¼ million but was beaten by another agent of Hooley's who offered £2 million! Such offers could, of course, only be based on Hooley's masterly capacity for exaggerating share values when at a later stage he sold the company through a public issue of shares. Potential shareholders seemed most ready to accept such inflation of values beyond what private businessmen would reasonably anticipate, when the general share price level had been rising and was nearing its peak: investment success in the boom bred speculative activity, at least until the bubble burst. Significantly the majority of merger issues by promoting syndicates were made precisely in such boom periods. The positive correlation between the level of share prices and the intensity of merger activity[38] is consistent with this hypothesis that financial factors played an important part in stimulating the amalgamations of this period. This view is also confirmed by the complaints of 'overcapitalization' which almost invariably followed the more unscrupulous or misguided merger issues.[39] Such complaints clearly suggest that the profits which were made subsequently to an issue were insufficient to service the larger amounts of capital which had been subscribed.

Thus on a number of fronts – technical, commercial and also financial – there were, in the closing decades of the nineteenth century, both strong pressures and new opportunities making for larger-scale enterprise. The result was that the merger waves of these years were far more intense than any which had been experienced earlier in the century.[40] Between 1888 and 1914 an average of at least sixty-seven firms disappeared in mergers in each year, and in the three peak years of high share prices and intense merger activity between 1898 and 1900 as many as 650 firms valued at a total of £42 million were absorbed in 198 separate mergers. The important turn of the century merger wave was particularly marked in the important textile finishing industry, in which a series of combines, with control over an average of 80 per cent of their respective markets, were floated: the Bradford Dyers' Association (1898, accounting for twenty-one firm disappearances), the Calico Printers' Association (1899, forty-five firms), the Bleachers' Association (1900, fifty-two firms) and the British Cotton and Wool Dyers' Association (1900, forty-six firms). There were further large mergers in other branches of the textile industry: the Fine Cotton Spinners' and Doublers' Association (1898, thirty firms) and the Yorkshire Woolcombers'

Association (1899, thirty-seven firms). In other industries also there were consolidations in this period, the more important among them being British Oil and Cake Mills (1899, sixteen firms), Wallpaper Manufacturers (1900, thirty firms), Imperial Tobacco (1901, twelve firms) and the Associated Portland Cement Manufacturers Company with its later subsidiary British Portland Cement (1900 and 1912, fifty-nine firms).[41] Almost all of these claimed, and many of them achieved, market shares of between 60 per cent and 90 per cent. Such large-scale multi-firm mergers were spectacular and gained as much attention from contemporaries as they have subsequently from historians; but scarcely less important were the less noticeable mergers that were also becoming commonplace. The larger firms in the brewing industry acquired several hundred smaller breweries in these years, and large firms like Vickers in the engineering industry and Levers in the soap industry were also growing rapidly both by internal growth and by merger.

This movement towards industrial concentration was historically unprecedented and it created manufacturing enterprises with capitals distinctly larger than the early nineteenth-century cotton lords could have aspired to. The movement in Britain was not, however, on as large a scale as the contemporaneous movement which was occurring for similar reasons in the United States.[42] At a time when the US manufacturing workforce was only slightly larger than the British, her larger manufacturing corporations were noticeably larger in terms of employment, and the gap was more evident in terms of capital or output. US Steel, for example, not only was more vertically integrated and had a broader management structure than any British steel company, but was very much larger. In 1902 the nominal value of US Steel's issued stocks and bonds was $1,322 million (more than £264 million) and the corporation employed 168,127 (125,326 of them in manufacturing).[43] Among British manufacturing companies by contrast, the largest employer, Fine Cotton Spinners and Doublers, had only 30,000 workers, and the largest by issued capital (Imperial Tobacco, £17.5 million) was also only a fraction of the size of US Steel.[44] The peak year for mergers in the USA was, as in the UK, 1899, but in both numbers and values the US merger wave far outpaced that in this country: in 1899 alone there were 979 firm disappearances by merger valued at $2064 million (over £400 million),[45] compared with 255 firm disappearances with a value of only £22 million in the UK. There is also evidence that the UK turn of the century merger wave affected fewer industries and created fewer large corporations with smaller market shares than their US counterparts.[46] The contrasting experience of the two countries is surprising, since they faced very similar technologies and were, arguably, at a comparable stage of industrial development. Hence a number of hypotheses have been advanced in explanation of the contrast. US management may have more successfully coped with problems of greatly enlarged company size.[47] Imperfections in the US capital market coupled with exceptional requirements for financial mobilization may have strengthened the hands of US financiers, like the Rockefellers and Morgans, in creating mergers.[48] Finally, Professor Payne has advanced a multi-causal explanation in terms of Britain's early start and technological base, the size and structure of the market for British goods, and the pride in self-sufficiency and anti-professionalism of the British industrialist.[49] None of these hypotheses are, by themselves, entirely convincing, though together they pose a formidable programme for further research, if providing no settled conclusions.

Whatever the reasons for the contrasting experience of the two countries, the results of these industrial developments in the UK are clear. By the decade before the First World War the structure of British manufacturing industry was already very different from that of three or four decades earlier. The foundations of the modern corporate economy were already discernible in the large firms that had been created, with many of the important companies of today (including Imperial Tobacco, Watney, Dunlop, GKN, and Vickers) already being established among the leading firms. If we look more carefully at the largest firms[50] and at their relationship with the rest of industry, however, it is clear that although many of the outlines of modern industrial structure were evident, many innovations we now associate with the corporate economy were yet to appear. It is true that the quotation of large manufacturing companies on the stock exchange and the widespread merger activity of these years were important innovations. Yet the industrial partnership and the family-owned factory remained the typical unit in most branches of manufacturing. The institutional innovations in company law, which strengthened tendencies to large scale, had also given a new lease of life to many smaller businesses. Partnerships and family firms adapted the new institutional form to their own purpose, and by 1914 as many as four-fifths of the registered joint stock companies were private rather than public companies.[51] Even amongst the public companies, moreover, the original family controllers frequently remained in leading managerial positions. It was a common practice, encouraged by the better company promoters, for the founding families to retain a major interest in a newly merged and publicly floated enterprise. This practice had a lot to commend it, for the separation and professionalization of management which we associate with modern corporations still had a long way to develop, and outside managers were not easily come by. Significantly, many of the firms which did not retain the services of the former owners (or which retained the services of owners lacking the managerial capacity to exercise overall control in an enlarged company) encountered serious managerial difficulties (see pp. 74–5). By contrast the three largest companies of the day – which were also among the most successful – J. & P. Coats, Imperial Tobacco, and Watney Combe Reid – were not built up around a new corporate management at all, but around old family firms with their senior management and directors recruited principally from among the founding families.[52] While this solved a fundamental problem of the corporate economy – that of maintaining managerial efficiency while divorcing ownership from control – it did so more by avoiding the issue than by devising new techniques of incentive and control.

In other respects also the large firms in the decade before the First World War were very different from those that were to emerge in the interwar period. The numbers of firms surviving is some indication of this – only a minority of the fifty largest firms in 1905 were still among the fifty largest in 1930[53] – but the contrast is even clearer in qualitative terms. Many of the large firms in 1905 were in a limited number of traditional industries: the brewing trade, for example, accounted for more than a third of them. Now the brewing industry was a very large one and this meant that the limitation of competition which we would normally associate with such a concentration of big firms was less likely to materialize in this industry. The typical large brewery still met significant competition not only from other large breweries in the metropolitan areas but from small and medium-sized local brewers throughout the country. Moreover, breweries that attempted to charge monopolistic prices would still meet some resistance from untied houses or other public houses on short contract terms. There were, of course, some large companies which more clearly dominated their markets – including Imperial Tobacco, Associated Portland Cement, and the textile finishing combines – but they were the exception rather than the rule among the largest companies in this period.

Furthermore, many of these prewar large firms were not involved in the modern sectors of the economy which we now associate with large corporations. Although many of them were prosperous at the time, they were principally engaged in the staple industries, which were shortly to face the strain of war and economic depression, and for many of them this was to mean a decline in their traditional markets. By contrast, the new and rapidly growing industries were poorly represented. There were only three chemical firms (two of them in stagnant or declining sectors of the chemical industry), one in electrical engineering and none in motor manufacture, among the top firms of 1905.[54] Of the chemical firms, the Salt Union and the United Alkali Company had been formed in 1888 and 1890 respectively, as defensive moves in traditional sectors of the chemical industry. Only Brunner Mond, using the Solvay process of alkali manufacture, represented a more recent development.[55] No British motor-car manufacturer had by then embarked upon techniques of assembly line production, which Henry Ford was at that time successfully introducing in America; and in electrical machinery the British market was dominated by subsidiaries of American and German parents and by imports from abroad.[56] There was, then, little sign of mass production techniques in the new industries, yet it was on these that the capacity to grow of the indigenous science-based corporations of the future was to rest.

It has been credibly argued that, during the general industrial stagnation of the years before 1914, Britain experienced a decline in industrial productivity and the lowest recorded rate of economic growth in her history.[57] The coincidence of this retardation of growth with the relative 'backwardness' in merger activity and industrial concentration raises a number of questions. If there is a causal link between the two phenomena, it is, however, difficult in the present state of knowledge to determine in which direction the relationship might lie. It might, for example, be argued that the new industries (on which the 'missing' growth would have been based) were typically highly concentrated, so that the low level of concentration in Britain was simply a function of her retarded economic growth. An alternative view would be that large corporations of the modern type would have been able to induce the adjustment in the structure of output (and particularly the growth of new industries) more efficiently than the multiplicity of small and medium-sized firms which the British economy had inherited. As contemporaries became more deeply concerned about their overall economic performance, they were more and more inclined to adopt this second view. Increasingly they saw the emulation of the industrial structure of the United States and Germany as the key to revitalizing the British economy. It was in self-examination in this critical vein that the 'rationalization' movement of the interwar years was to take root.

3

The rationalization movement

The rapid development of the idea of rationalization has
given rise to amalgamations at a speed and to a
degree which are altogether novel.
L. F. URWICK, address to the Economics section
of the British Association for the
Advancement of Science (1930).

ༀ

In the United Kingdom the First World War marked a watershed in
economic and business development as well as in political and social
life. On this much there is general agreement, but historians are
divided on the related issue of whether the changes of the war years
were uniquely a result of the war itself, or whether the same changes
would in any case very soon have arisen, since they stemmed from
growing social and economic pressures which were already evident
in prewar Britain.[1] Already in the late nineteenth century and the
first decade of the twentieth, there were, as we have seen, strong
inducements making for larger-scale enterprise, and it would not be
difficult to trace ideas about industrial organization which later came
to be dubbed 'rationalization' to an origin in the amalgamation
movements of the prewar years.[2] Yet only during the war and in the
years that followed did such ideas begin to attain wide currency and
gain the status of the conventional wisdom in some business circles.
The contrast between the pre- and postwar periods in industry was a
real one. Churchill's much quoted hope in 1914, that the war would
see 'business as usual',[3] was in fact to prove to be profoundly wrong,
for between 1914 and 1918 the pattern of production over a wide
range of industries was to be transformed as businesses strove to meet
wartime requirements. Many materials formerly imported from the
continent were cut off by the war, so that substantial growth of home
industries producing products such as magnetos (for vehicles and
aircraft) and dyestuffs (for the texile industry) was necessary.
However, private initiatives (both in such new industries and in the
established armaments industries) soon proved inadequate, and the

government, and especially the Ministry of Munitions, began to play an increasing role in planning, financing and directing the activites of manufacturing firms. The state, on a war footing, with a large and predictable demand for a wide range of weapons and general supplies, was in a unique position to influence business firms. In general, it used this position to induce them to adopt the most economical methods, particularly by discouraging product differentiation and by encouraging investment in long runs and mass production to meet government demand. Indirectly this resulted in more merger activity, as firms made acquisitions to expand their capacity. Mergers were further accelerated towards the end of the war, as firms like Vickers and Nobel (which faced a decline of demand for their military products in peacetime) strengthened their position by diversification and acquisition. The internal practices of firms were also profoundly changed by the war: interchangeable standardized parts were increasingly used in engineering trades; capital and unskilled labour took the place of skilled craftsmen; and there was increasing reliance on electricity as a source of power – during the war years electricity consumption doubled.[4]

Many of these wartime industrial developments – mergers, larger scale enterprise, new industries, standardization and mass production – were, of course, associated with the stirrings of what became the modern corporate economy. They were not forgotten after the war, for once the profitability of the new methods had been realized their impact was cumulative. The industrialist Sir Vincent Caillard typified the industrial mood when he looked back from the 1920s to the war years as a time of:

> cooperation on a marvellous scale when . . . manufacturers for the good of their country, threw away their old prejudices and put themselves unreservedly at the disposal of one another. Patents, secret processes, special methods, goodwill, were flung into the melting pot of the common weal.[5]

This was the authentic, exhilarated voice of a movement in business opinion which was growing in strength and which questioned the virtues of competition and championed the advantages of cooperation, merger and large-scale enterprise. Whilst many other wartime changes were abandoned,[6] the changes in business opinion which had accompanied them were, in general, more permanent. Indeed already, during the war, various committees sponsored by the government to enquire into wartime changes and postwar prospects betrayed a taste for continuing many of the wartime innovations in peacetime.[7] The war, so the contemporary optimism ran, had caused a 'New Industrial Revolution which is likely to have far greater results for good than the introduction of machinery 130 years ago'.[8]

Yet the situation faced by British industrial firms after 1919 was profoundly different from that which had been envisaged in the closing stages of the war. Instead of the anticipated postwar prosperity there was, after a brief inflationary boom, a fierce slump, and in 1921 the unemployment rate rose above 10 per cent, never to fall below that figure again before the Second World War.[9] Economic depression was, then, a central fact of the interwar experience: to the labourer it meant the dole, to the employer it meant overcapacity; for both it provoked a further re-evaluation of their political, social and economic beliefs and of the economic institutions they sustained. The effect of the depression in increasing political consciousness and stimulating the growth of the Labour Party, and its impact on the collapse of the classical paradigms of economic theory in the Keynesian revolution, have often been analysed by historians. Less well covered, but no less important, was its impact at the level of popular business philosophy, as more businessmen began to question the desirability of the configuration of firms and markets which they had inherited from the prewar era. The rationalization movement – which gained the attention of bankers, politicians and trade unionists, as well as of prominent industrialists between the wars – was an important aspect of the build-up of dissatisfaction with the market mechanism and of the movement towards greater reliance on large firms for economic organization. Though the Keynesian revolution ultimately demonstrated that the malfunctioning which they witnessed might also have a macro-solution, this did nothing between the wars to reduce the tenacity of the belief that the market economy was failing, and that it was the process of rationalization (essentially a micro-solution) that offered the way out of the predicament which this posed.

The word 'rationalization' lacked any precise meaning. As the *Economist* remarked: 'as often happens with a new immigrant to the language it is undergoing a vogue which has led to its use as a cloak for confused ideas, and sometimes as a badge of respectability for processes of doubtful value'.[10] To some prominent advocates it clearly implied horizontal amalgamation,[11] a view shared by some critics of the rationalization movement who described it, less enthusiastically, as 'a new fangled term to describe the old fashioned device of eliminating competition'.[12] 'I do not much like the word', wrote the economist D. H. Macgregor resignedly in 1934, 'but it has become necessary to use it. It is mainly a question of the scale on which private enterprise should be urged or compelled to reorganize itself by amalgamation.'[13] It is in this sense that the term is used here. However, we shall not lose sight of its wider implications, for the more intelligent apostles of rationalization were careful to stress the interdependence of the various aspects of their programme and the insufficiency of merger by itself as an automatic promoter of efficiency. Lyndall Urwick, for example (perhaps the most consistent and coherent advocate of rationalization), wrote that:

> The mere financial combination of businesses or the wider application of scientific methods of management to existing units of control, can neither of them by themselves contribute effectively towards equipping Great Britain with that reorganized national economy which is essential if she is to retain her place among the industrialized nations.[14]

The two were seen as complementary, not as competing, aims.

The call for experimentation in new forms of organization within the firm and for large-scale merger of interests was motivated by the failure of the market economy to produce prosperity and full employment, and as such was a worldwide phenomenon.[15] The British espousal of the doctrine of rationalization was more muted than that in Germany, where it was not only taken more seriously, but was more coherently developed and applied in a very wide range of industries.[16] Yet, given the strongly entrenched competitive, laissez-faire traditions in Britain, contemporaries nonetheless saw the developments in British opinion as 'a very remarkable change'. Before the First World War,

> while it was admitted that the old theory of competition was not working without disadvantage, it was believed that, all over, these were less than the disadvantages which might result from anything monopolistic. . . . The postwar tendency is to change this attitude.[17]

More complaints of 'overproduction' or 'underconsumption' were heard as one industry after another met problems of overcapacity; and competition was no longer widely accepted as essentially benign, but was increasingly referred to as 'cut throat', 'wasteful', 'unfair', 'destructive' or 'ruinous'. The world faced that 'gigantic paradox' later to be enunciated by Roosevelt but already stated neatly in 1931, by Urwick:

> Our control over natural resources is enlarged almost beyond the wildest dreams, even of each preceding decade. The world's capacity for production has been developed to a far greater degree than any corresponding increase in population, especially in the industrialized nations. Yet the peoples of those nations, by millions, are eye to eye with uncertainty, with want, with moral degradation and with despair. We meet under the shadow of the gravest economic crisis which has threatened the material well being of civilization for a century.[18]

The earlier belief in the inevitability of progress in an economy co-ordinated only by the 'invisible hand' of the market looked, in this interwar world, progressively less convincing. One justification on which the earlier faith in a competitive market system had been based was that 'the great complexity of effort necessary to maintain the world's material life cannot be organized, is beyond the control of any form of positive action which humanity can devise.'[19] But this belief crumbled in the face of evidence suggesting that the market also was incapable of that prodigious feat of organization which the world required. The market appeared instead to involve 'seventy-five per cent of our best endeavour . . . in unproductive competition, in overlapping and in confused striving'.[20]

In the place of the market's 'automatic' equilibration, which had once seemed to be its strength, it was suggested that men should substitute a *consciously* and *deliberately* fashioned 'rational' system of industrial regulation. 'There is abundant evidence', Harold Macmillan MP told a management research group in 1934, 'to prove that some form of conscious social direction will have to supplement the old system under which the regulation of our economy was entrusted to the method of trial and error in response to the price indicator',[21] and this sentiment was widely echoed by rationalizers. 'The belief that a more rational control of world economic life through the application of scientific method is possible and desirable'[22] thus grew in influence, amongst men pleased to believe in their creativity and potentiality as co-operators in extending their power of control over economic life by conscious and purposeful organization. Moderate and reflective economists such as Sir Henry Clay were increasingly concerned 'to discourage the hope that the problem, if left to itself, will cure itself, and to argue that the necessary reorganization of the depressed industries will not be affected unless the initiative is taken and the impulse given by some agency outside them'.[23]

The implication of rationality in the term 'rationalization'[24] emphasized that industry could conform to ideas and values whose proponents were growing in confidence and strength in contemporary society, and in particular to the growing awareness of, and faith in, things scientific at the level of popular philosophy.[25] Businessmen and statesmen accepted the common popular theme that advances in science and technology were giving men a growing control over the natural environment and pleaded for a greater recognition that the methods of scientific enquiry could solve social and economic difficulties also. Thus Josiah Stamp, economist, ex-director of ICI, and chairman of the LMS Railway, pleaded for 'a *science* of social adjustment',[26] and Lyndall Urwick in the peroration to his address to the British Association in 1930 challenged his colleagues to accept that:

It is time for a fresh step forward. Let us use the intellectual conceptions which have given us the great material advances of the machine age, to resolve the new difficulties which that age has created. Let us say as a scientific organization – 'it is intellectually possible; it is in line with our tradition'.[27]

The doctrine of progress through the rational application of scientific principles thus aroused expectations of amelioration in face of evidence of unemployment and instability, strengthening the motive to apply new methods to industry. 'Scientific management' thus attempted, within the rationalization movement, to match the growing success of science in other fields.[28]

In this respect, it provided for some businessmen an ideology to replace the doctrine of competitive free enterprise, whose ethical foundations and claims to be a gospel of human freedom were being undermined by socialism, a rival doctrine which in some respects overlapped the ideology of rationalization. Competition was disliked by both socialists and rationalizers, and they both stressed not only scientific and rational, but also humane, values: 'the glamour of the perfect, unselfish mechanism hangs about the system of rationalization.'[29] The business classes were, of course, very much aware of the need to provide a political and economic alternative to socialism. It was their position that was endangered by depression and it behoved them to revalidate it by showing that those parts of the market system which were causing trouble could be excised by the reorganization of private capitalism. The three-way promise of the rationalizer that 'it is intellectually possible . . . it is materially profitable; it will save our economic system from disaster'[30] was not easy to ignore. Rationalization readily became a defensive reaction to the challenge to the existing structure of power and ownership in industry, which was posed with increasing urgency by the rapid growth of trade unionism and labour socialism.[31] It was, then, no accident that in the Mond–Turner talks which marked the post General Strike rapprochement between moderate employers and union leaders, the employers' side laid great stress on the potential social benefits of rationalization.[32]

There was of course an alternative reaction. The inherited faith of members of the business classes in the 'theology of the market' could be self-validating. It was not difficult to prescribe a remedy for the deficiencies of the interwar economic system which was consistent with acceptance of a small enterprise system depending predominantly on competitive market mechanisms of economic co-ordination. Blame could be laid on the trade unions, for example, for introducing undesirable monopolistic elements into wage determination, or for causing inefficiency through 'ca' canny'. It could be said that government intervention and the expanding public sector had caused a malfunctioning of a private enterprise system which, had it been left to itself, would have been perfectly healthy. Indeed the very growth of monopolistic combines at the expense of small business could be pictured not as the cure but as the cause of the problem, preventing readjustment of supply and demand by creating price inflexibility. Moreover, all of these things were said, and said frequently, by private businessmen. Yet the flaw in such diagnoses was that, given the political and social situation, the industrial costs of the action they implied were felt by many to be unacceptable. The Geddes 'axe' and the May Report, lock-outs, the forced reduction in miners' wages, the Trade Disputes Act, cuts in local rating for businesses: all these were tried as remedies in this tradition, yet when it came to the point few businessmen viewed with pleasure the prospect of a protracted series of labour confrontations akin to the General Strike.[33] By the same token no government could safely contemplate either cuts in public expenditure larger than those of 1931 or the creation of more widespread distress in already distressed areas. By contrast the replacement of the moral economy of the market by an alternative modified system of economic rationality (which yet preserved something of the privacy of enterprise and the principle of profit) could seem attractive. Conscious action to rationalize industry or to plan the economy, especially when this involved some increase in monopoly power, thus became the vogue in advanced business circles. Many of their goals – profit maximization, the growth of their firms, or merely entrepreneurial exhilaration and empire building – were compatible with and reinforced by the doctrines of rationalization. A programme of merger, inter-firm agreements and 'scientific' management (in short of 'rationalization') thus became the common currency not only of a metropolitan élite of intellectuals (as some of its critics were inclined to imply) but also of businessmen who liked to picture themselves as successful and hard-headed.

The critics were correct, however, in pointing to quite virulent opposition to rationalization, an opposition for which in many cases the justification is readily apparent. There was clearly a faddist fringe to the movement, 'distinguished [as one rationalizer admitted] rather by moral enthusiasm than by effective methods',[34] which its critics could characterize as 'cheap, superficial and popular'.[35] The National Confederation of Employers' Associations (an organization strongly influenced by the many smaller and medium-sized businesses) felt it necessary to warn the Conservative prime minister that criticisms of the industrial structure and of businessmen emanated from 'a movement which seeks to discredit entirely the existing system for the conduct of industry', and others, too, felt that rationalization came perilously near to socialism.[36] To this criticism the rationalizers replied in kind, remarking that their philosophy 'has been met with in many influential circles by obstinate and destructive prejudice'.[37] The fear that large-scale organization was not growing as fast as they had hoped led rationalizers to examine 'the human forces which make for irrational, illogical, and inefficient organization'.[38] Entrepreneurs were accused of deriving psychic income from operating a system which was inefficient, a system which did not maximize profits, or growth. So the debate raged at a vigorous level of invective and argument, stoked not only by differing evaluations of the economic efficiency of large firms, but by radically differing views about the whole future of the enterprise system. Rival creative images of that future, and not only cost schedules, were at the heart of this controversy, and this circumstance accounts in good measure for its virulence.

Economic systems are organized by different societies not only in response to an objective assessment of the relative costs of alternative methods of satisfying given wants, but also on ideal grounds – that is, according to whether a particular economic system will produce as well as satisfy wants which are considered socially desirable in themselves. These factors are potentially as important as technical factors in determining the direction of innovation in economic organization, and thus in inducing movements in the relative costs of market and firm. The ideologies and self-images of businessmen, which can be studied in movements of fashion and opinion such as the rationalization movement, can throw light on this process, since rationalizing opinions would clearly tend to influence the direction of organizational innovations towards management within large firms. They did so not only directly, through businessmen who espoused them enthusiastically, but more widely as those less convinced found rationalization being put on their agenda by bankers, politicians, workers or others who were led by the climate of opinion to ponder on the possibility of merger and rationalization as a solution to economic difficulties. The greater number of decisions to merge or otherwise reorganize were no doubt widely and variously based and fundamentally *ad hoc*, rather than purely motivated by rationalization ideology, but the effects of the latter were none the less visible. Ultimately, moreover, it would not be the relative debating skills of rationalizers and anti-rationalizers which determined the structure of industry, but rather the objective changes in the relative costs of firm and market which the movement succeeded in inducing. Only if the *ex ante* desire for a more 'rational' control by the firm could be transformed into higher *ex post* net profits, based on increased revenues or reduced costs in large firms, could it be anticipated that the market would in the long run make its hoped-for retreat and yield to the rational brain of the administrator. As Chandler has shown in the case of America, the mergers which created lastingly dominant corporations were those where the economies of scale and integration were guaranteed by the real economies of using the 'visible hand'.[39] Increasingly British managers felt, or were encouraged to feel, that they could achieve more by extending their own organizational control. It was in this that the major potential of the interwar rationalization movement lay, for it was able to induce investment in innovating techniques of intra-firm organization, and thus motivated the cheapening of management within the firm relative to transactions in the market.

We shall return to the question of the management factor by large-scale firms in Chapter 6, but there were clearly other, non-managerial, changes in the relative costs of markets and firms which rationalizers did much to publicize. In particular, competitive market forms of organization required firms to forgo some of the economies of scale which could be achieved by aggregation. There is some compelling evidence of the existence of plant economies of scale in a significant number of industries (see Chapter 8), and rationalizers naturally stressed the access to such economies which merger could provide by aggregating the demand schedules of two or more firms in imperfect markets. Technical economies of plant size were not the only significant ones. Contemporaries frequently referred to the marketing economies of merger which were often considered to be the most important economies immediately available,[40] and there was also important financial economies (see pp. 66–7). The view was also gaining ground that only large firms could afford the research necessary in modern science-based industry:

> The small firms find it difficult . . . to pay for research laboratories [reported a committee of the Privy Council] . . . we believe that some form of combination . . . may be found to be essential if the smaller undertakings of this country are to compete effectively with the great trusts and combines of Germany and America.[41]

The experience of foreign countries, where industrialists had reaped (or were supposed to have reaped) the benefits of scale economies, was frequently held out by rationalizers as exemplary; and direct competition from German and American combines, which had already been a source of concern before the war, reinforced this message in the minds of many wartime and postwar merging companies. The house journal of Sperlings, the merger promoters, typifies this mood:

What has been drilled into us in Great Britain as the result of the general canvassing of our industrial position and prospects in the light of the war, is that there is far too little of 'Big Business' amongst us. While Germany and the United States have been developing huge industrial consolidations, with ample resources, specialized production, collective agencies for sale and distribution, and with a full equipment for scientific research, we in Great Britain have been trying to get along with a multitude of small, rather old-fashioned, manufacturing units, each maintaining its own selling and marketing organizations, not at all alive to science, stubbornly individualistic both in their products and in their attitude towards other firms in the same industry, conscious that the smallness of their installations made for inefficiency and waste and yet debarred from scrapping and rebuilding them on modern lines by the almost prohibitive cost. It is now being generally recognized that if we are to hold our own in future we must revolutionize our scale of doing things; in trade after trade.[42]

There was, throughout the period, a flood of literature praising German rationalization and American mass production, often contrasting Britain's industrial structure and performance unfavourably.[43] The evidence of merger abroad leading to economic expansion and successful competition with English firms in world markets weakened lingering memories of the great nineteenth-century development of English trade under small-scale competitive conditions. The conventional wisdom now suggested that, though in the past competition had yielded benefits for British industry, 'it is also true that a great increase [of production] took place in the USA and Germany under a condition of restricted competition and trade organization'.[44] Repeatedly the public rationale of mergers was the need to catch up with and to 'face on equal terms' foreign competing firms of larger scale.[45] As Marshall remarked, there had 'appeared a firm resolve to reconsider British methods in relation to the problem of the new age; and to the solutions of those problems which were being worked out in America, Germany and other countries'.[46] As a result of these industrial tendencies, Marshall went on to argue, 'the supersession of small businesses by large in many industries is inevitable'.[47]

This tendency was furthered by the more direct intrusion of

foreign influences on the British business scene. A remarkable, and significant, factor in many of the mergers of this period was the direct and indirect influence of persons or companies with American or German backgrounds. The recognized expert in large-scale organization in Britain before the First World War, O. Philippi of J. & P. Coats, was a German, and in the later rationalization movement leading industrialists such as Sir Hugo Hirst of GEC, the two Lords Melchett of ICI, and the Renolds of the Renold & Coventry Chain Company, were all of German origin or parentage and still strongly influenced by continental models.[48] Large combines abroad were also aware that they had a technical lead over their British competitors in large-scale organization and mass production, especially in the new industries. Some of the more enterprising among them, seeing their competitive advantage, sought to exploit it directly by entering the British market and establishing subsidiaries in order to expand their profits in this country. In some industries where they were unsuccessful they none the less frequently spurred their British competitors into consolidating into larger units themselves. Already before the First World War the Imperial Tobacco Company had been formed in such a defensive move against the invasion of the American Tobacco Company,[49] and such examples soon multiplied. It was an attempt by the German chemical giant I. G. Farben to extend its control by acquiring the British Dyestuffs Corporation which precipitated the company's eventual merger with three other British companies to form Imperial Chemical Industries, in imitation of the German combine.[50] American companies were generally more successful and thus contributed more directly to the rationalization movement both by acquiring British companies (which they then merged and expanded) and also by providing bank finance for rationalization.[51] It was the American General Electric Company, for example, which acquired and merged four electrical manufacturers to form Associated Electrical Industries; and General Motors of the US also acquired Vauxhall Motors and within a short time joined Ford as a dominant American firm in the British motor industry. Such intrusions from abroad, though frequently resented,[52] were none the less powerful reminders to British industrialists of the need to adopt the best practice scale and organization if they were to retain their independence in a period of severe international competition and relatively free movements of capital from America.

The tenor of business opinion had, then, changed greatly since before the First World War, both because of the enthusiastic espousal of the doctrines of rationalization and because of more direct pressure from foreign companies which had espoused them earlier. Of course, few industrialists thought that the creed of rationalization could provide a complete answer to the economic problems of the era, but influential businessmen were increasingly coming to accept that larger-scale enterprise could considerably strengthen the international position and the domestic prosperity of British industries. We will later suggest that the impact of this on the waves of merger activity and the rapid increase in industrial concentration in the decade or so after the First World War provide direct evidence of the significance of these movements of opinion (see Chapter 7). Yet already, in anticipation of such statistical confirmation, we can see from more circumstantial evidence that the rationalization movement was likely to exercise a strong influence on the managerial strategies of a significant number of important companies. In a catalogue of contributors to the contemporary debates on rationalization (such as has appeared in the notes to this chapter) appear some of the more prominent businessmen of the day. Sir Alfred Mond was involved in the Amalgamated Anthracite and International Nickel mergers; Sir Harry McGowan had presided over the creation of the Nobel combine and was instrumental in merging Joseph Lucas with its major competitors; together, the two men were the architects of ICI. Stamp, Barley and Mitchell were also senior managers in ICI and engaged in merging companies in the chemicals and metals industries. Lyndall Urwick was the founder of a pioneering and successful management consultancy which established itself as a leader in the field of advice on large-scale organization. Sir Mark Webster Jenkinson, the accountant, Reginald McKenna of the Midland Bank, and Dudley Docker, an ex-president of the Federation of British Industries, gave support to rationalization in engineering, shipbuilding, steel, and chemical manufacture, and they were particularly influential in the mergers with which Vickers were connected. Thus even the opponents of rationalization were constrained to admit that 'the blessed word, with its pseudo-suggestion of the scientific, has already hypnotized quite a number of important people'.[53] The support of 'important people' was in no way fortuitous, for the goal which the rationalizers had set before themselves was no ordinary one: the task was that of revitalizing the capitalist system of enterprise in Britain in what seemed to be its darkest hour.

4

Government: trustbuster
or promoter?

The function of the state is not to preserve
the competitive system.
J. H. JONES, *Social Economics*
(1920), p. 192.

ഌ

If the rationalizers were to succeed in persuading their fellow
businessmen to adopt their methods on a large scale, they would also
require the confidence of public opinion and of the governments of
the day. Yet it was far from clear that such confidence would
automatically be forthcoming, for rationalization could often present
its less attractive public face: that of monopolistic exploitation of the
consumer. Businessmen readily admitted that monopolization was
an important aim of the rationalization movement, and, as the
Economist remarked, 'the enhancement of profits by the elimination
of competition'[1] was often uppermost in their minds in planning
mergers. There was a justifiable public suspicion that manufacturers
aimed primarily to raise prices or reduce wages rather than to
achieve real economies in production. The peak of public disquiet
had already been reached in the 'Soap Trust' scandal of 1906, a
cause célèbre of the prewar amalgamation movement. William Lever,
together with other leading soap makers, had planned a merger
which would give the combined undertaking a near-monopoly of the
British market. Hearing of this, the *Daily Mirror* and the *Daily Mail*
ran a virulent campaign of criticism of the trust proposals,
suggesting *inter alia* that the trust would produce inferior products at
higher prices and provide less employment whilst doing so. The
public outcry and resultant bad will towards Levers and the other
companies immediately reduced the sales of their products and the
proposals for merger had to be hastily abandoned. Trial by press
thus successfully scuppered this early attempt at monopoly.[2]

It was, however, still possible for the soap firms to merge in a less spectacular fashion, and Lever himself quietly acquired many of his competitors on a piecemeal basis in the two decades following the initial scandal. The earlier debâcle had, however, pointed to the dangers which manufacturers faced when building up a monopoly position, for which the term 'rationalization' could be merely a politic circumlocution. Thus if rationalizers hoped to induce additional large-scale merger activity much would depend on the willingness of the press – and more crucially of the government – to permit businessmen the freedom in these matters to which they felt entitled. There was no shortage of precedents for government intervention to protect the public against monopolies. There was, for example, a long history of government regulation of the railways and similar 'natural monopolies'; and indeed, such regulation had often been requested by business groups themselves.[3] Nor was there a shortage of foreign models on which the government might base its policy. The Sherman Antitrust Act of 1890 in the United States, for example, had been strengthened to include powers to control mergers by the Clayton Act of 1914; and in Germany in 1923 the government had instituted a system of public supervision of monopolies and cartels.

In Britain, however, it was generally the case, at least until after the Second World War, that monopolistic schemes could proceed with little interference from the law. The common law had progressively abandoned its stance against 'restraints of trade' and many judges no doubt shared Lord Chancellor Haldane's view that competition could be undesirable since it 'may, if it is not controlled, drive manufacturers out of business, or lower wages and so cause labour disturbance'.[4] Thus monopolistic practices were freely tolerated and amalgamations could in general proceed without legal intervention. On one occasion, it is true, the aged Mr Justice Eve (a gentleman whose judicial acrimony appears to have descended impartially on all financial bureaucracies)[5] attempted to strike down a merger agreement on the grounds that it was 'a most villainous and mischievous form of finance' which was 'against the public' because it would raise prices.[6] However, though this populist stance had a certain attraction, he was so obviously misguided and ill-tempered in his judicial conclusions that they were reversed after only two days by the Court of Appeal:

the court was not concerned to see how the alterations would affect persons outside the company, and, so long as combination was not illegal, it was not for the court to enquire whether the interest of the purchasers would be injuriously affected.[7]

Any serious control of monopolies and mergers between the wars could not, then, depend on the common law; it would require the statutory creation of new powers. The nearest approach to such a government initiative came with the various committees on trusts which deliberated between 1918 and 1921. The first was the Committee on Trusts appointed early in 1918, by the Ministry of Reconstruction, to review the problem of trusts after the war. It noted the expansion of the power of combines both before and during the war, but recommended control by publicity only, a limited prescription which was also endorsed by the Committee on Commercial and Industrial Policy.[8] However, both committees also stressed the benefits of the activities of combinations and were impressed by the need for large-scale organization to meet German and American competition. They also praised the co-operation among manufacturers, for the purposes of standardization and production planning, which had been encouraged by the Ministry of Munitions in the war. This ambivalent approach to mergers and monopolistic arrangements, recognizing the existence of social benefits as well as social costs, was to be present in later discussions of monopoly policy, and, of course, remains today as the central dilemma of antitrust policy.

During the war a system of government price restriction and control of industry had grown up, as a necessary concession to labour in return for their efforts to transform the economy to a war footing. By 1918, however, there was a general feeling in govern-ment circles that such controls should be abandoned, typified by Churchill's statement, four days before the armistice that:

> Our only object is to liberate the forces of industrial enterprise, to release the controls which have been found galling, to divest ourselves of responsibilites which the state has only accepted in this perilous emergency, and from which, in the overwhelming majority of cases, it had far better keep itself clear.[9]

Although the price controls were a limited safeguard against feared public criticisms of profiteering and monopoly, then, most of them

were abandoned between 1919 and 1921.[10] However, in a new
initiative, the Profiteering Act of August 1919 made the earning of 'a
profit which is, in view of all the circumstances, unreasonable' a
punishable offence. The Standing Committee on Trusts, which was
set up to administer the new controls,[11] began its meetings in the
optimistic belief that it was the harbinger of wider legislation. Its
chairman, Charles McCurdy (formerly Food Controller, and a
Coalitionist Liberal MP), reminded its members at their first
meeting in October 1919 that 'we are asked to set up machinery for
the purposes of starting a general bureau of information on the
subject, and . . . the government have already started with
legislation on these lines which will be made permanent in the
Autumn'.[12]

Fifty-seven detailed reports on trusts and prices were to be
published in the next two years, but McCurdy's hope of permanency
was to prove illusory. As Beveridge judged,[13] the Act was essentially
a window-dressing device, and lasted only as long as it was useful in
that capacity, becoming a pawn in a political strategy which saw no
permanent place for government intervention in industry. With men
like Ernest Bevin, J. A. Hobson and Sidney Webb as members, it
served to placate the left, but the quality of the membership was a
guarantee of nothing more than the provision of information of a
usable kind. The Committee was maintained essentially as a safety
valve and, given its meagre powers, could provide no coherently
articulated antitrust policy. In the Lever Brothers case, for example,
it had no powers to reverse the process by which William Lever had
built up his dominant position in the soap industry by acquiring
competitors. The Committee pronounced not on the merits or
otherwise of this process of acquisition but on the demerits of the
subsequent price increases. With its initially small powers fast
ebbing away, it soon lost all credibility and even lacked the power
to require the production of information which it considered
relevant. Thus companies involved in mergers and rationalization
could, and did, effectively ignore the Committee with impunity.[14]

The history of the Committee on Trusts, though in itself an
abrupt historical *cul-de-sac*, is worth recounting because it does help
us to understand the basic political determinants of the peculiarly
retarded development of monopoly policy in Britain. The political
origin of control under the Profiteering Act had been a desire to

avoid the social unrest which would follow rapidly rising prices.[15] In April 1920 the Cabinet went on to consider a Trade Monopolies Bill and plans for extending and strengthening government powers in that field. Though the Bill was in fact deferred to a later session (and in the event never became law) the Cabinet debate on the subject is illuminating. It centred round two conflicting political pressures: on the one hand there was 'the widespread expectation of the public that the evils of profiteering would be vigourously [sic] handled' and, on the other, 'the effect of the newly introduced Budget on the business interests represented in the House of Commons and their attitude . . . generally, to any undue interference with trade'.[16] The balance of these considerations was calculated to favour acquiescence in labour demands for control of profiteering, for, as they had agreed at a previous meeting, they 'could not afford to take risks with labour. If we did, we should at once create an enemy within our own borders and one which would be better provided with dangerous weapons than Germany.'[17] By early 1921, however, food prices had been falling for some months and the political initiative was shifting away from the interventionist Liberal Coalitionists and their Conservative allies to *laissez-faire* and 'anti-waste' elements. The Profiteering Act was allowed to lapse in May 1921. The protests of the Standing Committee on Trusts[18] and subsequent pleas for the machinery to be resurrected[19] fell on the deaf ears of the ministers at the Board of Trade.[20] The Act had been part of the mechanism by which wartime controls were abandoned by a government which had no taste for intervention in the private sector except where decontrol would menace social stability. By 1921 many Conservatives were taking the view that 'propaganda' against profiteering was doing private enterprise more harm than good.[21] Thus, even if the government had itself had the will, it was increasingly undesirable politically to adopt an interventionist line in these relatively new areas of state activity.

The position achieved in 1921 was preserved intact throughout the interwar period.[22] Although the possibility of antitrust laws was considered, the Balfour Committee, which was appointed, *inter alia*, to enquire into 'the present extent of large-scale production, its possibilities and limitations',[23] concluded that 'the case for immediate legislation for the restraint of such abuses as may result from combinations cannot be said to be an urgent one', and pointed to the 'danger that a Bill, even if carefully constructed and safeguarded in its scope, might easily be so changed in Committee as to become . . . a formidable impediment to industrial development'.[24]

This unflattering appraisal of the skills of parliamentary committees in devising suitable legislation to protect the public against the potential dangers of monopoly was placidly received by a predominantly *laissez-faire* parliament, which acquiesced in this view of its own limitations. Throughout the interwar decades the business lobby, which had been prominent in the Cabinet's calculations on antitrust policy in 1920, remained important.[25] The Federation of British Industries maintained close links with between seventy and eighty MPs, seeking to neutralize criticism in the House of member firms such as J. & P. Coats which occupied monopolistic positions.[26] Industrialists such as Sir Harry McGowan of ICI regularly addressed the 1922 Committee of Conservative backbenchers on the virtues of large-scale enterprise, and the tradition of businessmen serving on a Board of Trade advisory committee was firmly established and welcomed by the Cabinet.[27]

In such an atmosphere of 'businessmen's government', *laissez-faire* and capitalism were naturally accepted as the ideal form of economic organization. The contemporary political debate on capitalism versus socialism generated myths and dogmas strengthening the uncritical adherence of the right to a belief in unfettered private enterprise. It was sufficient to express a bland faith in the virtues of the private enterprise system without enquiring too closely whether the competitive conditions necessary for the successful operation of such a system were present. Since socialists and trade unionists had been among the earlier advocates of antitrust and were now pressing for increased government intervention in the market economy, their opponents in government were unlikely to find these policies very palatable, and even a moderate suggestion that the government should sponsor a council to publicize monopolistic pricing could be characterized as a step on the 'slippery slope of socialism'.[28] As a contemporary regretfully recorded, the reaction 'has gone beyond all reasonable bounds, and inhibits the majority of businessmen from exercising any reasonable, intellectual judgement in matters where the action of a government department is concerned'.[29] With this convenient configuration of opinion, monopolistic firms could continue to rely on the spectre of state 'interference' with their monopoly position as a remedy which in the long run 'might be worse than the disease'[30] not only for them but for all businessmen.

No other pressure group with an interest in the control of monopoly or mergers really developed in the interwar years sufficiently to have an impact on policy. There was no well-organized consumers' movement, and both the co-operative movement and the Labour Party failed to gain acceptance for their proposals for the investigation of monopolies.[31] The press, though sometimes admitting the logic of a system of public control of monopoly,[32] emphasized also the value of rationalization and the need for a restructuring of industry. Mergers were generally welcomed as a positive sign of industrial vigour, and only in the later 1930s were doubts stirred, as opinion began to turn against schemes of rationalization which showed no regard for the public interest.[33] The general acceptance of the business viewpoint on antitrust was probably strengthened by the high level of unemployment and the declining prices of the time, as official and public opinion reacted with sympathy to the actions of producers trying to improve their lot in admittedly difficult times. 'Sympathies are more with the producer now', commented one economist, 'as with the consumer [formerly]'.[34] Economists, in general, were uneasy about applying their microeconomic work to real economic situations, and, whilst they accepted the economic logic of control, they generally viewed American-style antitrust legislation as ill-founded and ineffective.[35] 'Among the intellectual influences on contemporary policy', Robbins sadly noted in 1939, 'there are probably few which have been so potent as belief in the inevitability of monopoly',[36] and many politicians also believed, in the words of Philip Snowden, that 'trusts . . . are inevitable. They will continue, whatever obstacles we attempt to put in their path.'[37]

There was, then, for practical purposes, virtually complete acquiescence from government and press in the unfettered movement towards higher industrial concentration. The rationalizing or monopolizing businessman was free to pursue his ends even if the benefits were attained at the cost of the consuming public, and no rationalizer felt it necessary to offer safeguards to the public interest.[38] Furthermore, increasing industrial difficulties, and particularly the high and increasing level of unemployment, created a disposition in both business and government to view the rationalization movement with favour. It was but a short step from this to direct pressure on the government to intervene more positively to promote industrial change both by legislation and by providing finance for mergers and rationalization. There were precedents for such direct action in the government promotion of mergers in the dyestuffs industry during the war,[39] but this policy was implicitly based on the premise that government knew the appropriate structure of industrial firms better than private capitalists and businessmen themselves. Such a doctrine was, of course, a difficult one for the governments we have described, with their essentially *laissez-faire* outlook, to accept. Some government departments, which were already involved directly with industries from which they purchased supplies, did sometimes encourage rationalization by a policy of concentrating orders on a limited number of efficient firms, but such policies were not general.[40]

Pressure for the government to intervene in areas where it had no such direct interest soon mounted. Some of the younger Conservative MPs, and the government's own economic advisers, for example, pressed the view that there was scope for greater state intervention to change the structure of the more traditional industries.[41] At least one senior Conservative economic minister felt not only that more mergers and rationalization were needed, but also that industrial management was incapable, by itself, of solving the problems which they posed,[42] a view which was shared by some senior industrial managers with government contacts, who doubted the capacity of their colleagues in other firms.[43] Such criticisms could not, however, be publicly voiced by senior ministers for fear of alienating an important section of the Conservative Party's political support.[44] Instead the government tended to look hopefully to industrialists for evidence that they were hatching appropriate schemes, and industrialists glowingly obliged by pointing to their proven zeal for merger and co-operative schemes.[45]

Mergers were thus in general welcomed by government ministers, who (in the words of the President of the Board of Trade) saw 'before themselves the modest task of clearing away difficulties and of giving the necessary support and shelter to private enterprise to cope with its problems on sound principles'.[46] The only real concession to the rationalization lobby was to be not the wholesale promotion of merger but the removal of minor disincentives. In the 1927 budget the payment of stamp duties in cases where a new company was formed to merge two or more existing companies was remitted, a concession which was generally considered to accord with common sense and equity.[47] This relatively modest approach was supported by industrialists, many of whom were ardent rationalizers but felt that bankers rather than the government were the appropriate agency to bring pressure to bear on recalcitrant firms which would benefit from merger.[48] They often discussed their own larger mergers with ministers, both informally and through official channels,[49] but many businessmen feared accepting state money 'because they realized that government capital would be bound sooner or later to lead to government control'.[50] Even when less timid (or more impecunious) businessmen did make direct application to the government for financial assistance for schemes of rationalization, they were invariably refused, on orthodox Treasury grounds.[51]

However, the political pressure for a more forward policy on rationalization was leading somewhere, even if only in an indirect way. Montagu Norman at the Bank of England viewed it with increasing alarm and was particularly anxious to head off any attempt to renew the Trade Facilities Act for the purpose of providing government support for mergers.[52] He hastened to assure the government that adequate finance would be available privately for worthwhile amalgamation schemes in the basic industries, and began talks with the banks to canvass this object. The assurances fell on willing ears, and the government was grateful to Norman for taking the burden of forcing mergers on recalcitrant industrialists in the steel and cotton industries out of the government's hands and putting it into the hands of the banks. Churchill, then Chancellor, used Norman's assurances in his 1929 budget speech to nip criticism in the bud,[53] and his Labour successors, Snowden and Thomas, were able to develop this approach when Norman announced the formation, by a consortium of banks with Bank of England backing, of the Bankers' Industrial Development Company (see pp. 64–5).

The Labour government of 1929 to 1931 did not, of course, entirely share the Conservatives' ideological aversion to the belief that government decisions on industrial matters could be superior to private ones, yet Labour ministers, many of them with deeply conservative instincts on economic matters, went little further than their predecessors. Many Labour leaders, and their advisers, sympathized with the broader views of the rationalization movement,[54] but they had doubts about its implications for

monopoly power and industrial unemployment. Successful rationalization could, perhaps, through technical and organizational innovation, release economic resources – capital, labour, management
– from redundant uses and deploy them to new, higher productivity
uses. The release of labour was, however, a mixed blessing for a
government beset by social distress and cries for political relief from
near-derelict communities which already had vast labour surpluses.
Although some rationalizers argued that cost reductions achieved by
merger could increase aggregate demand (given a competitive pricing
response, income effects, and high price elasticities of demand),
most economists had grave doubts about the ability of mergers
through rationalization to solve the fundamental problem of mass
unemployment.[55] Thus the radical suggestion that the Board of
Trade should take over BIDC's functions and play a more effective
role in merger promotion was rejected.[56] Yet there was still some
pressure on the government to consider a more active role in
industrial reorganization, and to meet this Sir Horace Wilson, acting
as Chief Industrial Adviser, was charged with monitoring the
progress of rationalization in various industries. His brief was to
stimulate discussions between industrialists in which he was to
attempt, by the use of moral suasion, to induce them to merge.[57]
However, without the financial powers which gave the later
Industrial Reorganization Corporation its leverage, his initiatives
came to little; and, given the government's lack of a parliamentary
majority, it was obvious, as the *Economist* pointed out, that hints of
compulsory amalgamation if voluntarism failed were mere empty
threats.[58]

The fall of the Labour government in 1931, and the world
economic crisis of that year, brought the adoption of the 'great
policy' of protection in 1932. Tariffs were important for the
Conservatives in the National government in their effect on the
psychology of interventionism, for, through the Import Duties
Advisory Committee, more positive government pressure on industry was legitimized. In the steel industry, in particular, the IDAC
was able, through moral suasion and the threat of reducing the level
of tariff protection, to encourage restrictive agreements and mergers.
However, the approach remained a cautious one and the more
adventurous schemes of reorganization were shelved as the Committee trod the new ground of government usurpation of entrepreneurial decision-making powers warily.[59] The IDAC played a part in

'breaking down individualism and educating businessmen in many industries to work together',[60] but most of its ideas for encouraging the restructuring of industry do not appear to have been accepted. In the Lancashire cotton velvet industry, for example, the IDAC, despite its threat of withdrawal of duty, was no more successful in persuading industrialists to agree to mergers than Sir Horace Wilson had been in 1931.[61]

Though the National government maintained the policy of talks with industrialists which had been initiated by its Labour predecessors[62] and extended this policy through the IDAC, it continued to eschew undue dictation to private enterprise. Walter Runciman, the new President of the Board of Trade, and Leslie Hore-Belisha, his parliamentary secretary, were not enthusiasts for government intervention, and Runciman was sincere when he told the British Bankers' Association in 1934 that he would resist the pressure on him for more intervention, adding that:

> We may easily exaggerate the importance of mere size, and there are not wanting signs that in some quarters the limits to size have already been reached. . . . The truth is that in these days we have rather underestimated the value of competition. . . . It is in the preservation of competition . . . that we can . . . preserve the prosperity of our great commercial and industrial organizations.[63]

The views of interventionist businessmen like Harold Macmillan may have harmonized with the collectivist streak in Tory philosophy,[64] but their influence on government policy between the wars was minimal.

Essentially, then, the position of interwar governments was to eschew not only the role of trustbuster but also that of trust promoter.[65] Both of these policies are, we have argued, explicable in terms of the ideology and motivations of the governments of the day. They were for the most part more certain of their commitment to a capitalist system of enterprise, privately owned and as far as possible free of state intervention, than to the ideal of competition or the goal of planning through large-scale enterprise. When Stanley Baldwin told his Bewdley constituents at Worcester in 1929 that 'no one rejoices more than I do to see these industrial problems taken directly out of the hands of politicians, who have never been fit to handle them',[66] it was not mere political rhetoric but a genuine statement of his personal preference, and (making an allowance for the false modesty appropriate to such gatherings) an important strain of Conservative thinking. Many of his ministers shared this view and many of their supporters felt that it best served the interests of private capital. In this atmosphere, the ideal of *laissez-faire* – a *laissez-faire* that meant freedom from enforced merger as well as freedom from enforced competition – was still a powerful factor. If ministers were being forced by circumstances into a more forward interventionist policy in some spheres, many of them remained determined to limit it, and, in the case of the promotion of mergers and large-scale enterprises in manufacturing industry, they were largely successful.

Now these conclusions may appear to conflict with the conventional interpretation of the period as one of willing, extensive and increasing government intervention in the economy. Partly this interpretation arose because contemporaries were extremely sensitive to the extension of the powers of the state, and in many spheres the state was playing a larger role than it had before the war. It was thus a short but plausible step for free marketeers who disliked monopoly to assert that it arose because of political meddling rather than from tendencies inherent in the competitive system itself.[67] Even moderate organs of opinion such as the *Economist*, which recognized the undesirability of the extreme *laissez-faire* position in the conditions of modern industry, became convinced by the late 1930s that in many fields the government had gone too far.[68] In later years, then, it was natural for the government itself to be branded as the cause of the ills of increased industrial concentration. Some later antitrust campaigners believed, quite incorrectly, that the government had been a pliant tool in the hands of manufacturers seeking legislative sanctions for mergers.[69] This approach was also strengthened by the interpretive contribution of Marxist historians, who, wishing to establish the mutual support of private capital and the bourgeois state, have presented increased concentration as 'almost invariably fostered by a benevolent government'.[70]

The purpose of this chapter is not to deny the correctness of these views on government action over much of the economy. Had we been concerned with policy towards the electricity industry, the railways, oil supplies, mining or agriculture, our conclusions might well have coincided, for there was an increasing commitment of government finance and legislative support to these industries, whose special economic characteristics or strategic importance dictated government involvement.[71] In the case of manufacturing industry, however, it was sometimes admitted by even the most ardent free marketeers that they had little evidence of direct government involvement;[72] and the *Economist*, while criticizing proposals for legislative support of monopolistic cartels, even argued that stronger measures to promote large firms in manufacturing by compulsory amalgamation were required.[73] Thus, while it is true that the governments of the day, and a large section of public opinion, gave their general approval to the contemporary trend towards merger and large-scale enterprise, actual policy in this sphere was remarkably non-committal throughout the period.[74] One further reason why governments were happy to maintain this stance was that, even without the stimulus of government involvement, there was a substantial increase in merger activity and industrial concentration in these years (see Chapter 7). This movement resulted from the decisions of private and corporate entrepreneurs to expand, decisions taken principally in response to the signals of the market and the quest for private profit, rather than at government behest. Governments in general would give their encouragement and their blessing to these decisions (and this was welcomed by businessmen), but they would give little else.[75] In particular, they made it clear that the financial and managerial resources which the new larger scale enterprises required had to come from private financial sources and from the businessmen themselves. Ministers often opened their hearts and praised mergers, but the Treasury purse was firmly closed.

5

Capitalist ownership and the stock market

The divorce between responsibility and ownership worked out by the
growth and development of Joint Stock Companies . . . provide[s]
one of the clues to the future. Private enterprise has been
trying . . . to solve for itself the essential problem
. . . [of] how to establish an efficient system of
production in which management and
responsibility are in different hands
from those which provide the
capital, run the risk, and
reap the profit.
Liberal Industrial Inquiry, *Britain's
Industrial Future* (1928), p. 100.

ᏒᏕᏒ

In the nineteenth century the extent of the personal wealth and
credit of the owning family or partners usually established an upper
limit to the size of a firm. However, this constraint did not rule out
large firms, for the power of compound interest in building up a
single family's fortune over the years was considerable. Family firms
which had started business with assets worth only a few hundred
pounds could, over two generations or so of successful business,
become millionaire firms; and the capacity of such firms to borrow
funds for further expansion also expanded proportionately to their
assets. Those few owners who became millionaires several times over
– like the old established brewing families or the Wills family in the
tobacco industry – were able to finance from their own resources
companies which were among the largest in existence at the turn of
the century. However, the number of families amassing such large
fortunes was inevitably limited,[1] and small and medium-sized
enterprises remained more typical of manufacturing industry as a
whole. These groups of wealthy, and not-so-wealthy, capitalist
owner-entrepreneurs together held beneficial ownership of a large
proportion of the national capital stock. Some wealthy families, it is
true, had liquidated some of their interests and spread the ownership

of their firms more widely through the medium of a public flotation on the stock exchanges, but the majority of British manufacturing firms were still typically owned and controlled by single families or by partnerships. It is, then, hardly surprising that in 1911 the wealthiest 10 per cent of the adult population owned as much as 92 per cent of the total personal wealth in England and Wales.[2]

The further growth of large-scale enterprise, which the rationalizers were urging, would clearly require a modification of this regime of private capitalist ownership, since larger firms would in general imply the creation of industrial units, the ownership of which would effectively be beyond the financial resources of any single family. There were a number of possible ways of raising the additional finance. One of these was the recruitment of capital with legislative support from the state. This source had been used extensively by public utility enterprises, and one contemporary estimate suggested that by 1928 two-thirds of the capital required for large-scale undertakings in the economy as a whole had been raised with state assistance of various kinds.[3] In manufacturing industry, however, as we have seen, there was a firm political determination that the finance should come from private sources. Another option open to businessmen was the ploughback of internally generated profits into firms, thus enabling them to grow in the traditional manner of the family firm; the owners would thus be able to finance their own firms throughout if growth could be spread over an appropriately long period. There were many large firms between the wars which were able to rely principally on this option, including sizable old established family firms such as Pilkington in the glass industry, and new, rapidly expanding enterprises such as that of William Morris in the motor car industry. Morris, who began as the owner of little more than a bicycle shop, was able to expand on the secure financial basis of very high levels of profits (from his innovation of mass production in the car industry at Cowley) and he retained personal ownership and control, until in 1935 he floated Morris Motors ordinary shares on the London stock exchange. He had earlier refused a merger with both Austin and Vauxhall because his large private fortune would have been insufficient to gain full control of their capital, but even without such mergers, he gained a leading position in the British car industry, and was able to achieve many of the benefits of large-scale production to which the rationalization movement had drawn attention.[4]

Yet this pattern of growth could hardly have been widely adopted, for in other industries levels of profits and the capacity for internal growth were rarely as high as in the motor-car industry. Even if it had been possible in economic terms, the political consequences of the further concentration of an (already highly unequal) distribution of wealth in the hands of fewer owners would hardly have been attractive. Yet higher concentration in industry could not have been attained under a regime of direct capitalist ownership without such a shift towards still greater inequality in the ownership of manufacturing wealth. The way out of the dilemma posed by such financial and political constraints was provided by the further development of the stock market both as a provider of new funds and as a market in titles to existing industrial assets. Industrialists were able, through the stock market, to recruit capital in large amounts and from many sources. Provided that the prospects of large-scale enterprise were sufficiently attractive to call forth such investment, the capital resources of a number of moderately wealthy individuals could in principle, through the medium of the stock market, be aggregated to provide enough finance for the largest of firms. It was on this pattern, rather than in the nineteenth-century mould, that the financing of large enterprise was to be achieved.

This tendency was, of course, already exemplified in the quoted manufacturing companies of the late nineteenth century, but it was only from the 1920s that the consequences came to be widely remarked.[5] One widely quoted survey of a sample of the shareholdings in large companies in the interwar period, for example, showed that the average holding of capital was only £301.[6] There were still, of course, many quoted companies with less dispersed ownership, and some in which the original founding families held substantial shareholdings and were still able to secure representation on the board and effective managerial control. The transition to a more modern pattern was thus a gradual one, but many quoted companies soon had boards of directors who no longer held their positions by virtue of being the largest shareholders.[7] This trend has continued, and many of the largest firms of today – firms like ICI and Unilever with market capitalizations of over £1000 million – would effectively be beyond the personal wealth of any single individual.[8] The dispersion of ownership among many shareholders has thus become not merely a convenience but even a necessary condition of their existence.

This change has sometimes been dubbed the 'democratization of ownership', but it was not in fact accompanied by a very significant shift in the overall social distribution of property ownership. In 1960, for example, the wealthiest 10 per cent of adults still held 83 per cent of the personal wealth in England and Wales, and the vast majority of families still had no share in the ownership of industrial companies.[9] What had happened over the period since 1911 was not that a significantly larger proportion of families had become large shareholders, but rather that the minority of wealthy families no longer held their wealth in single companies in which they were also directors, choosing instead to spread their wealth over a wider range of assets. It is the divorce of ownership and control rather than the democratization of wealth, that has characterized the twentieth-century development of capitalist enterprise. Capitalists have changed their own patterns of asset holding, and the distinction between the *rentier* investors who provide capital and the directors and managers who organize production has in the process become more clearly articulated; but the general distribution of wealth in the community has remained remarkably stable.[10]

The motives which have led wealth holders to exchange a position of owning and controlling moderately sized enterprises for one of merely owning a diversified portfolio of shares in quoted companies[11] are many and varied. What seems to have happened in the case of the majority of family firms in manufacturing industry is that the family owners have at some stage taken the decision to sell out to an already quoted company, or, alternatively, to make a direct flotation of their company, possibly together with others, on the new issue market. The proceeds of these transactions have then typically been reinvested in a range of stock exchange and other securities, diversified over a number of industrial and commercial fields. We have already seen that the partial liquidation of family interests through company flotations became increasingly popular from the late nineteenth century onwards.[12] One possible explanation of this is that death duties, introduced in 1894, made it increasingly difficult to pass on total financial control of the family firm from one generation to another. However, estate duties were notoriously easy to avoid, and the Colwyn Committee, which considered the evidence, concluded that there were very few estates which did not have sufficient non-business assets to cover the cost of death duties incurred.[13] In cases where a business was sold on the death of the owner, then, this was more likely to be because of the wish of the family to diversify their holdings, or possibly to secure management succession, than because of inheritance problems.[14] Moreover, it is also clear that the vast majority of businesses which passed from the private to the publicly quoted sector did so not as a result of the death of the owner but rather as his explicit, considered and conscious choice. Whether we are thinking of inherited family firms or of relatively new enterprises (such as had been built up by Morris), owners voluntarily supplied a large flow of business assets to the expanding quoted sector, and death duties played little part in their motivation.

They were led to do so, we may safely conclude, because the private advantages to themselves of the new larger companies which could be created through the medium of the stock exchange were high. The gains in efficiency, to which the rationalization movement was drawing attention, were potentially large, and, in so far as these could be captured as returns to capital, they were attractive to capitalists. The returns from economies of scale and monopoly powers would accrue to wealth owners only if they were prepared to consolidate their assets into larger units through the medium of efficient quoted companies, and this in itself frequently required a divorce of ownership and control. But there were also special considerations which enhanced the private profitability of switching from direct ownership to portfolio investments. Partly this was a question of tax avoidance. Higher rate tax-payers – and most owners of family firms in manufacturing industry would be in the supertax bracket – generally preferred capital gains to income, since in Britain until 1965 most capital gains were free of tax. If they were able to capitalize the future income of their business, by selling out, the controlling family could thus frequently reduce their tax liability. The transaction could be profitable also to the new owners since, if they were paying a lower rate of tax, the effective rate of return on the future income flow would be higher: thus the transaction could be advantageous in these cases to both buyer and seller.[15]

A further advantage for family owners in selling out arose from the volatile conditions of the contemporary stock market. Keynes's unflattering comparison of the stock market to the casino[16] had its justification in the erratic speculative movements of share prices. The increased marketability of shares, coupled with serious informational imperfections in the capital market, laid the way clearly open for speculative activity.[17] For those who bought shares when the market was high only to be caught by a stock exchange collapse, this volatility would hardly endear them to the holding of assets in a general share portfolio. There is, however, compelling evidence that the majority of private companies sold out their business interests by more advantageous manipulations of the stock market. They were helped in this, as they had been before the First World War (see pp. 20–1), by company promoters who provided investors with 'advice'. These men persuaded industrialists to merge and publicly float their firms, ostensibly to gain access to economies of scale, monopoly power and other benefits. However, the promoters' profits were derived from the *ex ante* expectations of these benefits rather than from their *ex post* realization. Many of them therefore attempted to inflate the value of expected gains from post-merger integrations and to capitalize these in public issues at inflated prices which reflected these exaggerated claims, thus enhancing their own profits.[18]

The speculative booms were intensified by this activity, but this did create a clear profit opportunity for the important sector of owner-managed 'family' firms. It seems probable that the 'shadow' valuations of shares by owner-managers and other holders of stock in unquoted companies are in general less volatile than the valuations placed on titles to firms' assets by the stock market. This valuation discrepancy is positive in a boom and creates a margin of profit in a flotation for both the original owners and the promoters. It was thus in the fevered stages of stock exchange upswings that promoters were most active in their business of creating and exploiting speculative hopes by playing on the acquisitive instincts of investors and exaggerating the values of shares. There was a close, positive correlation between the sales of firms by their private owners and the level and rate of change of share prices. Contemporaries noticed that new issues to acquire existing assets were highest in stock market upswings and declined both absolutely and relatively to other new issues when the market slumped.[19] Further, it can also be shown that the level of merger activity (much of which consisted of unquoted firms being acquired by quoted ones, or merging with others in order to make a public issue economically) was positively correlated with the level of share prices throughout the interwar years.[20]

The existence of high profits in the mediation of the supply of firms and the demand of investors for securities, by the promotion of new issues and merger flotations, is also well documented.[21] Both the postwar boom of 1919–20 and the sustained stock exchange upswing of the later 1920s induced stockbrokers, issuing houses and *ad hoc* promoting syndicates to feed the speculative fever with dubious issues. 'Probably never in the history of modern trade and industry', suggested the *Economist*, 'was the net spread by the company promoter as it is today.'[22] Among them were many who could restructure industry to establish the basis of profitability which the high market capitalizations implied, and even promoters as unscrupulous as Clarence Hatry appear to have had a genuine faith in rationalization and some successful and logical mergers to their credit.[23] However, large profits could also go to the exaggerators and deceivers, and mergers offered a particularly fertile ground for such men, who could:

> realize the advantages that arose from manipulating, not a single company, but a group of companies. A 'parent company' with a number of subsidiaries at its command could do much to baffle the public as to its true state of prosperity. Not only could loans to, and investments in, subsidiaries be so manipulated that balance sheets concealed the true position of the whole group, but sales of rights could be so arranged that a subsidiary could show and transfer a dividend to the parent company which to the average investor may not have been indistinguishable [*sic*. distinguishable?] from a true trading profit.[24]

Thus developments in the stock market not only failed to improve the flow of information to investors but positively tended to distort it, and thus encouraged mergers of dubious economic logic.

While there were undoubtedly some legitimate and financially sound merger issues in booms, the new investors in many of them were inevitably disappointed. Postmortems usually revealed the wisdom of the original owners in selling out at boom values and in many cases laid bare the absence of any managerial rationale to the mergers that had been promoted. A number of the postwar boom promotions in the iron, shipbuilding, jute, glass and cotton industries (promoted in the main by Sir Edward Edgar's Sperling Combine and Clarence Hatry's Amalgamated Industrials) required wholesale reconstruction, and in some cases they disintegrated completely.[25] The new issue boom of 1928 also produced some spectacular casualties, and the average depreciation on the issues of 1928 was as high as 41–2 per cent by 1931.[26] To the extent that the former family owners had been paid in these shares (or invested the purchase price in similarly depreciated shares) they suffered along with other shareholders, but with their more direct experience of industrial trends, many of them had wisely demanded cash payments and made substantial financial gains from selling out. Even where they merely exchanged a portfolio of depreciated shares for their own companies, they still had the advantage of a more diversified, and hence less risky, investment. Of course all businesses carried with them risk in varying degrees, but it was extremely unlikely that a diversified portfolio of quoted company shares would do anything other than reduce this risk.[27]

The upshot of the new issue and merger booms was a substantial increase both in the total number of companies quoted on the stock exchange and in their total values. While there were only 569 firms in domestic manufacturing and distribution quoted on the London stock exchange in 1907, the number rose to 719 in 1924 and by 1939 had reached 1712.[28] Over the same period the market values of these quoted securities rose more than fivefold, from under £500 million in 1907 to more than £2500 million in 1939.[29] Already by the early 1920s, when 57 per cent of profits originated in public companies, those quoted on the London stock exchange included the majority of the more important manufacturing firms, and by 1951 a Board of Trade inquiry reported that quoted companies accounted for some 71 per cent of profits then generated by the corporate sector.[30] The great increase in both the range and the representativeness of stock exchange securities, which had enabled the former owners of family firms to diversify their holdings, also facilitated the formation of greatly enlarged manufacturing enterprises. In the interwar years, for example, we can safely say that enterprises which were valued on the stock market at £32 million or more would effectively have been beyond the resources of all but a few individual capitalists. Only one millionaire dying in the period left this much; Sir John Ellerman, the shipping and property magnate, left £36.7 million in 1933, but no one else even approached this level.[31] Without the facilities of the stock market for aggregating wealth, then, companies of this size could not have been formed. In 1919 there was only one such 'giant' firm, the J. & P. Coats sewing cotton combine, in which the family owners had been pioneers in diluting their ownership by a flotation of their capital three decades previously. By 1930, however, a further six companies – Unilever, Imperial Tobacco, Imperial Chemical Industries, Distillers, Courtaulds and Guinness – had attained this 'giant' size and the number of such companies continued to increase thereafter.[32]

The growth of these giant companies – and also of others in lower ranking (but still large) size categories – was in part the result simply of joining together existing assets which had previously been controlled by separate firms. However, some of their growth also derived from new capital issues to finance real growth in assets, a facility which the stock market could offer on favourable terms to established companies of this kind. Such capital issues were particularly useful to firms which did not have the cash flow to finance large and lumpy investments (such as frequently arose in mass production technology), and thus if they had not had this facility they could not easily have gained access to scale economies. Ford of Britain, for example, raised more than £4½ million in 1931 to finance the construction of the new Dagenham motor-car factory, then the largest such complex in Europe.[33] Like private firms, however, the large quoted firms of the interwar period relied principally on internally generated funds to finance their new capital projects. Between 1920 and 1938 some 28 per cent of earnings were on average ploughed back into new investment by British manufacturing firms,[34] and in 1924 it was established that some four-fifths of investment in home industry and commerce was financed by such business savings.[35] The system of self-financing had many advantages, particularly in avoiding the transactions costs and uncertainty of new capital issues in the stock market. Hence this source of finance was widely approved by industrialists,[36] and it was also tolerated by shareholders, presumably because of the tax and other advantages and because of the absence of a takeover mechanism to enforce higher payout ratios (see pp. 130–1).

Now self-financing can be an efficient system of allocating financial titles to resources in an economy where there is a direct relationship between the past and future qualities of management and between past profits and future investment opportunities. In this case firms which have in the past performed well will, from their own profits, gain a large portion of total new investment resources, and this may reflect the best use of those resources providing the highest social return. However, in a growing economy, with inter-industry shifts and single-industry firms, self-financing is likely to create immobilities, inhibiting the movement of capital to those new investment projects in which the marginal rates of return are highest. This had not been too serious in an economy of small firms where marginal adjustments in the capital stock by many firms could achieve substantial aggregate shifts. However, if only a few large firms dominate a number of industries in which substantial contractions are required, and there are only a few small firms in industries in which large new investments are required, the problem of immobilities could become a serious one. Companies recognizing this could and did overcome the problem by portfolio investment through the market in the quoted securities of other firms when the expected returns were high.[37] Another possibility was to diversify the firm's interests to include related fields and thus participate in the management as well as the finance of other firms. In the car components industry, for example, Joseph Lucas, which had surplus funds at its disposal, expanded its initially limited financial commitment to A. Rist Ltd into a controlling interest and ultimately in 1934 to full ownership.[38] The costs of such relationships were probably lower than for general investments through the stock market by the firm's shareholders, for several reasons in addition to the transactions costs of new issues (which could be high). Firms in the same or in a vertically related industry possess knowledge of each other's manufacturing skills, credit status and market position as part of their working stock of commercial intelligence, so that the costs to them in acquiring information on which to base decisions to acquire share participations are likely to be smaller than the costs to the investor. Furthermore the stock market was clearly ill-equipped to judge untried and especially science-based investment projects, in which *future* profit levels were the relevant factor in the assessment and *past* profitability could provide no guidance.[39] The commercial and technical intelligence departments of companies like ICI, by contrast, could perform such assessments more expertly, since they had closer knowledge than the institutions of the stock market of both the relevant production technology and the potential markets.[40] Large firms such as Vickers, GEC and ICI thus received a succession of proposals in technologies related to their own major fields of interest, from individual inventors and from smaller companies which needed the capital resources of a larger company for further development and expansion. Hence the continued flow of resources for new development was assured not principally by the stock market (which was generally unwilling to finance untried enterprises) but either by these large firms, or by the time-honoured methods of nineteenth-century innovators, using private sources of finance.[41] For the large firms such projects often laid the basis for future corporate growth and diversification, and in this sphere, as in others, such financing advantages were adding to the pressures towards larger firms.

For some smaller firms wishing to achieve the advantages of rationalization and large-scale production, however, neither large companies nor the stock market could supply the required financial resources. As the experienced accountant, Sir Mark Webster Jenkinson, explained to the Macmillan Committee, 'Some have got financial millstones round their necks, and do not know how to bring about fusion. Nobody will take them in.'[42] Often in such cases it was the banks and other creditors who provided the financial pressure, and the financial resources, for rationalization, sometimes against the will of the owners. Though the major banks frequently disclaimed responsibility for forcing bank debtors to merge, and officially ruled out joint action as a breach of the confidential customer-client relationship,[43] they did in fact participate in some enforced reconstruction schemes. In the steel industry, for example, Barclays forced the unwilling directors of Bolckow Vaughan to accept a bid from Dorman Long by the simple expedient of making the renewal of the company's £1 million overdraft conditional on the consummation of the merger.[44]

Such action by the banks was given a more formal structure with the creation, on Bank of England initiative, of the Bankers' Industrial Development Company (BIDC) in 1929.[45] This was intended to devise schemes to re-equip, and where necessary to amalgamate, companies in the staple industries which were often in financial difficulties. It appears to have been primarily an attempt to head off possible government intervention in the financing and reorganization of industry,[46] and, with financial backing from the Bank of England and other City institutions, and a high-powered staff, it aimed discreetly to catalyze the banks into action which was felt to be in their long-term interests.[47] An essential part of the BIDC's philosophy was that its capital should in no cases be used to relieve investors of existing financial burdens. Existing assets could not be bought for cash, and thus mergers involving cash acquisitions could not occur under its auspices.[48] Instead shareholders and creditors (including the banks) had to agree to pool their interests in return for a paper title to a share in any future benefits of the merger. Any new capital introduced into such schemes by the BIDC – which, of course, had prior rights – was intended to finance new investment only, and it was on these conditions that the bankers co-operated, some of them somewhat reluctantly. The most spectacular example of the BIDC's work was the formation of the Lancashire Cotton Corporation, which between 1929 and 1932 absorbed almost a hundred firms.[49] The majority of these were forced by their bankers, on the threat of withdrawal of overdraft and loan facilities, to accept the terms offered by the Corporation, though the bankers in fact delayed the process, ever hopeful that by dilatory quibbling they would gain better terms.[50] Though it is conceivable that mergers would have occurred in the industry in the absence of the BIDC (as they did in the fine spinning section of the industry),[51] the Corporation was undoubtedly larger and the operation more swiftly executed than would have been the case if the matter had been left to the directors of the individual companies. Smaller-scale mergers were also encouraged by the BIDC in the steel industry, though they were in large part due to the initiative of the British Iron and Steel Federation and individual companies and only partly to Montagu Norman's promptings.[52]

These developments in the stock markets and in banking institutions, then, both liberated firms from the size constraint previously imposed by the wealth of the individual owner and also created new pressures towards larger-scale enterprise. More generally, economies of scale in finance were added to the other economies of large-scale operations, and these may have been among the more important scale economies available to firms in some industries.[53] One of the financial advantages of scale came in the spreading of risks. This may seem to be a superfluous advantage, since we have already seen that capitalists were spreading their risks by diversifying their shareholdings over a wider range of companies. For directors and managers, however, risks were usually concentrated in the companies for which they worked, and since they, rather than the shareholders, took the major entrepreneurial decisions, the spreading of risk by diversifying their companies' interests remained an important consideration. More straightforward scale economies were created by the high transactions cost of raising capital by new issues on the stock market. The difficulty of raising capital in amounts of under £200,000 – the 'Macmillan Gap'[54] – was well known and must have inhibited many small firms from seeking a public issue. The basic expenses of issue – prospectuses, advertising, and the professional fees of accountants, brokers, bankers and solicitors – amounted to five figure sums and, as they were fixed costs, this could amount to as much as 20 per cent of the sum raised in a small issue.[55] Furthermore, the securities of small companies were less well known, less marketable and more risky investments, and were capitalized accordingly.[56]

Considerations of financial economies of scale appear to have loomed large for those entrepreneurs who perceived that these financing advantages could be added to the less spectacular financial economies available to large firms (such as the aggregation of inventories and liquidity and the benefits of cheaper overdrafts and internal banking).[57] The existence of such economies could itself induce firms to merge to achieve the appropriate scale. As Sir Josiah Stamp wrote:

> The average small unit will find it difficult to get finance for rationalization either cheaply or at all. But in as much as the agglomeration of such units may be big enough to command public company finance in London . . . the only hope for rationalization in the small unit industries is a further merging on a considerable scale.[58]

The only practical alternative to a public issue for the many small companies which required long-term finance beyond what they could provide from their own resources was to seek acquisition by an established quoted company (which could usually raise the finance more cheaply from its own funds or by a larger stock market issue). Either way the results of the financial economies were to accentuate the tendency towards the greater concentration of assets in fewer and larger firms.

In a developed stock market, it was also easier to reorganize capital into larger units in order to achieve other kinds of scale economies. Because the ownership of companies was increasingly divorced from control, and titles to assets were readily saleable on the stock exchange, a more fluid market in company control could develop. Instead of the delicate negotiations between family firms for consolidating their interests, more aggressive techniques of acquiring firms for restructuring an industry were opened up. E. R. Lewis, for example, a stockbroker who had floated the Decca company, suggested to its directors that they buy another record company, Duophone. When they refused he bought Duophone himself, and then, in 1929, suggested that they sell him the Decca company. Though not personally wishing to sell, the Decca directors realized the financial attractiveness of the offer and agreed to pass it on to their shareholders. It was accepted by over 95 per cent of them.[59] Similarly, Lord Leverhulme's offer of £13 10s 0d per share for the deferred shares of Knights in 1920 was so attractive that the company's directors, whilst themselves seeing no logic in the merger, advised their shareholders to accept on purely financial grounds.[60] Of course, financially profitable takeovers of this kind would often have been welcomed by closely held family companies also, but in the case of quoted companies neither the personal taste for continuing family ownership nor the practical difficulties of transferring titles intervened to complicate the amalgamation of assets into larger groupings.

In the case of Decca and Knights, although control and ownership were divorced, the directors took into account the financial interests of the shareholders who owned the company, and acted accordingly. This was not, however, invariably the case, as is witnessed by the insistence of some company directors on large side payments to themselves as a condition of agreeing to mergers.[61] Such practices were widespread and, had they developed into further conflicts of interest and affected the everyday running of quoted companies, they would clearly have created serious problems for the owners of industrial wealth. In general, however, a coalescence of the interests of shareholders and directors was achieved by a variety of expedients, drawn from the earlier experience of those family companies which had employed professional non-family managers in their businesses. The salaries of directors and managers were sometimes directly related to profits, and even where this was not formally so it was a common, and well understood, practice for bonuses to be granted to senior men when the company had had a particularly profitable year, thus creating a similar incentive. Nevertheless in some areas the interests of managers and shareholders did not necessarily coincide. The new generation of professional managers and quoted company directors was as likely to come from

the universities, the civil service or the professional classes as to have
inherited its managerial positions as a family right, and, though few
of its members were of humble origins, they were in general less
wealthy than the owning families whom they were gradually replacing on quoted company boards.[62] They relied more on their
current earnings than on *rentier* interest on inherited capital. Once
established in a senior position, moreover, they were jealous of their
rank and tended to regard it as a sinecure in much the same way as
the former family owners had done.[63] The growth of their firms (and
at the same time of their salaries and their prestige) appears to have
been a major objective of such managers. The entrepreneurs who
erected statues of themselves next to those of Nobel and Lavoisier on
the new Millbank headquarters of Imperial Chemical Industries
overlooking the Thames were, we may suppose, as much interested
in empire building and the glory it reflected on themselves as they
were concerned about the income of their shareholders.[64] Yet
another pressure towards larger-scale enterprise, in this case from
the managers themselves, was thus implicit in the stock market
developments of the period.

Whether from the point of view of financial economies of scale or
of the expansionist ambitions of managers, then, the rapid rise of the
corporate economy becomes more intelligible in the light of the
changing structure of capitalist ownership and the emergence of a
professional managerial class. However, these new developments
raised serious misgivings in the minds of many contemporaries. The
conclusions of the Liberal Industrial Inquiry (a body which was
strongly influenced by Keynes) typified these doubts about the
upper echelons of industrial management:

> the vast majority of appointments to Boards of Directors are made
> in effect . . . by co-option by the existing directors. Since the
> duties are indefinite and the privileges agreeable, the way is open
> to various kinds of jobbery. . . . A directorship . . . is apt to be
> awarded to influential people who . . . are without technical
> qualifications for the management of the business. . . . We do not
> think that the Boards, as at present constituted, of Public
> Companies of diffused ownership are one of the strong points of
> private enterprise. There is here an important actual and potential
> element of inefficiency.[65]

Moreover, shareholders and managers did not only have to face these consequences of the divorce of ownership and control, but, perhaps more crucially, had to meet the entirely new managerial and organizational problems presented by manufacturing enterprises which were larger and more complex than any that had previously been experienced.

6

Management and the limits to growth[1]

Be not frighted, trade could not be managed by those
who manage it, if it had much difficulty.
DR JOHNSON, *Letters*, ed. G. B. Hill,
vol. 2 (Oxford, 1892), p. 126.

ဘ

Even among the industrialists who supported the principle of
rationalization and were convinced that through it firms could gain
access to important scale economies, there were many who were prey
to doubts about the personal capacities of the men available to run
large-scale enterprises. 'The most difficult thing at present', the
Macmillan Committee was told by a banker, 'is to find a man who
can control 10,000,000 spindles. Find that man and I think you will
find five or six positions clamouring for him.'[2] As Sir Alfred Mond
told the House of Commons in 1926:

> The essential of the matter is 'management'. I have come to the
> conclusion that it is impossible for any human being efficiently to
> control any industry beyond a certain magnitude. At a certain
> point they begin to show the paralysis of red tape; they become so
> big that they are like a government department. In my view it is
> impossible to organize industries on a national basis and keep
> them efficient.[3]

This stress on the dangers of bureaucracy was rooted in a belief in
individualism in management, an idea that remained an important
part of the self-image of the business élite. If Mond himself was able
some six months later to embark upon the creation of Imperial
Chemical Industries, the largest merger in manufacturing (by market valuation) between the wars, it is none the less the case that the
fear of diseconomies of scale deterred lesser men.

That a merger did not automatically push back the barriers of
managerial diseconomies of scale was a problem often skipped by
those advocating rationalization, but central to the concern of

contemporary businessmen and observers. Though there are some increasing returns to relative size (in that increased market control both raises profits and reduces uncertainty, freeing entrepreneurial time for other tasks),[4] past and contemporary experience suggested that considerable managerial difficulties would be encountered when companies were merged. As the *Economist* sceptically remarked:

> The advocates of concentration and combination . . . are accustomed to dwell on the advantages in respect of efficiency and economy of production and distribution which are derivable from the promotion of standardization of output and specialization of works, the establishment of uniform costings systems, the interchange of information, the combined research, the collective buying of raw materials, and the joint marketing which are thereby facilitated. That such advantages are so derivable is beyond question; but, despite some very striking instances, the fact that they have been generally so derived is still far from established.[5]

Management was the crucial factor in the realization of economies of the type relating to the relative efficiency of firm and market in integrating economic activities. The gradual increase in the role of managerial bureaucracy in co-ordinating economic activity can be seen in the growing role of head offices in the development of large-scale firms. For many large firms before the war, the head office had been a relatively small adjunct to the main factory, and as such was typically based in the provinces rather than London. By the 1920s and 1930s such firms were building larger head offices, often in London with its central communications advantages and ease of contact with Whitehall and the City; and they were staffing them with increasing numbers of senior strategic managers and the accompanying clerical, and in some cases technical, bureaucracy. The contemporary Marxist who saw interwar mergers creating 'the monster office in which vast numbers of clerks are herded together for their daily work',[6] just as manual workers had previously been herded into factories, employed somewhat flowery language but the changes behind his observations were real enough. They can be seen most strikingly in the increasing proportion of employees in manufacturing industry who were employed in 'administrative, technical and clerical' rather than 'operative' jobs.[7] Before the First World War perhaps 8 per cent of UK manufacturing[8] employees were

The rise of the corporate economy

TABLE 6.1   *The rise in managerial overheads, 1907–48*

	Administrative, technical and clerical employees and working proprietors	Operatives	Col. 1 as % of total employees
All census industries			
1907	492	6492	7·6
Manufacturing industries only			
1924	567	4816	11·8
1935	746	4948	15·1
1948	1201	6107	19·7

Source: Department of Employment and Productivity, British Labour Statistics: Historical Abstract 1886–1968 (1971), Table 205.

involved in 'overhead' work rather than direct production; by the mid-1930s, the proportion had risen to 15 per cent and was continuing to rise (see Table 6.1). The transition from market relations to intra-firm organization did not, then, occur costlessly and automatically with an increase in scale: it required considerable investment of time, manpower, capital and skill in the creation of an efficient administrative structure. Only firms with this organizational investment capacity could embark on an extensive and sustained programme of expansion with reasonable prospect of success.

The reality of this awareness among businessmen and its effect as a constraint on the growth of the firm is shown strikingly in the business records of large corporations:

I contend [wrote a senior manager of Courtauld's on a proposal to acquire other rayon companies] that our present Board and *our present organisation* is and will be for a considerable time incapable of running a monopolized industry . . . Before therefore proceeding with the idea of trying to obtain control of either viscose or acetate producers or both, I consider that we should put our own house in order.[9]

On this advice the programme of acquisition was abandoned and it was not until 1957 that Courtaulds acquired its main competitor, British Celanese. Again, when the government was investigating the possibility of mergers in the light castings trade, it naturally looked to the largest merged firm in the industry, Allied Ironfounders, to act as a managerial nucleus, but, here too, the original merger of 1929 had imposed so great a managerial strain on the company as to rule out further acquisitions for some years. 'Any further concentration', it was reported, 'could probably best be carried out through this Company but they feel that it would be unwise to start negotiations for this purpose until they have consolidated their present position'.[10]

Two pieces of evidence, however, counsel caution in the use of managerial diseconomies of scale as a blanket explanation of the cautious approach of some entrepreneurs to mergers and company growth in the interwar years. First, there were a number of very large companies in various industrial fields which showed no evidence of chronically overstretched management. It was arguable that organizations such as the Post Office (with 200,000 workers) and the LMS Railway (with 250,000 workers) could function efficiently at a large scale, and, as W. H. Coates of ICI (which employed about 50,000 people in the UK) pointed out:

> There is no industrial combine, so far as I am aware, registered under the Companies Acts which has a number anywhere approaching those figures. The speeches of the Chairman of the LMS, and also the results of the Company notwithstanding statutory and other conditions under which they have to work, show that you can have efficient management for such an organization. It is hard to say that those economic units are too large.[11]

Second, and clearly related to the first point, there was a trend towards larger firms in many industries between the wars, and many of them could claim, with the Distillers Company, that 'this company has been a series of amalgamations. Its birth was the result of an amalgamation and the company has gone on amalgamating ever since'.[12] In the light of such evidence it would appear to be more realistic to postulate a managerial limit to the *rate of growth* (rather than the size) of the firm, a modification which is gaining acceptance in the theoretical literature.[13] Where managerial skills were highly developed it was realized that the managerial constraint on growth need not be a significant one at all.[14] The important variable was management. The analysis of the means by which barriers to growth were pushed back, as the skills of companies in digesting acquisitions and managing large extended organizations were evolved, therefore offers an important key to the merger process and the internal development of the modern firm.

The earlier experience of rapidly growing firms had not been promising. A very large proportion of the multi-firm consolidations of the turn of the century had encountered severe managerial problems, and this can hardly be a matter for surprise. In the majority of them there was no obvious 'parent' firm to act as nucleus or 'core' for the new managerial structure, for all the firms involved were, prior to the merger, of only small size. The rate of growth implied for the largest firm in the consolidation (i.e. the relation between its size and the sum of the sizes of the other firms) was, then, perhaps twenty times or more; that is, of an order of magnitude quite different from that experienced by firms in normal circumstances. The managerial stresses incurred by firms undergoing these rates of expansion were documented fully by the contemporary Fabian civil servant Henry Macrosty and have been tellingly re-examined by Professor Payne.[15] Almost invariably their promoters failed to pay sufficient attention to the problems of organizing large-scale enterprise and of integrating formerly independent and competing units. As a result many of the new combines were run more as debating societies than as industrial firms: one firm, the Calico Printers' Association, for example, had eighty-four directors, eight of them 'managing', and inevitably suffered from conflicting leadership. Such boards were too unwieldy to be effective, and the introduction of standard costings systems and other methods of maintaining efficiency was too often ignored.[16]

By the interwar years, then, the somewhat light-hearted abandon with which managers had entered upon these early merger agreements had been tempered by a more widespread awareness of the difficulties created by multi-firm consolidations and rapid growth, and large multi-firm mergers ceased to play a significant role in increasing concentration. This can be seen in Table 6.2, which shows the extinction of multi-firm mergers involving twenty or more firms, and an overall reduction in the average size of multi-firm mergers (defined as those involving five or more firms), in the first four decades of this century. The later multi-firm mergers were, moreover, small not only in terms of the numbers of firms involved but also in terms of their capitalization.[17] This abandonment of the large multi-firm merger did not, however, mean that fewer firms were being absorbed by merger in the interwar period; on the contrary the number of firm disappearances by merger actually increased, and in the interwar years overall perhaps as many as 4000 firms were absorbed in mergers and acquisitions (see Appendix 1). What happened was rather a change in pattern: firms, instead of seeking to convert an industry instantaneously into a monopoly, were choosing instead the path of sequential acquisition of smaller competitors and selective mergers with large ones, spacing out their growth more evenly over the years. This more balanced pace of growth not only enabled firms to bypass the chronic managerial stresses encountered by earlier multi-firm consolidations, but also offered the additional attraction of evading the opprobrium which had earlier accrued to the 'Soap Trust' and other attempts to create a monopoly instantaneously, rather than by gradual (and less noticeable) piecemeal acquisitions.

The significance of this new strategy in facilitating growth without managerial collapse is underlined by the experience of the odd man out of the 1920s in Table 6.2: the Lancashire Cotton Corporation. This consolidation of 1929 was disliked by many cotton mill managers but was forced on a largely unwilling industry by creditors and bankers acting through the Bankers' Industrial Development Company.[18] In its first year it acquired seventy companies and in the following year a further twenty-six, making it not only the largest merger (in terms of the number of firms disappearing) between the wars but the largest on record in Britain at any time. The problems of integrating many small and formerly independent cotton mills within one managerial organization were

TABLE 6.2 *The decline of the multi-firm merger in UK manufacturing industry, 1880–1939*

	Mergers involving 20 or more firms	*Mergers involving 5 or more firms*	*Average number of firms per multi-firm merger*
1880–9	1	5	19·6
1890–9	6	28	14·6
1900–9	4	20	14·6
1910–19	2	24	10·4
1920–9	1	40	9·1
1930–9	0	18	6·9

Source: L. Hannah, 'Mergers in British manufacturing industry, 1880–1918', *Oxford Economic Papers*, vol. 26 (1974), p. 14.

formidable. By mid-1931 it was evident to the financial backers of the Corporation that all was not well and an accountants' investigation into the management and organization was ordered. The resulting report was highly critical of the management, and these criticisms were reinforced in a further confidential report by Sir Eric Geddes, who had been sent to investigate by the BIDC. Geddes had gained a reputation as a skilled organizer by rebuilding the fortunes of the Dunlop Rubber Company after its collapse in 1921, and he was himself a keen enthusiast for large-scale organization and the rationalization of industry, a passion he shared with the managing director of Lancashire Cotton, Captain John Ryan. Yet, when he surveyed the company, Geddes could not conceal his belief that the task set for management by the initial amalgamation was super-human. He expressed these reservations in a letter to BIDC:

> I think the founders of the Lancashire Cotton Corporation underestimated the enormous difficulty of creating a great amalgamation of this kind without any real strong existing organization to take over control.
>
> It would have been difficult enough for any large organization with a loyal and tried staff to take over the industrial properties which have been acquired, but the task was immeasurably greater when one realizes that personnel had to be collected and a central organization created at the same time as the troublesome absorption of the Mills was taking place. It is easy to underestimate this trouble.[19]

Though this was wisdom after the event, there could be no more impressive testimony to the reality of managerial diseconomies of rapid growth than this assessment by a convinced rationalizer and successful entrepreneur when confronted with the results of a multi-firm merger which had ignored the dangers inherent in such consolidations.

For the majority of companies, however, the pace of growth was less hectic than this, and there were remarkably few mergers in the 1920s and 1930s which involved more than a doubling in size for the 'core' firm. Interwar entrepreneurs thus in general avoided the mistakes of their predecessors in this area, but they did not, on that account alone, banish all the managerial problems of rapid growth and large scale. The nature of these problems can be seen from the analyses of the co-ordination difficulties met by large organizations, which have been made by managerial theorists.[20] It is generally accepted that an executive can conveniently control only a limited number[21] of subordinates, and that expansion cannot efficiently be achieved by adding to the span of control above this number; instead an extra hierarchical level must be added. However, a very large firm employing this principle needs a long hierarchy of command, and control loss increases as the chain of command is extended, partly because of the decreasing efficiency of communication, and further because of the expanded field of discretionary behaviour for subordinates which is introduced. In some of the lower reaches of the firm, the adoption of standardized practices might help to widen the span of control (and thus shorten the lines of command), but at the level of senior management this is clearly difficult in view of the strategic and tactical decision-making required at those levels, especially in a growing firm. Generally, therefore, an increase in size will expand the strain on an organization and limit its efficiency.

Technical progress was reducing some of these problems of communication and control in large corporations between the wars. In particular the telephone, perhaps the most important new instrument of communication to become widely available to managers, provided a means of rapid communication between departments, or between geographically dispersed branches, and thus facilitated managerial control.[22] Technical advances substantially cheapened and improved the quality of telephonic communication, and the number of business telephones doubled between 1914 and 1930 and continued to rise rapidly in the 1930s.[23] In the case of other kinds of office machinery the rate of adoption was perhaps even more dramatic. Before the war such machines had been little used in business. In the works office of Stewarts & Lloyds in 1903, for example, it was later recalled that:

> The only piece of modern equipment was the telephone, with a private line to the Glasgow office . . . But there was no other office machinery of any kind – no typewriters, no adding machines, comptometers, pay-roll listing machines, etc. There were no women in the office. Everything was handwritten and the only duplication was by letterpress copying . . . No one trained in a modern office can have any idea of the crudity of office methods and organization at that time.[24]

In the interwar years, by contrast, typewriters, duplicators and accounting machines of various kinds were widely used in business, and mechanization of routine information gathering and processing was helping to overcome the problems of information presentation, and hence of co-ordination and control. While none of the interwar office machinery innovations had the same discontinuous effects on information and management in the large corporation as the computer (which was later developed from them), the claim of Powers-Samas in 1930, that 'without . . . mechanization of office accounting the rapid growth of business and the formation of large consolidations would have been difficult if not impossible',[25] clearly contained more than a grain of truth. Most important of these innovations were machines such as the Hollerith which could process accounting data with great speed, and which facilitated significant improvements in the collection and diffusion of information in large companies.[26] Furthermore, the effect of mechanization was not only to cheapen information processing, but, often more significantly, to stimulate new thought about systems of management control. At a Management Research Group meeting in 1937, for example, 'it was generally agreed by members after a short discussion (on office machinery) that of the saving in cost 10 per cent was effected through mechanization and 90 per cent by the general overhaul of existing systems'.[27] It was through such structural changes in management that the more significant organizational changes of these years had their impact on the growth of the firm.

The first reaction to the stresses of growth on company management was often the functional differentiation of managerial tasks. The increasing division of labour in management is reflected in the growth of specialized professional associations and institutions and in the expansion in the employment of specialist managers.[28] Apart from the well-established engineering and other industrially specialized institutions (which, however, showed some reluctance to introduce management and economics into their professional training), the Industrial Welfare Society and the Institute of Cost and Works Accountants were founded in 1919, the Institute of Industrial Administration in 1921, to be followed in the 1930s by groups such as the Purchasing Officers Association, the Works Management Association and the Office Management Association.[29] Most of the large companies which were members of Management Research Group No. 1, which had been founded in 1926, could send functional specialists occupying senior central office positions to group meetings to discuss specialized topics in personnel, finance, accounting and technical matters.[30] The recommendation to 'spread overheads' in much contemporary management literature refers, among other things, to the managerial economies of scale available in the use of such specialists, and also to the wider use of information, the cost of acquiring which did not increase with firm size.[31] The proliferation of functional specialists was important in that it enabled a central office to delegate managerial functions of an advisory or routine kind to specialists, whilst itself concentrating the efforts of entrepreneurial peak co-ordinators on the initiation and planning of general business policy and the efficient oversight of the manufacturing divisions of the firm.

Whilst such functional specialists could be trained in the new specialisms on the job, there was clearly a problem in recruiting as peak co-ordinators entrepreneurs and managers with experience of large-scale bureaucratic administration. Unlike the small firm, the large corporation was unable to rely exclusively on traditional sources of new recruits through social and family ties but had to develop a wider net of management recruitment.[32] The problems of managing large enterprises in manufacturing did, of course, have something in common with those of other large organizations, and the railways, early pioneers of large-scale organization, were one obvious source of recruitment. Sir Felix Pole, for example, moved from the Great Western Railway to become chairman of the new Associated Electrical Industries merger in 1928. More generally, manufacturing companies, usually lacking management training programmes of their own, proved adept at poaching young trainee managers from the railway companies.[33] The civil service was another source of recruitment to the expanding managerial hierarchies of manufacturing business. Sir Josiah Stamp, for example, had been trained in the Inland Revenue, and became influential in developing the advanced managerial structures of Nobel Industries (one of the largest manufacturing companies of the early 1920s) before becoming president of the London Midland and Scottish Railway.[34] A steady succession of civil servants from the Revenue followed Stamp into the higher echelons of the management of ICI (which had acquired Nobel in 1926), beginning with W. H. Coates, the right-hand man of the ICI chairman between the wars, and continuing with Sir Paul Chambers and other directors in more recent times. Other large businesses, notably Vickers, recruited

senior management from retiring military personnel, a practice
which had not only the commercially attractive overtones of *pan-
touflage* but also the advantages of recruiting senior men experienced
in bureaucratic procedures and problems of administrative control in
a large organization.[35] However, not all firms could rely on such
external sources of expertise, so managerial skills increasingly were
developed in the training of functional specialists and departmental
managers within the manufacturing enterprises themselves. As
Stamp told the Macmillan Committee,

> The kind of experience required in consolidating an industry . . .
> is a thing which, with a certain translation of terms, can be passed
> from industry to industry, and given men of the requisite
> knowledge and intelligence that experience can be cumulative,
> that type of man can be gradually evolved. . . . There are a few
> people who are born to do it, and who see their way through; there
> are others who could quickly learn from experience.[36]

One avenue of experience commonly followed was an accountancy
training, for it was particularly through developments in accounting
that the introduction of new methods for the oversight and assessment of subsidiaries was encouraged and facilitated. Cost accounting
had a long pedigree as a means of achieving efficiency through
managerial control in business,[37] but it could still be claimed in the
war that British businessmen had not adequately come to terms with
it,[38] and some of the most useful techniques of industrial accounting,
as Josiah Stamp pointed out in 1929, were 'almost entirely a
development of the last twenty years'.[39] Hence the demand for more
rigorous methods of financial assessment and management information from large businesses between the wars was mediated by a rapid
rise in the proportion of accountants working in industry: in 1913 a
substantial majority of English accountants were in private practice,
but by 1939 over half of them were in the direct employ of
business.[40] Accountants, who had previously only rarely taken
important positions in the directorates of large companies,[41] now
began to play a more significant part. At the Dunlop Rubber
Company, for example, F. R. M. de Paula (who had been Professor
of Accounting at the London School of Economics in the 1920s) was
invited to become Controller of Finance in 1929. He developed a
comprehensive system of internal audit, costing and forecasting, and
Dunlop's finance division was able to provide information for the

control of costs and investment, within a framework of annual budgets for subsidiaries. De Paula himself repeatedly stressed the relevance of these methods for overcoming the managerial diseconomies of scale sometimes encountered by merged enterprises, by securing centralization of control with decentralization of responsibilities.[42] The career of Francis D'Arcy Cooper at Unilever also indicates the expanding role of the accountant in solving the organizational problems of large enterprise. Coming to Lever Brothers from the accountancy partnership Cooper Brothers in 1923, he was largely responsible for consolidating the extensive and disparate parts of the empire built up by William Lever, and, after succeeding the founder as chairman of the company in 1925, he eventually became the chairman of the merged Unilever company and pursued his policy of consolidation and rationalization of subsidiaries there throughout the 1930s.[43] By 1936 7.6 per cent of all directors in a large sample of British companies were accountants, a larger proportion than any other professional group.[44]

The nature of the need for and the disadvantages of the centralized control that was being facilitated by these technical and accounting innovations was succinctly stated in 1930 by Lord Melchett (formerly Sir Alfred Mond and then chairman of ICI) when he said that 'the real problem of rationalization and merging of big enterprises consists in effective central control with sufficient elasticity lower down to allow action to be neither arrested nor delayed'.[45] In many companies this was to involve the splitting of activities on a regional or product group basis, and the creation of independent profit centres ('divisions') responsible for their performance to a peak executive, which controlled finance and capital investment. Since Melchett felt that ICI had attained these objects, that company is an appropriate one in which to study the evolution of a decentralized system of subsidiary management in harness with central office control.

At the time of its formation, in 1926, ICI was the largest merger in British manufacturing industry in terms of its capitalization, an amalgamation of four companies all of which had previously been extensively engaged in mergers. The two larger partners, Nobel and Brunner Mond, dominated the explosives and alkali sections of the chemical industry respectively, and, together with the British Dyestuffs Corporation and the United Alkali Company, they formed a diversified chemicals and metals group which had a market value at the time of its formation of over £60 million.[46] The company continued to grow both internally and by acquisition, and no insurmountable managerial barriers to expansion seem to have been reached. The managerial structure of ICI should, then, offer some indications of the expedients by which large organizations were able to overcome managerial limits both to the absolute size and to the rate of growth of the firm.[47]

Its managerial structure seems to have owed most to the largest partner in the merger, Nobel Industries Ltd. Brunner Mond, which was in the throes of a managerial reorganization at the time of the merger, envisaged a somewhat looser framework of control, but already in the provisional agreement to merge it was accepted that the new company would adopt a Nobel type of structure. Nobel had its origin in the British end of the Nobel Dynamite Trust which, having been split off from its German counterpart in the First World War, amalgamated with its main British competitors, some thirty or more companies in all, to form Explosives Trades Limited, the company changing its name to Nobel Industries Limited in 1920. Centralization of these separate interests was first required and it was for this purpose that the Nobel structure was originally devised. Within six years of the merger, a central research department had been established at Ardeer, and production had been centralized in the most efficient factories, the remainder being closed down and sold off or transferred to other uses. This was achieved by the efforts of H. J. Mitchell, aided by John Rogers and Josiah Stamp, in creating a central office structure at Nobel House in London which could handle the managerial problems of consolidation and growth. Routine functional responsibilities such as central purchasing, personnel, publicity, legal, taxation and investment matters were centralized at Nobel House. The legal form of control for the original subsidiaries and for new acquisitions (of which there were many) was for Nobel Industries to become the sole director and for a delegate board to be appointed, responsible to the Nobel board, the management committee and the finance committee. The assessment of the performance of the subsidiaries was facilitated by a unified system of merger accountancy which was developed by Josiah Stamp at a central secretarial department. This was fully operational by 1923, showing the financial results of all companies in the group on a common basis. Two other central departments, the development department under Todhunter (which investigated proposals for diversification and technical innovation) and the central executive and advisory department under Mitchell (which acted as the board secretariat and supervised trading agreements and commercial intelligence), had important entrepreneurial roles. In particular they jointly (and sometimes with the assistance of outside accountants) assessed potential acquisitions in their financial, commercial and technical aspects. The skill of their pre-merger assessments, together with the central post-merger control, facilitated the assimilation of acquisitions and the release of synergy in the mergers which were undertaken. Growth was thus self-sustaining as the financial and managerial 'surpluses' generated were made available for further expansion.

When this centralized system had been successfully established it appears that some devolution of responsibility onto the manufacturing units was attempted, Mitchell aiming at 'the retention at HQ only of the ultimate control and of certain specialized service departments'.[48] The metal manufacturing subsidiaries were organized from Birmingham rather than from Nobel House and, although financial control and rationalization of capacity were enforced, they were kept on a loose rein. Although the major ingredients of a financially centralized group with decentralized divisional management, which later developed in ICI, were present in this structure, they were there only in germ. It was only with the increase in size after the ICI merger that a full system of divisions emerged. Even then, however, full centralization of ICI itself was to precede the programme of decentralization.[49]

Although Sir Alfred Mond became the first chairman of ICI when it was formed in 1926, men from Nobel occupied strategically important positions in the new company. The considerable managerial 'surplus' of the Nobel group (indicated by the reported drying up of attractive investment possibilities in its development department's reports) was now released upon the task of organizing the larger company. Investment management was soon centralized in the finance committee, and an executive committee, consisting of directors with functional responsibilities, controlled all new capital expenditure and provided a central forum for policy-making. Banking, purchasing, commercial, staff, and statistical control policies were very quickly standardized and centralized. In short, an enlarged central office of service departments and strategic entrepreneurial committees was developed similar to that which had obtained in Nobel. The rationalization of production capacity on the basis of technical and financial reports on subsidiary factories had by the late 1920s been applied to the whole range of ICI manufactures. Expansion continued as the manufacture of new products was initiated and new subsidiaries were acquired (after investigation by the central development department) in the metals, fertilizer, dyestuffs and general chemical fields. The system of regional sales offices originally developed by Brunner Mond was taken over by the group and became the sales offices for the majority of ICI products.

This centralization brought lower costs through enhanced buying power and rationalized production, joint distribution and selling, better financial control and improved cash flow, and better use of scarce research, commercial intelligence, and other managerial talent. Nevertheless the structure soon showed signs of the weaknesses of centralized decision-making, and between 1928 and 1931 manufacturing was decentralized to eight 'groups', each with a chairman and a delegate board consisting of local executives and liaison officers from head office. The model for the groups was the Birmingham end of the business which had been inherited from Nobel and had subsequently grown by the acquisition of further nonferrous metal companies. Traditionally independent within Nobel, this group was reorganized in 1928 and each of the four companies in it was also decentralized. This was soon recognized as an appropriate model for the larger chemical subsidiary companies also, and the other groups were set up in the following year.

Inter-group policy was co-ordinated by a central administration committee on which the group chairmen sat together with the senior ICI functional officials. Formally, two subcommittees of the main board, the finance committee and the general purposes (formerly executive) committee, exercised ultimate control. Channels of communication were thus established through the common membership by central and 'group' (i.e. local) executives of central committees and 'group boards'. The main board's authority was exercised through control of capital expenditure on the basis of past results (assessed by the unified accounting systems and interdivisional market pricing which had been introduced during the centralization phase), and of future prospects (assessed by technical and commercial experts). Finance thus remained centralized and, through performance measurement and annual budgets, controlling.

By the 1930s, then, the company had clearly developed into a modern decentralized corporation with a functionally specialized head office exercising overall financial control and providing managerial and financial services to the divisions ('groups'). It could be seen as a federation of semi-independent firms with the central office providing a highly efficient capital market, management consultancy, and service agency. The logic of such a structure had not by the close of the interwar period been fully worked out at ICI. The chairman, by now Baron McGowan of Ardeer, maintained autocratic central control and insisted, for example, on central office control over pricing policy, so that individual profit centres were not in fact wholly autonomous, and the 'groups' themselves could not therefore be held fully responsible for commercial results, which largely emanated from company rather than 'group' policy. The 'groups' were thus concerned principally with efficient works management and it was in the sphere of production rather than of commercial affairs that decentralization was really effective. None the less, for all its limitations the structure clearly approximated to the paradigm of the multidivisional corporation.[50] Aided by more favourable demand conditions and more successful participation in cartels than many less fortunate companies experienced in the depressed 1930s, ICI was able with this decentralized structure to undertake profitable expansion, both internally and by acquisition, without the operation of the serious managerial constraint which, as we have seen, had limited the rate of growth of other corporations of comparable size.

ICI appears to have advanced further with its multidivisional management structure than most companies, and it would be quite wrong to take its success in solving problems of diseconomies of scale as typical, but a few other companies were feeling their way along similar organizational lines. Spillers, the flour milling combine, established a regional divisional structure in 1926, with four regional groups whose general managers had full executive authority; a fifth group for Scotland was subsequently added. Turner & Newall established product divisions in 1931 to consolidate its diversification within the asbestos industry, with separate units for the management of its mining, asbestos textile, asbestos cement and magnesia insulation interests. Dunlop, although it ran its central Birmingham rubber tyre factory and associated businesses directly on functional lines, decentralized its other operations into four divisions specializing in general rubber goods, footwear, garments and sports goods.[51] A full analysis of how typical these cases were must await a definitive study on the lines of Alfred D. Chandler's classic description of the evolution of enterprise structure in the United States,[52] but it would appear that (as Chandler found for the United States) the general adoption of a divisionalized structure was delayed until the postwar period in Great Britain.[53]

What is clear is that, within their varied management structures of the 1920s and 1930s, British manufacturing companies were directing a good deal more resources to management problems than previously. The ratio of administrative staff to operative workers (which had been substantially lower than in the USA before the First World War) was, by the 1930s, very similar to the US level.[54] Much of this represented a strengthening of centralized, functionally differentiated management rather than a divisional structure. Even so, some companies were adopting aspects of the managerial structure implied in the multidivisional hypothesis, without yet adopting the structure in its pure form. Interwar management literature and inter-firm contacts helped to spread knowledge of budgetary control and divisionalization. Accountants were quickly familiarized with the problems of imposing uniform accounting on a merger and of controlling capital expenditure by forward budgeting[55] and management specialists frequently discussed the desirable level of decentralization.[56] The experience of American decentralized management was well publicized,[57] and large British businesses interchanged information on management methods.[58] The creation of a central office and the adoption of a divisional structure with central financial controls was by no means universal, and in smaller and medium-sized companies direct centralized control of all subsidiaries seems to have remained impossible and decentralization of responsibility was limited.[59] Even among larger companies a decentralized system was adopted as much by default as by choice. Where no deliberate strategy of decentralization on the ICI model was developed, the holding company form of control of subsidiaries was most commonly used and internal competition of an administered kind was allowed to persist with only minimal policy and financial controls being exercised from head office. In this sense a decentralized system was the natural form of management in a company growing by acquisition and it was widely adopted,[60] though there was great variation, both between companies and within the same companies at different points in time, in the degree of central control which was exercised. Associated Electrical Industries, which had been formed in 1928 by the consolidation of British Thomson-Houston and Metropolitan-Vickers, continued to run them separately for many years, with loose connections through staff meetings (for exchange of information rather than managerial co-ordination) and a central financial control which was very much at arm's length.[61] Other leading companies described as loosely run confederations of subsidiaries with little central control include Tube Investments, Imperial Tobacco, Tootal Broadhurst Lee, Hawker Siddeley, Guest Keen & Nettlefold, and Electrical & Musical Industries.[62] If this looser structure prevented the full realization of all the organizational economies of rationalization, it nevertheless gave them access to the benefits of pooled overheads, risk spreading, the interchange of commercial and industrial methods, collusive pricing policies, and some degree of co-ordination of new investment.[63] Provided that no problems resulted from their large scale, these firms could grow rapidly by reaping such benefits without encountering serious managerial diseconomies of scale or of growth.

However, many firms which failed to develop an appropriate balance of centralization and decentralization failed to create the managerial surplus and profits stream which was necessary if acquisition activity was to be sustained, and the rate of growth of large firms was still significantly constrained by the management variable. Though Nobel was able to double in size in 1918 through a multi-firm merger, then continue a programme of consolidating and diversifying acquisitions over the next eight years, and subsequently, by merging with three other companies, triple in size to become ICI (which then itself expanded by further acquisitions), the majority of companies had to accept a more leisurely pace of growth. Even mergers on a more modest scale than those of the earlier multi-firm mergers could run into grave problems. In 1924, for example, a committee of enquiry into Crosse & Blackwell (a merger of seven companies) had to recommend the writing down of the capital by £2¾ million, finding:

> serious duplication and overlapping in management [and] that benefits which had actually been derived from combination were so few as to be practically non-existent; and, worst of all, that the associated firms had been competing with one another as strenuously as ever.[64]

Those involved in rationalization could still, it seems, give far too little attention to the management factor for the subsequent health of their creations.

Chandler has diagnosed relative managerial backwardness in many large British firms, and has explained it largely in terms of the persistence of conservative family management, even in publicly-quoted enterprises, in Britain.[65] The failure to centralize and rationalize production and marketing after merger certainly seems to have been common where the individual units were formerly family businesses and the new board contained mainly family representatives who preferred things to remain that way. Such firms also found it difficult to create professional management structures and, indeed, in some cases they eschewed that objective in favour of continuing existing family perquisites and traditional organization.[66] Even public company boards retained strong controlling family elements, and the peculiar British tradition of (in cricketing terms) excluding professional 'players' from board positions in favour of 'gentlemen' amateurs died slowly.[67] No more than a dozen major British manufacturing companies had developed management training schemes for university graduates in the 1930s; and the traditional method of recruitment, where it was not confined to family, was still often by patronage of a director or senior manager rather than openly competitive.[68] Other avenues of entry into management via professions such as engineering or accounting were also closed to many potential entrants by the requirement to pay a 'premium' for apprenticeship training. Even for those able to surmount these barriers, a business career perhaps did not attract the ablest minds, for the social prestige of British business remained low.[69] It is striking that, at a time when university training (sometimes in subjects closely related to business) was becoming the norm for management in the USA, Germany and Japan, only a small minority of senior British managers possessed any form of university degree.[70] The suspicion must, then, remain that the potential for increased efficiency in large-scale bureaucratic co-ordination of economic activity was less professionalized and possibly less competently executed in Britain than may have been the case elsewhere.

Even so the firms which did solve the problems of large-scale organization and of discontinuous digestion of acquisitions were, in Britain as elsewhere, able to achieve high growth rates through merger, involving a doubling or tripling of firm size in a year. Companies like ICI, Reckitt, Fison, Metal Box, British Plaster-

board, Distillers, Tube Investments, and many other leading acquir-
ers in the large and medium company size ranges could, and did,
grow rapidly between the wars, though they rarely attempted to
acquire more than one large or three or four small or medium-sized
companies in a year, preferring to keep their rate of growth to a
manageable level. Such companies, especially those like ICI which
had solved the current organizational problems of merger, were
already approaching rationalization, monopolization and company
growth with increasing confidence. They were active in important
sectors of the economy, and other industries were exhorted to follow
their example. In 1935 a research group sponsored by Political and
Economic Planning was claiming that:

> Now that the technique of large-scale production is much nearer
> solution owing to the realization that the advantages of centralized
> control can only be achieved through functional and administra-
> tive decentralization it cannot be overemphasized that the [cotton]
> industry must face up to the necessity of further amalgamations.[71]

The management developments which we have described were thus
both an inspiration of and a response to the merger waves, an
integral part of the rationalization movement as well as a condition of
its success. As managers solved these problems, economic co-
ordination by competition and the market could begin its retreat. If a
misquotation from Burke be permitted, sophisters, economists and
calculators were coming in the large decentralized corporation to
supplement and partially to succeed the more inchoate signals and
disciplines of the market.

7

The rise of the corporate economy: dimensions

How much? how large? how long? how often?
how representative?
J. H. CLAPHAM, 'Economic history as a discipline',
Encyclopaedia of the Social Sciences,
vol. 5 (New York, 1931), p. 327.

ဢ

By the interwar decades circumstances were in a number of respects
more favourable to the development of large-scale business organizations than they had been during the earlier, and sometimes abortive,
movements towards higher concentration of the turn of the century.
Managers had previously, in smaller firms, often been able to take
questions of organization for granted, devoting their attention to
marketing and other policy problems. Now they found that they
were to a considerable degree involved in organization making. This
was a natural requirement of a movement in industry which aimed at
supplementing, and to some extent replacing, co-ordination by the
'invisible hand' of the market by the organization, planning and
execution of economic activities by the 'visible hand' of bureaucratic
hierarchies within firms. This in turn was increasingly desirable as
economies of scale and of integration in production technology,
marketing and finance were developed, and it was favourably
regarded by a benevolent government and by public opinion. The
growth of the stock exchange and the transformation in the ownership of enterprise provided the financial wherewithal for
economies to be realized by the groupings of assets into large firms.
Thus, whilst evident difficulties remained, increasingly it seemed
that the governmental, financial and managerial constraints on the
growth of the firms had been loosened sufficiently to produce
substantial growth. The foundations on which the large-scale corporate economy could be built were already firmly laid.

This process was, of course, a gradual, evolutionary one which had its roots firmly in earlier manifestations of capitalism and enterprise. It was not – any more than was the industrial 'revolution' before it – a sudden revolutionary overthrow of established economic structures and relationships, though it was eventually to transform the economy from which it grew. We have already seen that the prewar birth of the corporate economy was troubled and its early growth exceptionally slow. In the interwar rationalization movement, however, there was a strong and growing body of opinion which believed that its progress should be accelerated. The aim of the present chapter is to identify the time pattern of the growth of large corporations which followed, and in particular to identify the period during which they grew most rapidly to achieve a state which resembled the corporate economy of today and diverged significantly from the nineteenth-century structure of enterprise. In order to establish whether such a period of rapid transformation in the structure of manufacturing industry can be pinpointed, it will be necessary to examine the dimensions of industrial concentration and of merger activity over the first eighty years of the present century.

For the manufacturing sector overall, estimates of the share of the largest 100 firms in manufacturing output between 1907 and 1978 are presented in Figure 7.1.[1] The points for the years for which data are available are plotted on a semilog scale to facilitate comparison of the rates of growth in the share of the largest 100 firms in each period. All of the estimates, and especially those for earlier years, are in some degree conjectural, so too much emphasis should not be placed on slopes that do not significantly differ from the horizontal: the 'decline' from 1939 to 1948 could, for example, be accounted for entirely by errors in the data.[2] There are however, some important movements in concentration which stand out very clearly in Figure 7.1. First, after several decades of perhaps slightly increasing concentration, there was, in the decade following the First World War, a sustained and rapid rise in industrial concentration, as a result of which the largest 100 firms gained control of perhaps one quarter of manufacturing output. That level of concentration is very similar to the level in the United States at the same time, though this high level had been achieved earlier in America.[3] The 1920s rise in British concentration levels was followed by several decades of stagnant, or possible even declining, concentration, so that the level of 1930 was probably not exceeded until the early 1950s, by which time the second substantial upward movement was clearly under

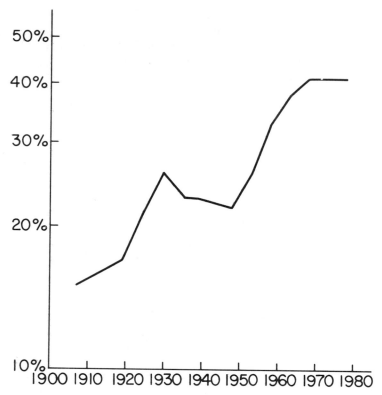

FIGURE 7.1   *The share of the largest 100 firms in manufacturing net output*
1907–78 (semilog scale)
Source: Appendix 2

way. The rapid rise in the share of the largest 100 firms then
reasserted itself, and (in contrast to the United States, where
concentration rose more slowly) it continued into the 1960s at a rate
comparable with that of the 1920s. This second surge also tailed off,
and the share of the largest 100 firms settled at about 40 per cent of
manufacturing output in the 1970s.

    This chronology provides a clue to the dynamic process by which
the corporate economy developed: a clue revealed by comparison of
these changes in concentration with the time pattern of merger
activity shown in Figure 7.2 below. (The nature and source of the
merger statistics are more fully discussed in Appendix 1.) Over the
period from the turn of the century to the present a broad correlation

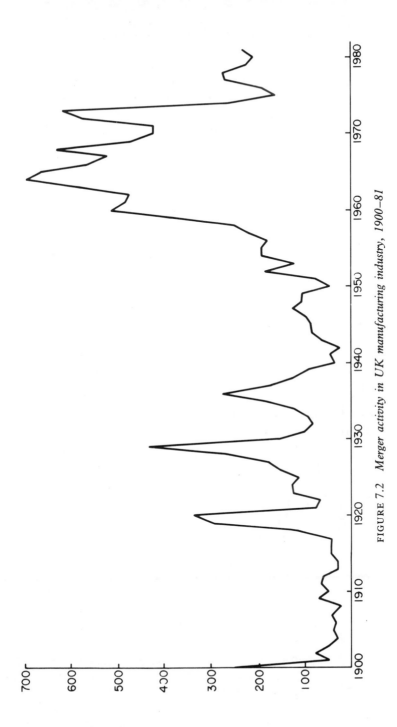

FIGURE 7.2 *Merger activity in UK manufacturing industry, 1900–81*

between merger movements and changes in concentration is evident. In particular the two periods when merger activity was at its most intense – the 1920s and the 1960s – correspond to periods in which the largest 100 firms were increasing their share of output, while the lulls in concentration in the 1930s, 1940s and 1970s are paralleled by decades of relatively low merger activity.

The 1920s appear as the first merger-intensive decade, with the average annual level of 188 firm disappearances by merger over three times the average of the preceding four decades, and the peaks of 1920 and 1929 not again equalled until the merger waves beginning in 1959. Then in the 1960s the annual average of 564 mergers per year suggests a further substantial increase in merger activity, but this subsides in the 1970s and early 1980s. Much the same pattern is shown in the values of the firms disappearing in mergers, converted for changes in the price level (see Appendix 1), though in this case the minor peak in the 1930s is more muted than in Figure 7.2.

A further indicator of the level of merger activity is available for some of the years which we wish to compare and is presented separately in Figure 7.3. This shows the proportion of the total

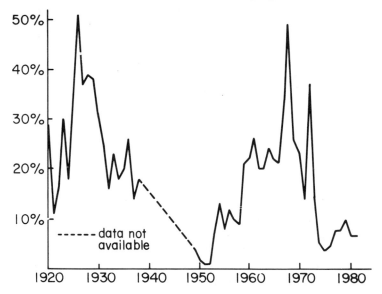

FIGURE 7.3   *Merger values as a proportion of total investment expenditure in manufacturing industry, 1920–81*
Source: Appendix 1

investment expenditure of manufacturing firms which is accounted for by their expenditure on acquisitions and mergers. Such an indicator is particularly useful since it provides a measure of merger activity relative to other sources of the growth of firms. Firms may grow either internally – that is, by investing in new factories and plant – or externally – that is, by acquiring existing firms. Investment in internal growth is usually the most important source of expansion for firms in general, and Figure 7.3 confirms this, but in some years mergers were also very important. In the peak years of 1926, 1968 and 1972, for example, mergers accounted for about one half of total investment spending. These figures confirm the previous suggestion that the level of merger activity in the 1920s and 1960s was significantly higher than in the intervening decades. However, a contrast with the previously presented measures is that the level of merger activity is not, according to this relative measure, higher in the 1960s than in the 1920s; in the earlier decade, overall, mergers accounted for 32 per cent of investment expenditure, a figure similar (within the probable margins of error in the data) to the 28 per cent of investment expenditure for which mergers were responsible in the 1960s.

Now all of these estimates of merger activity, and especially those for the periods before the 1960s, are in some degree conjectural. Differences in the methods by which the series for the various decades have been compiled and linked render comparisons between the level in widely separated years (of the kind we have just hazarded) extremely speculative. Given the changing conventions of compilers, the vagaries of the reporting of mergers, and the varying stringency of legal disclosure requirements, it is difficult to assess precisely the degree to which series covering such a long period are comparable. The number of mergers is undoubtedly greater in each period than the level actually recorded in Figures 7.2 and 7.3, but we cannot tell by how much. Moreover, in contrast to the case of the iceberg (whose visible tip always bears the same relationship to its submerged portion), the various peaks seen in the merger statistics may represent a changing proportion of total merger activity, and this would clearly imperil our conclusions. A more detailed analysis of the merger waves at the level of individual firms can, however, be used as an independent check on the impression gained from the aggregate merger statistics. We have a very full record of the merger activity of the largest firms because their major mergers are regularly noted in the financial press, and also many of them have published company histories in which we can follow their development. It is therefore possible, for each large firm, to discover in which decade its founding merger or more substantial growth by acquisition occurred. On this basis an intertemporal profile of merger activity can be constructed which will be less subject to the vagaries of reporting that detract from the comparability over time of the aggregate merger statistics. The results are shown in Table 7.1.[4] The right-hand column confirms that the impression in the aggregate statistics

TABLE 7.1   *The decade of the major mergers of the leading companies in UK manufacturing industry*

	The top 82 companies of 1948	The top 100 companies of 1970
1890–9	7	2
1900–9	6	4
1910–19	6	2
1920–9	19	14
1930–9	10	6
1940–9	3	4
1950–9	–	4
1960–9	–	21
(Unclassified*)	(31)	(43)

– Not applicable.
* Firms whose major mergers could not be allocated to particular decades or whose growth was primarily internal.
Source: see page 228, note 4.

(of the predominance of the 1920s and 1960s in merger activity) is an accurate one. Of the largest companies in 1970, fourteen had their major merger in the 1920s and as many as twenty-one in the 1960s, both of these figures being well above the number experienced in other decades. There is, however, a tendency for later merger waves to expunge the effects of previous ones and this may create a new bias in the results. The GEC, AEI, English Electric merger in 1967–8, for example, is chosen as the major merger for that company, though each of the three component companies also had earlier 'major' mergers which, had they remained independent, would have been recorded in the table. A counterweight to this effect is therefore provided in the left-hand column of Table 7.1. This is based on the largest firms in 1948, and thus shows the role of mergers in the 1920s more clearly, without the overlay of subsequent merger waves.[5] The table as a whole leaves little room for doubt that there was a substantial merger wave in the 1920s which perhaps rivalled in importance that of the 1960s. The contrast between this and the experience of the United States is particularly striking. A similar study of the largest 100 US manufacturing corporations showed that over half of their major mergers occurred before the First World War.[6] Thus the picture of British firms 'catching up' in the rationalization movement of the 1920s with a structure of industry which had been created earlier in the United States is confirmed.

The pervasiveness of increased concentration and the widespread impact of the merger movement throughout manufacturing industry[7] in the 1920s can be seen in Table 7.2, which unlike the previous merger and concentration figures, relates to a restricted population of relatively large and mainly quoted firms. It is possible to calculate the size (measured by the market value of their capital) of around 600 firms, which by 1930 probably still accounted for less than a half of manufacturing net output, though they had absorbed around 600 additional firms in mergers during the 1920s. The resulting size distribution, though it is confined to the upper ranges of firms,[8] does enable us to calculate the share of the largest five companies within each major industrial classification. Between January 1919 and December 1930 the five-firm concentration ratio rose in all fifteen industry groups, the rise being in most cases a substantial one. In this population the 100 largest firms' share rose from 53 per cent to 77 per cent of the total market valuation of the firms, and this may understate the overall rise in concentration, because the sample as a whole was gaining at the expense of the under-represented smaller and unquoted firms.[9]

In order to separate out the relative importance of mergers and internal growth in the increased concentration, it is necessary to make some assumption about what the level of concentration would have been in the absence of merger. Suppose that in 1919 there were two firms, A and B, each with one half of the market. If A acquired B early in 1919, thus becoming the only firm, and if by 1930 the market had grown by 50 per cent, two views might be taken about what had caused the increase in concentration. One view might be that the merger of 1919 accounted for an initial increase but that the

TABLE 7.2   *Concentration in industry groups, 1919–30*

	Shares of the largest five firms			
	1	*2*	*3*	*4*
				Proportion
			Counter-	*of the*
	1919	*1930*	*factual*	*increase*
Industry	*population*	*population*	*'merged'*	*due to*
	(%)	*(%)*	*population*	*mergers*
			(%)	*(%)*
Food	39·0	74·0	67·7	82
Drink	25·7	40·6	33·9	55
Tobacco	94·5	99·7	97·7	62
Chemicals	61·3	86·3	84·0	91
Metal manufacture	28·7	45·9	42·7	81
Non-electrical engineering	46·3	56·2	53·7	75
Electrical engineering	43·8	51·9	56·8	160*
Shipbuilding	64·6	89·7	84·9	81
Vehicles	34·1	66·5	41·2	22
Metal goods not elsewhere specified	68·0	87·1	80·8	67
Textiles	47·4	64·0	51·3	23
Clothing and footwear	33·1	58·0	40·1	28
Building materials	59·5	83·0	81·4	93
Paper and publishing	40·8	73·8	64·6	72
Miscellaneous manufacturing†	49·2	84·8	70·5	60
	Share of the largest 100 firms			
All manufacturing	56·4	77·4	72·5	77

Notes:
* A merger contribution above 100 per cent implies that, but for merger activity, concentration would have declined in this industry.
† Includes industry groups conventionally listed separately as 'leather, leather goods and fur' and 'timber and furniture' in addition to the conventional 'miscellaneous manufacturing' category.
Source: Calculated from the data described in L. Hannah and J. A. Kay, *Concentration in Modern Industry* (1977).

rest of the increase in A's size by 1930 should be accounted internal growth. An alternative, and perhaps more plausible view[10] would be that it was the merger of A and B that caused the whole of the increase in concentration (since if that merger had not occurred B would have shared the subsequent growth of the market, and the share of the two companies in the larger market of 1930 would have been the same as in 1919). It is this assumption that is adopted in calculating the percentage contribution of mergers to the increase in concentration which is shown in the fourth column of Table 7.2. The calculation requires the construction of a hypothetical population, reflecting an adjustment to the real firms of 1919 to show them as they would have been if all the mergers which occurred between 1919 and 1930 had occurred instantaneously, in 1919. By comparing the level of concentration in this hypothetical or 'counterfactual' population (column 3) with the level actually observed in 1919 and 1930 (columns 1 and 2), we can estimate the proportion of the increase which is attributable to merger activity (column 4). For all manufacturing industries taken together, more than three-quarters of the increase in concentration is due to merger.[11] In all but three of fifteen industry groups mergers were more important than internal growth in increasing the level of concentration.[12] The rise of the corporate economy was, then, strongly conditioned by the unprecedented merger movement of the 1920s, which significantly increased the rate of growth of leading firms over a wide range of industry groups.[13]

A number of the important dimensions of the rise of the corporate economy do, then, support the conclusion that in the 1920s concentration was rapidly increasing as a result of a merger wave of unprecedented proportions and of permanent significance. What is thus revealed in the statistics is broadly consonant with the shifts of opinion amongst businessmen, financiers and politicians which we have chronicled in earlier chapters. The heightened faith in 'rationalization' generally, and in the achievement of economies of scale and co-ordination in large combines particularly, was clearly being acted upon in these years. The disadvantages of the inherited structure had been perceived and there was an attempt, showing clearly in rising concentration and merger activity, to remedy some of its deficiencies. Processes of this kind are, we began this chapter by conceding, of necessity gradual. Sometimes, it is true, they are hurried on by waves of fashion, but usually they require many years of trial and error, of learning and teaching, before their effects become pervasive and irresistible. To attempt to identify 'stages' in such gradual, evolutionary processes is perhaps arbitrary, but in this case we have good reason for settling a label on one important 'stage'. The years after the First World War clearly saw an acceleration of structural change and it is to the interwar decades, and particularly to the period 1919–30, that the 'rise of the corporate economy' is most naturally dated.

These interwar decades have in general been painted by historians in melancholy shades; and that the underlying depression in the staple industries and the widespread unemployment of able-bodied adults represented a blight on industrial life, a deeply unacceptable face of capitalism, can hardly be gainsaid. It has, however, become increasingly clear that against this gloomy backcloth Britain witnessed in the interwar period a rate of economic growth higher than that of some major competitors, and certainly better than the growth rate that had been achieved in Britain in the decades of stagnation before the First World War.[14] This change in trend growth performance clearly required rapid and substantial readjustments in the structure of industrial output.[15] and the question naturally arises as to whether the evolving structure of firms which we have described was an integral part of this shift. Economic growth, involving the expansion of new industries and the contraction of old ones, can in principle be achieved by the multiplication of new firms coupled with the bankruptcy of firms in the old industries. However, the changes in the composition of output between the wars did not occur exclusively in this way but rather evolved in parallel with substantial internal and external growth by large firms. Hence it is possible that the merger waves and the growth of large firms were integral parts of a common process of economic change. In the next chapter, therefore, we must examine more systematically the course which the large corporations were steering: the directions of their expansion, and in particular their role in the new industries.

8

The rise of the corporate economy: directions

*It may be that the influence of Mass Production upon the
Destinies of Great Britain will be far greater than
that of the Wars and adventures from which
the British Empire grew.*
SIR ERIC GEDDES, *Mass Production* (1931), p. 5.

ꜩ

The merger waves and increased concentration levels documented
quantitatively in the previous chapter were quite pervasive, affecting
old industries and new, the relatively small-scale industries and the
industries with mass production, big firms and medium-sized ones.
It was, arguably, the biggest shake-up in the corporate structure of
British manufacturing to have occurred this century. The degree of
change and the modernity of the structure created can be glimpsed
in the changed roll call of the top fifty firms (measured by the market
value of their capital) in the manufacturing sector at the end of the
great merger wave, in December 1930, shown in Table 8.1. The
largest firm twelve years earlier, J. & P. Coats, the sewing thread
manufacturer, had a market capitalization of only £45 millions in
1919;[1] by the end of 1930 (when Coats itself was only a little bigger)
five more firms – Unilever, Imperial Tobacco, ICI, Courtaulds and
Distillers – exceeded that value. The largest of them – Unilever and
Imperial Tobacco – had a market capitalization in excess of £130
millions. The whole group of fifty firms in Table 8.1 were over twice
as large in real terms in 1930 as the top fifty in 1919.[2] The increase in
terms of number of employees in the leading firms is less spectacular
than the increase in their capital values, but is nevertheless striking.
In 1907 the largest manufacturing employer (Fine Cotton Spinners
& Doublers) employed only 30,000 people and few other firms even
approached that figure. By the 1930s there were at least ten
manufacturing businesses employing 30,000 or more people, the
largest of these, like ICI and Unilever, employing 50,000 or more.[3]

TABLE 8.1   *The fifty largest manufacturing companies of 1930*

Industry	Name of company	Estimated market value (£ million)
Food	Unilever	132·0
Tobacco	Imperial Tobacco	130·5
Chemicals	Imperial Chemical Industries	77·3
Textiles (rayon)	Courtaulds	51·9
Textiles	J. & P. Coats	47·4
Drink	Distillers	45·5
Drink	Guinness	43·0
Rubber	Dunlop Rubber	28·2
Publishing	Allied Newspapers	27·6
Vehicles	Ford Motor Co. (subsidiary of US Ford)	21·2
Metal manufacture/ engineering	Guest Keen & Nettlefold	20·3
Shipbuilding/engineering	Vickers	19·6
Drink	Watney Combe Reid	18·5
Publishing	Daily Mail Trust	15·6
Electrical engineering	General Electric Company	14·5
Building materials	Associated Portland Cement	13·9
Chemicals	Reckitt & Sons	13·4
Drink	Bass Ratcliffe Gretton	13·3
Chemicals	Boots Pure Drug (British subsidiary of Liggett International)	12·8
Asbestos	Turner & Newall	12·6
Food	J. Lyons	12·1
Engineering	Babcock & Wilcox	11·0
Food	Bovril	10·8
Food	British Cocoa & Chocolate (Cadbury-Fry)	10·3
Metal manufacture	Mond Nickel (British subsidiary of International Nickel)	10·3
Tobacco	Carreras	10·0
Drink	Walker-Cain	10·0
Drink	Mitchells & Butler	9·9
Electrical engineering	Associated Electrical Industries (British subsidiary of International General Electric)	9·8
Metal manufacture	Dorman Long	9·8
Textiles	Fine Spinners & Doublers	9·8
Food	Tate & Lyle	9·3
Publishing	Daily Mirror Newspapers	8·8
Footwear	J. Sears (Trueform Boot Co.)	8·5

TABLE 8.1   (*continued*)

Industry	Name of company	Estimated market value (£ million)
Matches	British Match Corporation	8·1
Paper	Wallpaper Manufacturers	7·9
Drink	Hoare & Co.	7·6
Vehicles	Morris Motors	7·6
Electrical engineering	British Insulated Cables	7·5
Drink	Taylor Walker	7·5
Food	United Dairies	7·3
Drink	Barclay Perkins	7·1
Metal manufacture	Stewarts & Lloyds	7·1
Textiles	Bleachers Association	6·9
Food	Liebigs Extract of Meat	6·9
Textiles (rayon)	British Celanese	6·8
Metal manufacture	United Steel	6·7
Drink	Allsopp	6·4
Textiles	Combined Egyptian Mills	6·3
Chemicals	Pinchin Johnson	6·3

Source: see Appendix 3.

It is the argument of this chapter that the giants created in the 1920s were, by and large, enduring features of the British corporate economy, and that this derives not only from their large relative size, but from significant changes in their managerial strategies in the interwar years.

This shift in strategy was perhaps most difficult to achieve in the old industries. Many of the large firms in these industries, formed in the faltering prewar moves towards a corporate economy,[4] such as Armstrong–Whitworth, the naval shipbuilders, or the Bradford Dyers Association, had by 1930 slipped to lower positions in the league table of firms. Indeed fourteen of the largest fifty firms of 1919 had not only failed to hold their own relative to other firms but their market capitalization had by 1930 declined in absolute terms also.[5] None the less Table 8.1 and the listings of large firms in 1948 and later[6] do suggest that firms with a base in 'old' industries could evolve strategies adequate for survival. Firms like Watneys and Imperial Tobacco – very much creations of the pre-First World War merger boom, but consistently among the leaders in subsequent listings – had the rather special advantages of entrenched market positions selling addictive goods in markets in which there were substantial barriers to new entry, and, in the case of brewing, still substantial room for growth by merger. However, less fortunate old industries, such as textiles, iron and steel, and shipbuilding, faced a loss of overseas markets, substantial competition in the home market and a weak financial position, which in some cases was aggravated by overcapitalization in the postwar boom of 1919–20.[7] It was important in these industries to tailor output to demand, and to maximize productivity by gaining access to economies of scale, rationalization and integration; and there is some evidence that attempts of this kind were being made. Both merger activity and increases in concentration in the metal manufacture, shipbuilding and textile industries were, for example, as marked as in the new industries, and substantial improvements in productivity were also achieved in these industries in the interwar period.[8]

In some cases it is possible to pinpoint particular areas in which economies flowed from the enlarged scale of firms in the staple industries, but much of the evidence currently available is impressionistic rather than conclusive. Firms like Allied Ironfounders, the Renold & Coventry Chain Company, and Jute Industries are known to have been making acquisitions and rationalizing production afterwards.[9] Cases of vertical integration were also becoming increasingly common, particularly in the iron and steel industry, and although not all firms seized the opportunities, some were able to gain economies by vertically linking the output of steel from the ore to the finished product, minimizing heat losses between the interlinked processes.[10] Stewarts & Lloyds, when building a large new integrated steel tube plant at Corby, was also able to internalize some of the external economies of its expansion there by buying up local ironstone companies, and this in itself encouraged, and increased the profitability of, such ventures.[11]

Perhaps the highest contemporary hopes for gains from rationalization were those entertained by the critics of the extremely depressed cotton trade, in which the typical unit still remained small. The logic behind these hopes was described by the Balfour Committee:

The effects of concentration and combination on the elimination of the most inefficient plant are not altogether simple. There can be no doubt that the operation of free competition is a very slow and costly method for the purpose of securing such elimination. The tenacity of life shown by businesses working at a loss is somewhat extraordinary. Plant and buildings are often highly specialized, and there is a reluctance to incur an almost total loss by dismantling them where there is a chance that a favourable turn of the market will for a time at least put the business on a profitable basis. But the results of the prolonged competition of inefficient undertakings react on the more efficient, and tend to depress the whole industry; and an operation of cutting out the dead wood may be essential for the speedy restoration of prosperity and the resumption of growth from the more vigorous branches. It seems unquestionable that this operation can often be performed more speedily and 'rationally' and with less suffering through the mechanism of consolidation or agreement than by the unaided play of competition.[12]

Clearly, however, such a process of rationalization could only make a contribution to economic growth if it enabled firms to free redundant resources for transfer to other, higher productivity sectors of the economy. The Balfour Committee reflected a widespread contemporary view that this could be done more efficiently by management within a consolidated enterprise than by the alternative, traditional (but it was felt, socially undesirable) method of long-term competitive attrition, with capitalists and workers gradually transferring their services elsewhere under the threat of bankruptcy and unemployment. The crux of this case was what might, by analogy with the more familiar economic concept of entry barriers, be thought of as 'barriers to exit'.[13] Such barriers, which induce firms to stay in an industry even though its prospects in both the long and the short term are poor, could arise from over-optimism about future prospects, or a mistaken belief that they would survive whilst their competitors would not. In the cotton industry, where these problems were met in the most extreme form, managers were able to sell output at a price below marginal cost by calling on unpaid capital from their shareholders, and even, it seems, in some cases by attracting loans from bankers. Such actions can only have diverted funds from capital formation which could have been more effectively used in the new industries, but mergers such as the Combined Egyptian Mills (fifteen firms in 1929) and the Lancashire Cotton Corporation (ninety-six firms in 1929–32) aimed instead to cut back the capital stock of these industries and release resources in the process. Despite considerable difficulties experienced in the attempt to combine many small, competing enterprises (see pp. 75–6), the Lancashire Cotton Corporation, in particular, was able to close a number of mills, unseat the incumbent management, scrap large numbers of redundant spindles, and raise prices to marginal costs or above. British textile firms were among the largest in the world, as they had been already before the First World War, but they were not amongst the most successful in integrating the various vertically related activities to achieve cost reduction and marketing success.[14]

The extent to which concentration and contraction on the part of the 'old' industries enabled the 'new' industries to grow can, moreover, easily be exaggerated. There remained many old industries in which rationalization had made little progress. The problem of creating new strategies for old industries was particularly strong in regions such as Scotland, which were overcommitted to the slow-growing staple industries. While there were moves towards rationalization of some firms in these industries, the shifting of resources from old to new industries was relatively rare.[15] Even without the transfer of resources from old industries, the basic factors of production were often in ample supply elsewhere. It was an overall deficiency in demand, rather than supply constraints, that held back the further growth of the new industries. The supply of labour, for example, was not a bottleneck to growth in this period of widespread unemployment, and even if skilled workers were released by rationalization of the linen or cotton industry, their skills were very specific and hence their contribution was unlikely to be more valuable to the new industries than that of the unskilled, unemployed workers who were available in large numbers. Capital, too, was fairly industry-specific, and whilst factories could be, and were, transferred from old to new uses, a scrapped spindle or a redundant shipyard produced little but scrap metal. Thus the use in the new industries of redundant capital resources from the older trades, where it occurred, was more a convenience than a necessity. Much the same can be said about the supply of managers and entrepreneurs. While some managers undoubtedly transferred to the new industries, management still tended to be industry-specific, and the 'steel men' or 'cotton men' who transferred did not take with them more than very basic skills. The situation was, then, very different from that in the period after the Second World War when, given full employment conditions and capacity constraints on growth, the transfer of resources from the old industries was a prerequisite of the growth of the new.

The most hopeful strategy for large firms in the staple industries was to diversify into alternative products for which demand was growing and in which their existing financial, technical and managerial skills gave them a comparative advantage. In a sense Nobel and ICI were the prime exponents of this strategy, for, from an initial base in stagnant sectors of the chemical and metals trades such as alkali, explosives and ammunition, they rationalized their production facilities in these fields and diversified into new ones, thus achieving rapid rates of growth (see pp. 109–10 below). Yet in industries in which managerial skills were not adaptable, perhaps for reasons inherent in technologies with little spin-off between the various branches, this strategy was not always successful. Vickers, for example, based on iron, steel and shipbuilding and, like Nobel, facing declining postwar markets, saw the need to diversify into peacetime products and in fact entered the 1920s with subsidiaries involved in electrical engineering (Metrovick) and motor vehicles (Wolseley), and also manufactured aircraft, aluminium, and scientific instruments.[16] The common dependence on metals technology does not, however, seem to have provided as useful a technical core of growth as in the Nobel case, for, despite a substantial programme of acquisition, the market value of Vickers' capital hardly increased at all between 1919 and 1930. By the later 1920s the company had abandoned much of its earlier strategy – Metrovick was sold to AEI and Wolseley to Morris – and it began to concentrate more on achieving economies in its traditional spheres of operation. The result was a series of horizontal mergers with competing firms in the major heavy engineering industries: Vickers-Armstrong consolidated Vickers' shipbuilding interests with those of Armstrong-Whitworth; and the English Steel Corporation and Metropolitan-Cammell Company consolidated their steel and railway carriage interests with those of Cammell Laird. The mergers were justified by the Cammell Laird board in a letter to its shareholders, in the classic terms of the rationalization movement:

> The development of elaborate and costly machinery, the growth of mass production, the stationary if not contracting condition of the basic industries in this country, and the example of our principal

competitiors abroad point irresistibly to the need for far-reaching reorganization. . . . The arguments in favour of these proposals appear to us to be conclusive, for they render possible economies in production, improvements in technical efficiency and sales organization and a development of research which can be achieved in no other way.[17]

These initiatives with which Vickers was connected were by no means the only ones of a similar kind. More generally, in the steel industry, amalgamations such as Lancashire Steel, Colvilles, and British (Guest Keen & Baldwins) Iron & Steel involved the demerger of steel companies from vertical groups formed earlier, but now abandoned in a period when it was generally thought that the advantages of horizontal amalgamation were the greater.[18]

It is the growth of firms themselves principally based in the new industries, however, that is most striking. Rapidly growing industries such as rayon, motor-cars, electrical engineering and the modern sectors of the chemical trade experienced significant changes in the structure of their firms.[19] Before the First World War, there had been a failure to invest in the new and potentially rapidly expanding sectors, so that for products like dyestuffs and motor-cars imports had exceeded domestic production.[20] In the First World War and after, however, a dramatic shift in the pattern of world trade, and a realization of the potential profitability of a pattern of production more akin to that in America and Germany, seems to have induced a substantial shift; and in the eleven years 1920–30 one third of gross capital formation was directed to five major growth industries: rayon, electricals, motors, chemicals, and paper.[21] In many of these industries, therefore, the growth of firms was rapid and as the new capacity often incorporated mass production techniques it also tended to be concentrated in relatively few firms. Thus William Morris was able, by reaping economies of scale, to expand his modest 5 per cent share of the motor-car market in 1919 to 41 per cent by 1925, increasing his annual production from only 387 cars to 55,582 in the same period. Other car manufacturers, notably Ford (a subsidiary of US Ford) and Austin, also grew substantially in the 1920s, as did the major domestic supplier of motor-car tyres, Dunlop Rubber.[22] In the rayon industry, in which Courtaulds had already attained a dominant position by 1919, there was also substantial further growth, and by the later 1920s the company was providing a substantial proportion of the world's greatly enlarged output. At the same time its major competitor in the rayon industry, British Celanese, was also growing rapidly and joined the list of the fifty largest firms.[23] The mass production methods introduced by these firms enabled them to make substantial price reductions. The average factory price of cars fell from £308 in 1912 to £259 in 1924, £206 in 1930, and to £130 by 1935–6, while the price of a hank of viscose yarn fell from a postwar peak of 19s 3d to 4s 6d in 1929, and 2s 6d in the later 1930s.[24]

The innovation of mass production methods, which was so clear a feature of the manufacture of rayon and motor-cars, was less readily apparent in the science-based, and rapidly expanding, electrical engineering and chemical industries, but here also the size of the firms greatly increased. Whilst there were still opportunities for small specialist firms in many branches of these industries, a number of large corporations developed, with widespread interests diversified over a range of manufactures. The formation of such companies appears to have owed a lot to the merger waves between the closing years of the First World War and the early 1930s. Imperial Chemical Industries, for example, was formed in 1926 as a consolidation of four of the largest fifty firms of 1919: Nobel Industries, Brunner Mond, the British Dyestuffs Corporation, and the United Alkali Company.[25] All except the latter were themselves recent groupings of chemical companies – Nobel was the merger of thirty explosives companies in 1918 and had since made a number of further acquisitions in an attempt to diversify. Brunner Mond, already large before the war, had acquired a number of rivals and integrated backwards during the war. British Dyestuffs, which controlled 75 per cent of British dyestuffs output, was the result of a merger backed by the government during the war in an effort to expand the British production of dyestuffs. After the main ICI merger this pattern of consolidation and diversification by merger continued, and further significant purchases were made of firms in the fertilizer, metals and dyestuffs fields.

The advantages of such a grouping are to be seen partly in the classical motives for the reduction of competition and the achievement of scale economies. Competition was reduced not only by the increased market dominance of ICI in areas such as dyestuffs, but also by forestalling the possibility of new entry by one of the other merger partners which did not at that time directly compete, but which had the technical ability to diversify competitively in the future. Economies of scale were achieved partly by the rationalization of old plant and partly through new investment in larger plant. Six months after the initial merger, for example, Nobel had closed 55 per cent of its explosives capacity and was producing for the lower postwar demand at a cost reduction of 16 per cent. Similar rationalization appears to have followed the main ICI merger: the alkali production of the United Alkali Company and Brunner Mond was, for example, concentrated in the more efficient plants, with resulting cost savings overall. Such concentration could, in principle, have been achieved without a merger by competitive forces (as in the motor-car industry), but in practice competition in these branches of the chemical industry was so imperfect that in many cases merger was probably a prerequisite of such cost savings and certainly speeded up the process. New investment projects on a large scale were also undertaken by the new ICI group: the Billingham complex, for example (which Brunner Mond had had difficulty in financing alone), was significantly expanded, though it in fact proved to be an unprofitable investment. More relevant to ICI's longer-run success was the synergy involved in bringing together the commercial and technical expertise of firms in heavy chemicals, organic chemicals, chemical engineering and non-ferrous metals in a unique complementary combination. It had been the fear of Nobel (which brought its expertise in nitrocellulose and non-ferrous metal technology to the group) of 'having no technical and economic groundwork on which to build'[26] that had been one of the original motives of the ICI merger. With the benefit of the merger, the diversified expertise of the constituent firms was applied to a wide range of products, including paints, metal, leathercloth, plastics, solvents, dyestuffs, fertilizers, and high pressure engineering, and the collaboration was generally a fruitful one. Whilst not all the resulting spin-offs and new investments were profitable, many were, and the grouping made a significant contribution to the diversification and modernization of the mix of output in the chemical industry in which ICI had a dominant share.

In the electrical engineering industry concentration was less marked,[27] but three principal groupings came to fill a role similar to that of ICI in the chemical industry. The largest of these – the General Electric Company – had its origins in an electrical merchanting business of the 1880s and, after substantial prewar growth, embarked upon an important programme of expansion in the war, taking control of the Osram Company (which had been cut off by the war from its German parent), and Chamberlain & Hookham (a meter manufacturer). However, the claim of the company to manufacture 'Everything Electrical' was only really assured with the acquisition during the war of Fraser & Chalmers, which secured a place in the heavy electrical industry. The company's Witton works were also extended and a 50 per cent interest was taken in Pirelli-General Cables. Between 1918 and 1922 GEC's issued capital was increased from £1½ million to almost £9 million, so that the stage was set for the company's expansion from a workforce of 15,000 in 1919 to 40,000 twenty years later. Somewhat less successful was English Electric, another wartime grouping of electrical companies manufacturing a range of specialist electrical products, based on Dick Kerr & Company of Preston. After purchasing the Coventry Ordnance Works from a consortium of shipbuilders, this group was floated as the English Electric Company, with a capital of £5 million, in 1919, in which year it also acquired the former Siemens Dynamo Works at Stafford for £1 million. Athough the company subsequently experienced serious financial and managerial problems (and hence was not among the largest fifty firms of 1930) it became a major rival for GEC after reorganization in 1931.

The origins of the third leading electrical manufacturer, Associated Electrical Industries, are bound up with American influences. The British Thomson-Houston Company was already owned by the General Electric Company of America (no relation to the British GEC), and Gerard Swope, the president of the American parent company, was anxious to extend his influence in Britain. Hence in 1926–7 he acquired Ferguson Pailin and Edison Swan and in 1928 added the Metropolitan-Vickers Company (which, though originally under the control of the American Westinghouse Company, had passed from them to Vickers during the war), consolidating all four British subsidiaries under the name of Associated Electrical Industries.[28] As a result of this merger activity, GEC, English Electric and AEI came to control some 35 per cent of the electrical engineering industry, and, on the heavy plant side (where fixed costs were large and competition fierce during the periodic depressions in demand),[29] their market share was as high as 60 per cent. The motive of greater market control and the control of competition was certainly an important one in the mergers, and whilst some economies of operation were possible, integration within the merged companies was very slow. In AEI, for example, the BTH and Metrovick interests were run as virtually independent subsidiaries on the manufacturing side for many decades, with only loose co-ordination of commercial and financial policy. There were benefits in the mergers from the bringing together of commercial manufacturing and technical experts in the electrical industry,[30] but despite this advantage there remained great scope for the smaller specialist firm in many areas. In domestic electrical appliances, for example, production expanded rapidly in the 1930s, but subsidiaries of foreign firms such as Hoover and Electrolux and new British enterprises such as Morphy Richards played the leading role.[31] In the field of electrical sound and entertainment, however, a large British company, Electrical & Musical Industries (a merger in 1931 of the Gramophone Company and Columbia Graphophone), was a conspicuous success.

What both ICI and the leading electrical manufacturing companies had in common was a commitment to, and a developed expertise in, a specific, but wide, area of modern technology. Such specialization was a logical extension of the division of labour in an increasingly complex industrial environment. Moreover, since in many of their individual product lines they faced competition from smaller rivals, we may perhaps infer from their continued growth[32] that there were real advantages to the possession and development within the firm of such a core of technical expertise.[33] This strategy of development could also be successful in narrower technical fields. Dunlop, for example, achieved substantial growth in the rubber industry not only on the basis of the greatly increased interwar demand for its traditional product, motor-car tyres, but also by integrating backwards and forwards and by diversifying within the rubber indus⁺ry. Hence it became involved in rubber plantations, in the production of cotton and wheels (both related to its tyre production) and in the marketing of tyres and retreading services, and also acquired the Charles MacIntosh group and other companies in the general rubber goods trade.[34] Similarly, Turner & Newall, initially a merger in 1920 of four manufacturers involved in the asbestos trade, pursued a policy of diversification and integration, acquiring in 1925–30 Ferodo brake linings, a group of asbestos cement companies, and a substantial interest in Rhodesian asbestos mines.[35]

Many of these technically-based firms in the new and expanding industries were also developing sources of future growth by heavy investment in research and development.[36] There are significant economies of scale and advantages to the diversification of risks in corporate research, and it was generally felt that a firm employing less than 1000 people was unlikely to mount a significant research effort. Hence the growth of larger firms did much to stimulate this kind of expenditure, and, in consequence, accelerated the rate of technical innovation. The constituent firms of ICI, for example, had all financed research laboratories, but within four years of the merger of 1926, their collective research expenditure was, as a matter of deliberate policy, quadrupled to reach £1 million by 1930, and, after a cutback in the depression, it rose again to £1.4 million by 1939. This represented perhaps three-quarters of the total research effort of the chemical industry and extended over a wide field of chemical products from fertilizers and dyestuffs to the high pressure chemical engineering technology of Billingham. Similar expansion took place in other industries. GEC, which had set up a research group just after the First World War, built its large Wembley laboratories in 1923, and by 1927 was employing 200 research staff there. British Celanese, Courtaulds' major rival in the rayon industry, revealed in 1932 that in the previous seven years it had spent over £1 million on research into the acetate process. Many others among the leading firms also established research laboratories and even in the older established industries firms began investing more in research than had been common in the past. The United Steel Companies, for example, opened their large central research department at Stocksbridge in 1934.

In 1926, when Harry McGowan of Nobel had speculated on the future of the chemical industry, he had felt that 'organized research lies at the root of our prosperity', and he referred explicitly to the need to copy the German example.[37] Seven years later, when he had implemented this policy within ICI, he was well satisfied with the results: '[The] benefits [of research] are continuous. They may be summarized as more economical manufacturing processes, improved outputs, finer products, more efficient technical services . . . and the development of new commodities.'[38]

These favourable sentiments were also echoed by Lord Rutherford, in his last report as chairman of the Department of Scientific and Industrial Research:

The historian of the future [he wrote in the mid-1930s] will probably point to the last five years as a period marking an important development in the industrial outlook of this country. These years have seen the fruition of the policy adopted by several large undertakings of setting well-balanced teams of research workers to solve a particular problem or to develop a new product. . . .

Cooperation, team work and extensive organization on the technical side are essential for success.[39]

Out of the investment in corporate laboratories came new products such as television and plastics, and improvements in fuel utilization and electric lamps; and the success of such innovations had a strong bearing on the commercial survival and growth of the inventive firms concerned. Patent applications from companies (as opposed to individuals), which had accounted for only 15 per cent of the total before the First World War, had risen to 58 per cent by 1938, and a study of individual major inventions also shows the increased role played by industrial laboratories both in the original invention and in the development and marketing of new products.[40] Among the many 'springs of technical progress' which improved the productivity performance of British firms in the interwar years, then, organized research in corporations with a specialist core of technical knowledge was certainly one.[41]

In addition to new products and new techniques based on scientific developments, there were also opportunities for corporate growth based on specialist skills in marketing. This is reflected in the growing number of large enterprises which were based in the consumer goods market. Firms that had already developed skills in advertising in the nineteenth century, like Guinness, continued to show a high rate of expansion, and further consolidation of other nationally advertised brands of alcholic drinks occurred: Bass, for example, acquired Worthington for £3 million in 1927, and the Distillers Company integrated forward to acquire the two major blended whisky groups, Johnnie Walker and Buchanan-Dewar, for £20 million in 1925. The foremost exemplars of corporate growth based on marketing were, however, in the food industry. The importance of branded goods and advertising was well established by the First World War, and the forward integration of manufacturers into distribution and wholesaling (which branding often entailed) was given an additional boost by the increasing competitiveness of motor lorry transport, which was replacing the railway system on which prewar marketing had been largely based. The diverse Anglo-Dutch Unilever empire perhaps best exemplifies the type of integration and diversification based on the logic of marketing skills which such developments made possible.[42] This firm, the result of a series of mergers culminating in the merger of the Margarine Union and Lever Brothers in 1929, had been created primarily because of the need to co-ordinate the raw material purchasing policy of the constituent firms, and it held extensive interests throughout the world in oils, fats, soap and margarine markets. Yet its core of skill in marketing was also an important part of the process by which it maintained its position as an integrated food and proprietary products marketing group. In addition to consolidating the accumulated marketing experience of the constituent partners in the mergers of 1918–29 which built up the group, the company consolidated much of its road distribution network into the S.P.D. Company, developed its own advertising agency, and, through its Allied Suppliers subsidiary, controlled a large chain of retail grocery shops including the Maypole, Home & Colonial and Liptons groups. It was essentially by developing the skills that had been learnt in marketing soap, margarine and other traditional products that the company was later able to continue its growth by developing products such as frozen foods and a wider range of branded household goods.

Whilst no other group pursuing a strategy of marketing-orientated growth could rival Unilever in size, there were many others which were developing an expertise in marketing and distribution in similar though not identical ways. Among the largest fifty firms of 1930, for example, there were Reckitts (which was to merge with Colmans in 1938), United Dairies, Boots, J. Lyons, and Cadbury-Fry. To assess the net benefits of these developing skills would be a difficult task,[43] but in so far as they achieved economies of scale in marketing and the more efficient integration of manufacturing with distribution and retailing, they represented an improvement on earlier marketing methods which had been based on a greater number of middlemen and less integrated company operations.

These categories have by no means exhausted the full range of directions in which the corporate economy of the interwar years was expanding. This was also the period in which press barons, such as

Lord Rothermere and the Berry brothers (later Lords Kemsley and Camrose), gained control of a large share of the national and local newspaper market. Whereas in 1921 the big press chains controlled only 15 per cent of newspaper output, by 1929 this had risen to 44 per cent, and the chains also integrated backwards to the manufacture of newsprint and introduced more aggressive marketing methods.[44] Whatever the social and intellectual losses these moves involved – and they were no doubt considerable – there were substantial financial gains from limiting the number of competing local newspapers, thus reducing the overlapping activities of staff, which had been a consequence of competition between many newspapers to report the same news.

Among companies ranking below the top fifty shown in Table 8.1, there was also substantial growth, both internally and by merger, in the interwar years. The Metal Box Company, Tube Investments, Joseph Lucas, and Fison, for example, all owed their dominant market position to merger activity between the end of the First World War and the 1930s, a period in which they were also undergoing rapid internal growth.[45] Other groups based on marketing expertise were also being formed in this period – Beecham, for example, which was to become a leading manufacturer of proprietary articles, made important acquisitions in 1925 (Veno) and in 1938 (Eno and Macleans).[46]

Much of the technical and marketing expertise on which the growth of these large and medium-sized firms depended was generated within the firms, from their own experience of mass production and marketing and from their own research and development efforts. Yet, in view of the lagging development of Britain in some of these industries, imported expertise could also play its part and large companies were also involved in introducing new techniques in this way. The foreign influence was in some cases direct. In 1930, for example, four of the largest fifty firms – Ford, Boots, AEI, and International Nickel – were under North American ownership,[47] and smaller firms also provided a vehicle for American expansion; US General Motors, for example, acquired Vauxhall in 1925 and Procter & Gamble acquired Hedley in 1930, thus gaining important UK footholds. Whereas in 1914 there had been perhaps seventy US companies operating in the UK, by 1936 this had risen to 224 and many of these were now among the dominant firms in their industry.[48] Even where direct foreign ownership was not the avenue for transfer of technology and expertise, less formal means could be used to import technology from Germany and the United States. ICI, for example, had a patent-sharing agreement with Du Pont and I. G. Farben (bolstered by a general agreement to divide the world market between themselves), and many of the company's ideas for diversification can be traced to a technical logic initially explored by Du Pont in the American context.[49] Among other leading firms, English Electric had a substantial licensing agreement with the American Westinghouse Corporation, Austin used American consultants when he set up his Longbridge factory for the mass production of cars, and Morris himself, when introducing the mass production of steel plates for his cars, went into partnership with an American company to finance the Pressed Steel Company.[50] It appears, then, that some of the technical progress and improved productivity of the period can be ascribed to imported technology. The large firms which were developing their expertise in these fields were playing an important part in this process, as they were also in the development of indigenous research and marketing skills.

The logic of the development of these skills was not only that large firms should import technology, however, but also that they should themselves expand overseas, to exploit their comparative advantages in wider markets. As corporations successfully attained large scale in Britain and developed a transferable expertise, therefore, they often developed a strategy of expanding through overseas manufacturing subsidiaries.[51] The more oligopolistic markets created by mergers and patented research, and by the growing tendency to protectionism, also helped stimulate firms in domestic oligopolies to acquire a stake in factories abroad. Overseas activities by British corporations – already well-developed before the First World War – thus saw significant further expansion in the 1930s,[52] albeit on a less grand scale than the overseas expansion by US corporations at the same time.[53] The natural direction of expansion for many companies in the interwar context was the Empire. The title Imperial Chemical Industries was, for example, no accident, for, as the founders said:

> The British Empire is the greatest single economic unit in the world. . . . By linking the title of the new company to that unit, it is intended to lay emphasis upon the fact that the promotion of Imperial trading interests will command the special consideration and thought of those who will be responsible for directing this new

company . . . and it will be the avowed intention of the new
Company, without limiting its activities in foreign overseas mar-
kets, specially to extend the development and importance of the
Chemical Industry throughout the Empire.[54]

Large firms like ICI, Unilever, EMI, Cadbury-Fry, Amalgamated
Press, and Dunlop did develop an extensive network of overseas
subsidiaries in the Empire,[55] but neither they, nor other British
firms, confined their attention to imperial areas. Unilever, for
example, had extensive European and American interests, and
Courtaulds, through its American Viscose Corporation subsidiary,
was a dominant rayon producer in the United States, while EMI
owned some fifty factories in nineteen countries, principally in
Europe. By 1934 British firms had accumulated assets in US
manufacturing industry valued at $305 million,[56] and much of this
was a result of expansion and new acquisitions in the 1920s. In the
world as a whole, it is difficult to estimate total UK direct investment, but very rough estimates for the later 1930s suggest that it
amounted to a significant portion of total UK overseas investment by
that time, aggregating between £500 and £1500 millions.[57] No
systematic study of the contribution of such overseas direct investment to the British economy in this period is available, but in 1927
the chairman of GKN gave some indication of the potential contribution to a leading company's prosperity: 'Our interests [he said]
are worldwide, and I can assure you that it is only on account of that
fact that we are able in what have been twelve months of general
depression, to maintain our profits on such a scale.'[58]

In contrast to the return on the mass of overseas assets accumulated by (mainly) portfolio investment in the period up to 1914 –
valued then at £4000 million – the rate of return on the smaller sums
directly invested abroad by large firms was probably greater, since it
captured not only the *rentier* returns of the portfolio investor, but
also the profits which accrued to the innovating entrepreneur with
technical and managerial skills, of the kind now increasingly embodied in the framework of the international company. Of course, not
all such ventures met with success – Morris, for example, made a
disastrous attempt to enter the French motor-car industry[59] – but
direct investment was looked upon with increasing favour in business and official circles. The Macmillan Committee, for example,
which included eminent economists, bankers and businessmen,

noted that 'industry is yearly becoming more internationalized' and gave its stamp of approval to this trend, contrasting it favourably with the dominant nineteenth-century forms of investment:

> in the realm of the foreign investment it is primarily towards British-owned enterprises abroad that we should wish to see our energies and capital turned rather than merely towards subscribing to foreign government and municipal loans, which absorb our available foreign balance while doing little for our industry and commerce.[60]

This examination of the historical record of the directions of corporate expansion in the interwar period suggests that the quantitative changes charted in the previous chapter were matched by important qualitative innovations in corporate policies, which marked a significant break with the past. It is, of course, true that many of the characteristics of the corporate economy could already be seen in the larger companies before the First World War, and the discontinuity is not by any means a total one. Kynoch, for example, had been prewar pioneers of diversification, and the United Alkali Company had had an advanced research and development programme, and both companies eventually joined ICI.[61] Firms like Lever and Bovril were developing modern techniques of advertising and marketing well before 1914, and it was on those techniques that many interwar corporations were based.[62] Some firms had also developed overseas manufacturing subsidiaries, and already in 1899 Sir Archibald Coats claimed that the greater part of J. & P. Coats' profits were derived from overseas interests.[63] Yet, wherever quantitative assessment of trends in these developments is possible, the case for a clear shift in industrial practices in the 1920s is overwhelming. In the statistics of mergers, industrial concentration and overseas acquisitions, we have already seen that structural changes were occurring at an unpredentedly high rate. These can be paralleled by statistics on mass production at the plant level: in 1914, for example, Ford, then the largest UK motor-car manufacturer, produced only 6000 cars, whereas by 1939 six firms all had substantially higher outputs.[64] In the case of the strategy of integration and diversification also the statistics indicate a shift; between 1880 and 1918 only 8 per cent of mergers were of the diversifying or vertical kind, whereas by 1919–39 the proportion had risen to 37 per cent, and absolutely by an even greater amount since mergers in general were then more common.[65] Interwar corporations were also investing significantly more on research: total industrial expenditure on research and development in the later 1930s was at least £6½ million annually, compared with under £1 million before the First World War.[66] Many of the larger firms of the turn of the century merger wave had very narrow product lines and aimed primarily at the restriction of competition and the raising of prices; in the interwar period the more obvious social benefits of economies of scale and accelerated rates of technical innovation were increasingly in evidence. Imperial Chemical Industries was, in short, much nearer to the archetypal modern, diversified, multidivisional corporation than the single-product, badly organized Calico Printers Association, which might be taken as typical of the prewar stage of corporate immaturity.

The newly invigorated strategies of diversification, large-scale plants, multinational expansion, and investment in research and development and marketing were not uniformly successful, but, when they were successful, they often established their exponents firmly among the top-ranking firms in the economy. The firms in Table 8.1 (pp. 102–3 above), which formed the basis of the new British corporate economy by 1930, have remained the mainstay of Britain's corporate structure. There have, of course, been changes. Some of the firms, committed to old industries, have failed to maintain their position, others have only done so by merger with stronger rivals. The chance of dropping to a lower rank did, however, decline as the quantitative and qualitative changes we have discussed made their mark; neither large absolute size nor new management strategies could guarantee permanence but they did greatly improve a firm's chances. Table 8.2 shows the increased stability of the industrial leaders. In the decades prior to 1930, around half of the top 100 firms disappeared each decade[67] (and many of these were ranked relatively high at the beginning of the periods); after 1930 the stability of the population increased, and dropouts tended to come mainly from the lower-ranked firms or from firms being acquired by other firms in the top 100. It was still possible for dynamic newcomers to displace existing leaders, but the major leaders were firmly established, as they had been at an earlier stage in the US corporate economy.[68]

None the less, it could plausibly be argued in the 1930s that further opportunities for rationalization and economies of scale still existed, and many contemporary critics felt that, however far the

TABLE 8.2   *The fate of the leading 100 firms, 1919–69*

	Surviving in top 100	Acquired by firm remaining in top 100	Dropout to lower rank
Status of top 100 firms of 1919 in 1930	52	17	31
Status of top 100 firms of 1930 in 1948	71	5	24
Status of top 100 firms of 1948 in 1957	71	3	26
Status of top 100 firms of 1957 in 1969	68	22	10

Source: L. Hannah and J. A. Kay, *Concentration in Modern Industry* (1977), p. 104.

corporate economy had advanced, it was not far enough. In some industries it could be pointed out that British firms were still substantially smaller than their American or German counterparts. In the steel industry, for example, although by 1930 the twenty largest firms controlled 70 per cent of the British output of iron and steel, their combined output of steel was still less than one third of that of the US Steel Corporation and about the same as Vereinigte Stahlwerke of Germany.[69] Again, in the car industry, while the six largest firms accounted for 90 per cent of total output by 1939, they still manufactured forty different engine types and even more chassis and body models; and, despite opportunities for cost reduction through further standardization, they had tended to increase, rather than decrease the number of models in the 1930s.[70] Management in this, and other industries also left much to be desired: Courtaulds, for example, despite its prosperity and dominance of the rayon industry, had an inadequate managerial organization and was technically unenterprising.[71] The Balfour Committee bemoaned the absence of managers with a capacity to understand the technical developments which were transforming the nature of firms in the science-based industries:

> It needs to be much more generally recognized [the Committee concluded] that the requirements of industry in this respect include not only the intensive training of the expert, but also the widespread diffusion among future industrial leaders of the capacity to appreciate the value of science to industry.[72]

The economic benefits made possible by larger-scale enterprise were thus neither complete nor were they to be achieved in isolation. They required complementary investment in scientific and business education and, more generally, a change also in social and managerial attitudes. To attempt to unravel such complementarities would be a formidable task, and this, coupled with the absence of much of the required data, makes it difficult to assess in precise quantitative terms the proportion of contemporary economic growth which can be attributed to the structural and organizational changes which were occurring. There is, however, a strong circumstantial case for believing that the structural changes and productivity improvements of the period are linked,[73] and the impressionistic evidence which we have been able to cite here tends to confirm this case. Closer studies of individual industries and firms may, in the future, provide us with more precise estimates of the gains, but for the moment we must be content with the weaker, but still significant, conclusion that the growth of large companies in the interwar years contributed substantially to the underlying productivity improvements in British manufacturing industry between the wars.

9

From the 1930s to the 1950s:
continuity or change?

Private Enterprise has had the great advantage . . . of being able
to put forth a considerable range and variety of systems and
to try them out in practice . . . it has provided us with
a fine laboratory and many experiments, the results
of which, for good and, sometimes, for evil, we
are just beginning to reap. The task . . . is to
take full advantage of what has been
going on, and to discern in
the light of these manifold
experiments which
ideas are profitable
and which
unprofitable.

LIBERAL INDUSTRIAL INQUIRY, *Britain's Industrial
Future* (1928), p. 100.

When it was suggested to Briggs that his new combination should
be called by some such title as Universally Combined General
Industries he was speechless with rage. 'We'll have the
word "Briggs" in it,' he gasped at length, 'or we'll
cancel the whole thing.'

JOHN LEE, *Letters to an Absentee
Director* (1928), p. 40.

৩৩

Many of the features that distinguish the modern corporate economy
from the Victorian economy of small family firms were, then, firmly
established in Britain by the early 1930s. Over large sectors of
manufacturing industry the position of large integrated firms had
been strengthened by vigorous internal growth and by the unprecedented merger waves of the dozen years following the First World
War. These firms were also diversifying their product ranges
through the acquisition of businesses in related fields, and some of
them had laid the basis for continued growth by investment in new
technologies and well-equipped research laboratories. The possibilities of expansion through vertical integration at home and abroad,

and through overseas manufacturing subsidiaries, were also being more fully explored than they had been in earlier decades. Typically the large corporations were quoted companies and their shareholdings were widely dispersed beyond the entrepreneurial families to which most of them owed their Victorian origins. Some of them, like ICI, had begun to solve the problems of maintaining efficiency through management decentralization, and this enabled them to sustain the rapid pace of expansion, which the reduction of financial constraints on firm size and the diversification of their activities had made possible.

There are thus clear lines of continuity between the corporate economy of the 1930s and that which we now know. Moreover, the temptation to see the expansion of large corporations progressing in gradual, but decided, steps towards the high levels of concentration of today is a strong one, for the taste for rationalization and merger often seems, like a crystal dropped in a supersaturated solution, to be producing a cumulative effect of ever-increasing concentration. There are a number of *a priori* considerations which lend plausibility to this view. The process by which expanding markets create new possibilities for the division of labour is a self-sustaining one, since divisions of labour also operate in their turn to expand markets, and we would expect this process, once started, to continue to open up new opportunities for economies of scale. Furthermore, given the trend towards higher market coverage, vertical integration, and diversification, the economies of such innovations would increasingly tend to be internalized by large firms. Hence external economies of scale would become progressively less important, and the repeated divisions of labour would operate more unambiguously in the direction of increasing firm size. It might also reasonably be expected that there would be some learning effect: the attractions of monopoly power, for example, would be more widely appreciated by entrepreneurs, as the experience of some firms of successfully raising profits by monopolistic consolidations became more widely known. For many reasons, then, we might expect the more rapid growth of large firms to continue. Even if no such tendency were present, however, overall concentration could still increase, owing to the operation of the 'Gibrat Effect'. If large firms only grow as fast on average as small and medium-sized firms, there may (if there is a diversity of growth rates *within* these size groups) still be a tendency for concentration to increase, because of the operation of this effect and the absence of any compensating regressive tendencies (see pp. 6–7).

In the light of these theoretical considerations (which are also rendered plausible by the casual observer's impression of continually increasing concentration) any data which suggest that concentration has actually fallen, in any recent period, are understandably regarded with some suspicion. It was, then, natural that when, in the 1950s, British economists first attempted to measure changes in concentration over time, they reported their findings that concentration may have actually decreased in the years prior to 1950 with repeated warnings that their figures should be interpreted with caution.[1] Yet, as further evidence has accumulated, the view that the strong upward trend of industrial concentration which had been established in the 1920s did not continue in the following two decades has gained plausibility. Indeed, the share of the top 100 firms in manufacturing output, which was as high as 26 per cent in 1930, appears to have declined to 23 per cent in 1935 and remained at that level or possibly even lower until it began to rise again in the 1950s (see Appendix 2).

These results are confirmed by the analysis of changes in concentration among the larger (mainly quoted) firms shown in Table 9.1. Between 1930[2] and 1948, in this sample of larger firms, the share of the largest 100 firms declined from 66 per cent to 57 per cent of the market capitalization of the population as whole. Declines were shown in thirteen of the seventeen industry groups and the rises in the others were only marginal. Evely and Little, using *Census of Production* data for 1935 and 1951 to examine individual industries at a more disaggregated level, were unable to come to a similarly clear-cut conclusion about the general direction of concentration change, but their data are consistent with the view that concentration was not increasing.[3] The statistical record of merger activity in this period also suggests that dramatic changes in industrial structure were on the whole absent. In the 1930s expenditure on mergers by manufacturing firms was running at only half the level of the 1920s, and in the 1940s there was a further decline in merger activity, so that it was then more subdued than at any time since before the First World War. This level of merger activity did slightly increase concentration, but this effect was overwhelmed by the more general tendency of internal growth to reduce concentration, thus producing the net effect shown in Table 9.1. Not until the later

TABLE 9.1   *Concentration in industry groups, 1930–48*

Shares of the largest five firms

Industry	1930 population (%)	1948 population (%)
Food	65·9	57·7
Drink	37·2	38·8
Tobacco	98·7	96·8
Chemicals	70·4	66·3
Metal manufacture	34·3	30·9
Mechanical engineering	36·6	21·4
Electrical engineering	41·7	42·0
Shipbuilding	84·4	79·2
Vehicles	47·8	36·1
Metal goods, n.e.s.	37·2	41·0
Textiles	53·8	38·9
Leather	57·9	54·1
Clothing & footwear	32·8	32·9
Building materials	53·2	50·4
Timber, furniture	35·8	34·7
Paper and publishing	56·5	37·5
Miscellaneous	77·3	64·3

Share of the largest 100 firms

All manufacturing	65·7	56·9

Source: Calculated from the data described in L. Hannah and J. A. Kay, *Concentration in Modern Industry: Theory, Measurement and the UK Experience* (1977).

1950s was the merger intensity of the 1920s again equalled (see Appendix 1). While the various historical statistics of both mergers and concentration can, individually, pose serious problems of interpretation (which are more fully discussed in the Appendices), their collective weight again makes it difficult to evade the view that the trends established in the 1920s were interrupted for several decades thereafter. In the 1930s and 1940s the tide of the corporate economy had certainly ceased to flow; it seems likely that it had actually begun to ebb, perhaps significantly so.

Of course this does not imply that large firms actually contracted in size; on the contrary, they would have had to grow in absolute terms, in this period of expanding output, just in order to maintain their relative position. The industries of the second industrial revolution, with their typically large firms, expanded vigorously. The 1930s saw motor-cars becoming a typical middle-class possession; and the cheapening of electricity and the building boom meant that two-thirds of British homes had electricity by the end of the decade; the new industry suppliers expanded correspondingly. The 1930s was also a period of growth for important industrial firms such as British Plasterboard, Beecham, Bowater Paper,[4] Hoover, Colvilles,[5] Allied Bakeries, Morphy Richards, and Reckitt & Colman, and the postwar years saw important consolidations such as the merger of two cable companies in 1945 to form British Insulated Callenders Cables. In the tinplate industry, also, there was the long awaited merger of the Richard Thomas, Baldwins, Guest Keen, and Llanelly interests to form the Steel Company of Wales in 1947. What was absent, however, was a vigorous, general, and sustained merger movement leading to a substantial further concentration of output in the larger firms, such as had been experienced in 1919–30.

Outside the sector of large firms, in which we have seen the origins of the modern corporate economy, however, there were substantial movements towards greater concentration of output in fewer firms. Firms employing less than 200 people, which had accounted for approximately 38 per cent of total employment and 35 per cent of net output in manufacturing industry in 1935, accounted for only 24 per cent and 20 per cent respectively by 1958;[6] and much of this decline in the small firm sector must have occurred in the 1930s and 1940s. Yet this trend is not reflected in the statistics of concentration presented earlier, for these were based on the top firms in manufacturing or on the quoted sector only, and thus they could not capture changes in the lower range of the size distribution of firms. What appears to have happened is that, by a combined process of competitive elimination by rivals, acquisition by other firms, and internal growth to larger size, the population of smaller firms contracted over the two decades, and births of new small firms were insufficient to redress the balance. Since the share of the largest firms in manufacturing output was also stable or declining in this period, it follows that firms in the middle ranking size ranges must have been growing in importance, and it may be inferred that it was in this sector that much of the real growth in output over the period occurred. Although the large corporate sector showed little movement towards higher concentration in these years, there were, it seems, important changes making for increased consolidation and larger scale among the smaller and medium-sized ranges of firms.[7]

Any such consolidation was, of course, welcomed by rationalizers, but, in general, contemporary observers, at least in the 1930s, regretted that the movement was not more widespread, and there were numerous calls for further consolidation among the larger firms. On the whole, however, this pressure was resisted by industrialists, and the stereotype to which this gave rise has become well known, for it became the standard critique of the conservative British businessman. He was (so ran the conventional wisdom) either ignorant of or irrationally averse to the potential benefits of rationalization, mass production and merger because he feared that they would lead to a loss of personal dominance and control. There is an abundance of examples of firms, especially family-owned firms, which might have derived financial benefits from larger scale but refused to do so for such reasons. Kenricks, the Midlands hardware firm (one of the few medium-sized companies to have been effectively scrutinized by a business historian), is a case in point. The owning family commissioned a report from their management consultants Peat, Marwick & Mitchell, which recommended that they should seek a merger with rivals. However, when the report arrived, it was rejected with the remark 'that it was a very good report but that no action should be taken', and, with friendly bankers, Kenricks were able to survive a period of low profitability without either merging, or going public.[8]

Such businesses especially disliked the prospect of being exposed to the scrutiny of the public and of financiers whom they generally (and often with justification) distrusted. As an accountant closely involved in mergers commented:

> Men who have been accustomed to personal domination almost amounting to dictatorship in their own businesses, do not take kindly to a change of circumstances whereunder they merely become members of a Board of Directors, and may find themselves subject . . . to the control of others.[9]

The capitalist market ethic inherited by businessmen of this mould stressed individualist competition, rather than mutuality, in the conduct of inter-firm relations; the moral foundations of the case for capitalist entrepreneurship implied that the individual's character and skill determined relative rewards. Their 'individualism' is

hardly surprising in view of this ideological background. Sargent
Florence well summed up its implications:

> What it actually means is, that they prefer power over their own
> little works to having a small share, with possibly very little power,
> in a large amalgamation. Secondly, they rather enjoy, as far as I
> can make out from talking with them and listening to them, the
> little game of competition; they love the secrecy of *private*
> enterprise and the sense of playing for a side; it is possibly a very
> British instinct; and they feel there is more zest in fighting against
> a rival than in combining with him. Thirdly, they like the feeling
> of running a little property; it is rather a *petit bourgeois* point of
> view, but after all, men in the Wool Industry or, say, the Brass
> Industry are *petit bourgeois* and have been since the middle of the
> Victorian era in England. Finally, the most important reason for
> their wishing to cling on to their own little business is the feudal
> idea of handing it on to their family.[10]

For such men – and they were represented in large areas of British
industry – an increased autonomy from competitive forces in the
product market, and an improved access to capital or economies of
scale, both of which could become available in an enlarged quoted
firm, were but poor substitutes for the greater personal autonomy
and direct command relationships in their own firms.

Even in larger firms there could be a determined resistance to
change based on the belief that, whatever the proven benefits in
other industries, mass production and rationalization were inappropriate to their firms. Rationalizers, who complained that there
was 'a national bias on the part of industry to regard its troubles as
merely temporary',[11] felt that industrialists were conservatively
wedded to ways that had worked in the past but were inappropriate
in the present, and industrialists did sometimes act with remarkable
conformity to this caricature. 'There is, nothing to recommend the
mass production of standardized ships,' thundered Viscount Inchcape, 'that is a method which may be described as the communism
of ship construction,' and he went on to advocate 'the widest
imaginable diversity of detail and assembly',[12] a course which would
effectively have prevented the achievement of scale economies and
thus have cut right across the work of other industrialists who were
attempting to introduce engineering standardization.[13] Bankers
could also impede reorganization, by supporting potentially bank-

rupt firms in order to protect their frozen overdrafts in the hope of eventual recovery of profitability. It was, in principle, open to entrepreneurs who wished to promote standardization, merger and mass production against the 'conservative' elements to acquire competitors in order to 'rationalize' their industry. However, the opportunities for entrepreneurs to act as midwives to new developments in this way were not as great as they were subsequently to become with the development of the takeover bid. In the case of private firms, of course, little could be done if the owner-directors of a firm standing in the way of rationalization did not wish to sell their assets. A sufficiently high offer could, it is true, be persuasive; and some of the more colourful press barons also used the threat of uneconomic price cuttting and competitive attrition (subsidized by their other newspapers) as a means of persuading family owners of provincial newspapers to sell out their interests. Such tactics were, however, probably exaggerated in the telling, and were certainly an untypical form of takeover.[14]

In the case of publicly quoted companies, with widely dispersed shareholdings, by contrast, it might be supposed that an appeal directly to the shareholders by a bidder would be sufficient to overrule directors who refused merger negotiations which offered real economic advantages. In practice, however, takeover bids contesting the views of incumbent directors were virtually unknown before 1950.[15] The position of directors in potential bid situations was strengthened by the inadequacy of the information possessed by shareholders about the asset and profit position of their companies. This greatly weighted the advantage in favour of negotiating mergers through the directors, and even in the few cases in which direct bids were made, the shareholders invariably accepted their directors' recommendation to refuse. So remote was the possibility of a successful contested bid that it seemed quite natural for a contemporary account to insist that 'the negotiations must obviously be conducted by the Directors. In order to preserve proper secrecy, it is not possible for the Directors to acquaint the shareholders of the matter.'[16] This did not necessarily prevent mergers between quoted companies, for the directors (especially if they were themselves offered suitable 'compensation') might agree to a merger, and if they did so it was almost certain to go through without opposition. As the *Investors Chronicle* commentator advised: 'if the directors decide that the business should be sold it is difficult to make any other suggestion'.[17] On the other hand, where a prospective bidder could *not* convert the directors of a quoted company to his view, he was for practical purposes no more able to enforce his view in a takeover bid than he would have been in the case of an entirely private family-owned company. Indeed, the point may be made more strongly, for, while a family company might accept a generous offer because it was financially profitable to do so, directors could and did refuse offers which their shareholders would have been glad to accept. Hence, in this sense, it was more rather than less difficult to induce a quoted company to merge, and this is reflected in the merger statistics: less than 5 per cent of the firms quoted on the London stock exchange in 1924, for example, were acquired by other quoted firms in the following fifteen years, a much lower percentage than that which has prevailed since the development of takeover bidding.[18]

An entrepreneur who was convinced of the potential benefits of rationalization and mass production was, then, in a difficult position if he could not persuade other industrialists to agree to his proposals. The one option that remained open to him was to build his own plant on a large scale, and, by competitive price reductions (made possible by the use of superior, low-cost plant), to drive out his competitors (or force them eventually to accept a merger). This is precisely what happened in some industries. William Morris, for example, acquired a number of small competitors and suppliers, but owed his successful introduction of mass production not to this but to his ability, through cheaper prices, to win new markets and force small-scale specialist motor manufacturers out of business. More generally the disappearance of many small firms over manufacturing industry as a whole is in part the result of such a process of natural selection through competition. Yet such a strategy for introducing mass producton was not always possible, for it depended on the existence of special conditions. In the car industry, for example, rapidly expanding markets meant that the majority of consumers were 'new' and had no initial loyalty to any particular make of car; it was, moreover, a highly competitive market. Hence Morris and the other major mass producers of cars could be confident of finding customers for their output.[19] In many other markets, however, there were imperfections of competition, resulting variously from branding, advertising, consumer loyalty, restrictive agreements or, in the case of some products, from vertical integration between a manufacturer and his suppliers or retailers. The classic case of the latter type of market imperfection was in brewing, where the tied house system and legal restrictions on the licensing of new pubs tied the brewer to a limited number of pub outlets. Any conceivable price reductions made possible by scale economies in new plant would not, in this industry, be able to capture more than a small proportion of the trade of the publicans already tied to other breweries. In this and other industries facing imperfect markets, therefore, an entrepreneur introducing mass production could not, unless he made economies large enough to permit very substantial price reductions, hope immediately to win a sufficiently large market to justify his investment. A precondition of the building of a large plant in such a market would, then, be a merger of interests with existing manufacturers, amalgamating, as it were, not only their assets but also their consumer demand.[20] In these conditions, then, the absence of a takeover mechanism might seriously inhibit desirable structural changes.

In the light of these factors, the view that British businessmen were in general forgoing the potential social benefits of reduced industrial costs through mass production (and, for that matter, the potential private benefits of monopoly profits) becomes more intelligible, for the economic mechanisms which are conventionally thought of as penalizing such ignorance or irrationality operated only perfunctorily in the interwar context. There are, however, alternative, quite plausible explanations of the apparent aversion of large numbers of entrepreneurs to larger-scale enterprise. We must, then, pause before accepting the condemnations of the rationalizers – who frequently had little knowledge of the conditions faced by the industries they criticized – to ask whether the actions of industrialists can rather be explained, in part at least, as a rational response to the economic conditions of the time. It is, for example, worthwhile recalling that the 1930s and 1940s were an exceptional period in economic history, encompassing the most serious world depression and the most destructive world war ever experienced. It is conceivable that such upheavals interrupted the long-run trend towards increasing competitive advantages for larger-scale enterprises, and that this, rather than entrepreneurial irrationality, explains why the corporate economy changed down to a lower gear. Closer consideration suggests that this might indeed be the case.

If world economic conditions rather than an outbreak of irrationality had temporarily halted the trend towards higher concentration, for example, the effect would have been widespread and other industrial nations would have experienced declining or static concentration: the evidence for the United States confirms that such a trend was also found there.[21] The expectation of a downward movement in concentration is also supported by a consideration of the likely impact of a world depression on the determinants of concentration which had been identified. In markets in which demand had contracted, for example (such as those faced by the British export industries in this period), the scope for economies of scale may have been attenuated, given the classical proposition that the division of labour is limited by the extent of the market. Several of the large-scale investment projects planned by the industrial leaders of the late 1920s, for example ICI's Billingham chemical complex and Ford's Dagenham motor-car plant, proved to be too big for market demand and caused considerable financial embarrassment.[22] Firms that saw in their market environment no prospect of a sufficiently large demand to enable them to reap the scale economies of low-cost mass production could sensibly reject, on marketing grounds, mergers which on technical, engineering grounds would have been appropriate.[23] Financial economies of scale, which had also been acting to increase the size of firms, were also reduced as the collapse of international investment in the 1930s led City institutions to turn their attention to the financing of British industry.[24] Thus William Piercy, who had in the 1920s advised a company to seek outside capital only at the £250,000 level, could in the 1930s advise them to start at £100,000, or even at £40,000 on the provincial exchanges; and later in 1945 the foundation of the Industrial and Commercial Finance Corporation, explicitly to cater for the smaller companies, further improved their position.[25]

Of course, depression had not limited markets and reduced the potential economies of scale everywhere, and there were many markets in the 1930s in which demand was growing, but even here, economies of scale were not leading inexorably to large-scale enterprise. Some economies of scale could, for example, be achieved by the collective action of independent firms rather than by further consolidation. Industrial research associations, jointly financed by industry and government, were in this period allowing smaller firms to gain the advantages of research which, acting independently, they would have been unable to afford.[26] In marketing also, there remained advantages for the small specialized unit which was quick to respond to changes in consumer tastes, and in the production technology of many industries economies of scale were unimportant or had been exhausted at quite a small size.[27] Some technical changes of the period, moreover, were reducing the need for large scale. Electric power was, for example, much easier than steam power for small users to adopt, and the completion of a national grid in the 1930s greatly cheapened electricity in most parts of the country.[28] Hence it may well have been that many industries had, by 1930, achieved a position in which many of the major economies of scale related to firm size were exhausted.

One of the factors that continued to limit overall economies of scale was the widespread experience of management difficulties in coping with large amalgamations, and this continued to militate against rapid company growth. Firms tried in a number of ways to avoid these difficulties, for example by eschewing multi-firm amalgamations and developing new organization structures (see Chapter 6), but such managerial initiatives were not universal amongst large firms, and those which did not devise appropriate structures could encounter very serious managerial problems. Some large companies found that they had expanded more rapidly than could conveniently be handled by their existing managerial organization, and demergers to cope with this were sometimes necessary.[29] In more serious cases bankruptcy or financial reconstruction was forced on firms which suffered from overcapitalization and an over-rapid rate of expansion. Evidence of such cases is not readily available, for failing firms leave few records, but one recent study[30] which examined seven of the larger mergers of 1919–28 (each of them involving five or more firms disappearing, valued at over £3 million) found a high incidence of failure, and one difference between the successes and the failures was the ability of the successful firms to create a viable management structure. In view of these experiences, and more general managerial disquiet at the problems of rapid expansion, it is hardly surprisng that there were in the 1930s only two mergers of comparable magnitude: the acquisition by Wallpaper Manufacturers of five of its competitors in 1934, and the consolidation of six sugar beet processing firms to form the British Sugar Corporation in 1936. Significantly these had the additional advantages of, respectively, a well-entrenched monopoly position and a large government subsidy, and this no doubt in part accounts for the willingness of the industrialists involved to embark upon them.[31] In other cases, however, businessmen were increasingly wary of new, poorly planned merger schemes, and those companies which had been able to expand rapidly in the 1920s often had their hands full with the problems of establishing managerial controls over their already enlarged enterprises. Hence for many large companies the managerial constraint on their own growth remained a real one.

This is not, of course, to say that the advantages of merging were no longer sought after; on the contrary, the perennial attractions of monopoly power were still much appreciated by industrialists. There was, however, a shift in emphasis in the 1930s, a shift which can be seen both in the rationalization literature and in business policy. The shift may be broadly characterized as one away from merger and the growth of large firms towards the restriction of the market by collective agreements.[32] This option had the added attraction that it bypassed the managerial problems of enlarged companies since it maintained the independent status and the existing size of firms intact, but it could, through an efficiently organized cartel, gain the monopolistic advantages of market control, allowing firms to restrict output and increase prices above competitive levels. Of course, this option had been open to businessmen for a long time and had been extensively used in the past, but a number of factors increased its attractiveness and viability in the 1930s. The common law, which had for some time tolerated restrictive agreements, showed increasing favour to such agreements in the interwar period: 'a definite movement from the protection of individual economic freedom to the recognition of the legitimate purposes of group control'.[33] For reasons very similar to those which had gained the rationalization movement support for larger-scale enterprise, collective action by producers through trade associations was increasingly represented as being in the national interest. Rationalizers often stressed the virtues of 'organized marketing' and there were pressures on the government to give more support to private restrictive agreements, including the portentously named proposals for the 'self-government of industry' canvassed by Political and Economic Planning and The Industrial Reorganization League.[34] The latter was backed by Lord Melchett of ICI, but industrialists could not agree amongst themselves that the general enabling bill which he proposed was desirable, and the Cabinet in fact rejected the proposals (which had the support of Conservative backbenchers) because it 'would have the effect of checking industrial enterprise and development'.[35] Nevertheless, the National government did give some support to more limited restrictionist schemes. The 1935 budget granted a tax concession to voluntary schemes designed to restrict capacity.[36] This encouraged many private schemes on the model established by the National Shipbuilders Security scheme, which had earlier been encouraged by the Bankers Industrial Development Company in order to rationalize capacity in that industry.[37] Also, in the cotton industry, where there had been a decade of largely unsuccessful private experiments with schemes for cutting down capacity and reducing competition, the government gave legislative sanction to a levy for the scrapping of spindles.[38] The Import Duties Advisory Committee also fostered schemes for the control of investment and pricing in steel and elsewhere, sometimes using the threat of withdrawal of the tariff as a means of enforcing its views on the industry.[39] This supportive policy reached its zenith in the war, when the government gave more solid sanction to trade associations and restrictive agreements as part of wartime output planning.[40] Whereas in the First World War wartime pressures had led to increasing concentration, the system of physical controls, raw material rationing, and output planning in the Second World War, by contrast, was designed 'to alter the basic structure as little as possible'.[41]

Even where positive government initiatives were lacking, the private associations and industrial cartels which were formed in the 1930s and during the war appear to have been both more permanent and more successful than many of their predecessors, which had often foundered in trade depressions, as secret price shading developed and dissension between members mounted. Partly they owed their new-found prosperity to the adoption of a general tariff in 1932, which reduced the threat of import competition from abroad that had previously inhibited monopolistic pricing[42] and thus greatly strengthened the position of cartels in the home market. Partly also they were strengthened in the 1940s because wartime and postwar shortages created a sellers' market so that there was little competitive pressure to act as a disruptive force on the cartels. But in addition to these factors it is surely no accident that the new success of restrictive agreements followed on the rapid increase in concentration which industry had experienced in the 1920s. It is a commonplace that the difficulties of organizing a cartel increase in proportion to the number of its members: if there are many firms in an industry the costs of policing an agreement are high, and there are dangers that 'free riders' will enjoy the benefit of high prices without reducing their production proportionately. With more mergers between firms and increased concentration, however, both formalized cartels and informal oligopolistic collusion were substantially simplified and the risks of failure were reduced.[43] In other respects, also, the large corporate firms of the 1930s were better placed than their predecessors to reap the advantages of oligopoly situations. Because of improved techniques of market research for example, they were better able to exercise price discrimination or to raise prices to a profit-maximizing level, without a further movement to a full monopoly position, or even, perhaps, without a formal price agreement.[44]

The significance of this increasing reliance of British companies on market control through formal cartels or informal oligopolistic collusion, rather than through larger-scale companies, can be seen in the contrast between industrial attitudes in Britain and in the United States, where, despite increasing official tolerance during the 'New Deal', cartels still remained unpopular and were conducted with difficulty and often in secret. The contrasting national attitudes were revealed in the negotiations in Britain of the American industrialist Gerard Swope, of the International General Electric Company. When Swope (who already controlled AEI) approached the other major British electrical manufacturers with a view to acquiring control of their undertakings, his financial advisers found it difficult to see why he should prefer this to the alternative of a monopolistic cartel. Vivian Smith, his English adviser, put the matter clearly in a note to the Lazards banking house (which was advising one of the companies on Swope's 'shopping list'): 'Personally [he wrote], I am not at all sure whether instead of having one great octopus in the trade it is not better to have several big companies with a close working arrangement.'[45] Such an arrangement would, of course, have all of the monopolistic advantages of a merger, yet it would avoid the organizational problems which would be created for the management of a 'great octopus'. In the event, the other major English companies – GEC, AEI, and English Electric – appear to have agreed with Smith: certainly the industry was organized on this basis for almost three decades, before the cartel finally collapsed and was eventually replaced by a merger in 1967–8.

It is because of the great expansion in the number of successful cartels and restrictive agreements in the 1930s and 1940s that that period has been commonly seen as the highwater mark of the restrictionist and anti-competitive forces in British industry. On the whole this view is a just one,[46] but the stronger version of it, which goes on to ascribe many of the ills of inefficiency in British industry to the euthanasia of competition, is more problematical, for, despite much contemporary evidence of inefficiency, it is by no means obvious that this was uniquely concentrated in the monopolistically organized industries.[47] Moreover, it is a moot point whether the extreme competitive struggle which, in the absence of cartels, would have been forced on industries suffering from overcapacity would have served these industries better than collective schemes for capacity reduction. In cotton spinning, for example, the financially weak firms were often those which had suffered from speculative company promotions and not necessarily those with uneconomic equipment; in this industry, therefore, the competitive process working through bankruptcy might have had adverse effects on overall productive efficiency, had it not been tempered by planned scrapping of the uneconomic equipment.[48] Equally the pessimistic view of the period is not entirely borne out by the evidence of further improvements in the management of large companies, the rationalization of plants, and the move towards standardized mass production methods in British firms of the 1930s. English Electric, for example, which had languished between its formation in 1919 and 1930, was revitalized in the 1930s under new management.[49] Other large corporations were also reaping the advantages of their earlier investments in research: in 1933, for example, ICI's research chemists discovered polythene, and EMI was at the same time developing television technology, which led in 1936 to the setting up in Britain of the first electronic television system in the world.[50] The trend towards mass production on the plant level also shows clearly in the statistics for these years. In manufacturing industry as a whole, the proportion of total employment in the largest plants (those employing 1500 or more workers) rose from 15 per cent in 1935 to 24 per cent in 1951. The number of smaller plants (those with 200 or fewer employees) declined proportionately: the percentage of employment in these plants fell from 44 per cent in 1935 to 35 per cent in 1951.[51] The trend to larger plants was particularly noticeable in the chemicals, metal manufacture, building materials, aircraft and engineering industries, where literary evidence confirms that there were substantial economies of scale. Even without a further concentration of output in fewer *firms* then, there was a clear trend towards the concentration of output in fewer *plants*; and, from the point of view of production economies of scale, it is these latter changes, rather than the earlier changes in the structure of firms, that have the greater significance. Moreover, the two phenomena are surely not unrelated. When large firms were first created by a merger the management would be able to reap some of the advantages within a very short time. The cost of specialized central services could be spread over all the subsidiaries, competitive price cutting by different branches of the firm could be prevented, and hence perhaps market prices could be raised. It would sometimes also be possible to 'rationalize' sales forces, product ranges, advertising budgets, and the internal financial and accounting functions. Sometimes small plants could be closed down and production concentrated in the efficient (and usually larger) plants, which had previously been working below capacity. Other scale economies, however, could only gradually be reaped, since they were not matters of rearrangement of existing assets and working practices, but had rather to be embodied in new investment on a larger scale. Of course, it might be argued, from an engineering point of view, that a merger cannot make any difference to such an investment decision, since all firms, large or small, face the same long-run production function, and will thus choose to build their new plants of the optimal size, irrespective of their own initial sizes. However, there are a number of reasons, implicit in our earlier analysis, which would lead us to expect a merged firm which had successfully attained larger scale (such as those formed in 1919–30) to build larger plants than would have been planned in the investment programmes of the constituent firms, had they been acting separately. Given widespread competitive imperfections in the product market, for example, a single firm which built a large new plant in order to gain access to economies of scale could not be sure of an appropriately enlarged share of the market. Hence in some industries, where economies of scale existed, but the resulting price reductions were not sufficient to enable a firm to wrest established market shares from competitors, a merger was a precondition of larger plants (see p. 132 above). Moreover, given imperfections in the capital market, and the extensive reliance on the ploughback of profits for the finance of investment, a larger merged company would also be better able to finance the capital investment required for large plants.[52] We may, then, expect the consequences of a substantial increase in the number of larger firms (such as had occurred in the 1920s) to be seen not only in immediate efficiency gains (and monopolistic exactions) but also in the longer run, as such larger plants, bringing with them new economies of scale, are being built. Some indication of the delay between the initial merger wave and the reaping of such efficiency gains can be seen in the statistics of the proportion of manufacturing net output produced in small plants (defined as those with less than 200 employees). Between 1924 and 1935 (when the intitial direct effects of the 'rise of the corporate economy' were presumably being felt) the share of output produced in such plants was only reduced from 42 to 41 per cent. In the following sixteen years, however, this share was substantially reduced, so that by 1951 small plants accounted for only 32 per cent of manufacturing output;[53] and much of this can be ascribed to the building of larger plants by the larger firms created in the merger wave of the 1920s. The rapid recorded increase in industrial productivity in the 1930s[54] and the resilience of productivity in the 1940s may, then (in so far as they were due to plant economies of scale), be an important, but delayed, benefit of the earlier industrial movements which had led to the rise of a corporate economy of firms capable of making larger-scale investments.[55]

A favourable account of the industrial developments of the 1930s and 1940s might, then, be constructed from the evidence of structural change in these years. It would be admitted that large firms were no longer gaining relative to others, but this could be represented as a rational entrepreneurial response to the managerial difficulties of large-scale enterprise and to the exhaustion of the economies of scale available to them at the level of the firm. At the level of plants, however, the benefits of the earlier consolidations were being pursued and larger-scale plants were producing continuing productivity gains. Yet such a favourable view would be unlikely to be universally accepted, and a very different picture, with a pessimistic viewpoint, can also be drawn. On this view, firms were not pursuing the rationalization of capacity and the introduction of mass production methods as vigorously as they might properly have done, because of the absence of a competitive spur. Between 1935 and 1951, for example, industrialists commonly met an increase in demand by increasing the total number of plants in operation (rather than, as later, by building new plants on a sufficiently large scale to permit a net decrease in the number of plants), thus presumably forgoing greater economies of scale.[56] Instead of seeking profits in mass production economies, the pessimistic argument might run, they increasingly sought higher returns through monopolistic restrictions, and the cartels they formed could only secure the private advantages of monopoly power, rather than those benefits which also corresponded to a social advantage, such as economies of scale in production. The prevalence of restrictive practices, and of large firms which were little more than loose confederations of subsidiaries, lends weight to the view that it was a desire for monopoly, rather than for real economies, that was behind the industrial developments of these years.[57]

That we have found evidence for both of these views can hardly be surprising for it is unlikely that such generalizations can be anything other than oversimplifications of the diverse experience of many entrepreneurs, with varied levels of skill and working in a range of industries, each with different economic conditions. The game can be played of producing examples of poor performers and of highly successful ones, but an objective assessment is only possible if adequate yardsticks for performance can be devised and if full evidence is available on the conditions faced in each industry. In the absence of such studies, we must rest content with the limited conclusion that, while there are intelligible reasons for expecting poor performance in this period – monopolistic imperfections and the absence of the takeover bid mechanism for disciplining quoted companies, for example – there is also some indication that some of the longer-run benefits of the earlier merger movement were being exploited as new investment in larger plants embodied improvements of productivity. For the more restless contemporary critics, however, such a limited and fence-sitting conclusion was unconvincing, and in the later 1940s the view was again gaining ground that the available economies of scale had not been sufficiently exploited. Again American methods seemed to point to changes in British technique. It was this view that stimulated Sir Stafford Cripps to establish, in August 1948, the Anglo-American Productivity Council. Selected teams of businessmen and trade unionists were sent to view US industry under its auspices, and they unanimously stressed the need to emulate American methods. At the same time academic research was confirming that US industry achieved considerably higher levels of production per head than UK industry, and it was noted that the US superiority was most marked in the mass production industries. Whilst differences in size of plants as such could not in general account for the gap in performance, US firms were found to be more conscious of the need for long runs, standardization and expenditure on research, and the businessmen on the postwar productivity missions were in general impressed by American achievements, as their predecessors in the rationalization movement of the 1920s had been.[58] If critical self-analysis is a virtue, then virtue was once again widespread in the later 1940s, as business criticism of Britain's industrial structure mounted. As in the 1920s, this reassessment was again to have profound implications for industrial practices and the structure of firms.

IO

The modern corporate economy

There was a need for more concentration and rationalization
to promote the greater efficiency and international
competitiveness of British industry. The
changes which had so far taken place
in this direction . . . did not yet
match the economy's
requirements.

INDUSTRIAL REORGANIZATION CORPORATION, *First Report
and Accounts* (1968), p. 5.

Size in itself is no solution – indeed it is not
without its disadvantages.

INDUSTRIAL REORGANIZATION CORPORATION, *Report
and Accounts for the Year ending
31 March 1969* (1969), p. 7.

ဢ

From the later 1940s the interest of government policy-makers in the
subject of industrial organization quickened, and the significance of
past changes in the structure of firms (and the possibility that the
trends established earlier would become even more marked) increasingly attracted the attention of economists and of businessmen
also. From this time on, the growth of large firms and the rise in
merger activity is paralleled by an equally rapid rise in the volume of
literature devoted to the subject. The impact of this literature has
been wide. It has led to a re-evaluation of the Labour Party's
approach to business and a new interest in planning through
large-scale enterprise.[1] On the theoretical level, traditional models of
economic behaviour have been questioned, and attempts have been
made to modify them to take account of the development of
'managerial' capitalism.[2] There has also been a great deal of
empirical work on the dimensions of merger activity, industrial
concentration and business behaviour.[3] Yet contemporary writers,
understandably impressed by the sheer weight of information produced on postwar mergers and increasing concentration, have
sometimes concluded from it that modern developments were
historically unprecedented. As we have seen, this view is erroneous.

It is, therefore, worth while reviewing the evidence for recent years in the light of our earlier analysis.

There can be no doubt that, after the pause in the 1930s and 1940s, concentration again increased at a rapid pace in the 1950s and 1960s. The share of the largest 100 companies in manufacturing net output, which in 1953 (as in 1930) stood at 26 per cent, had by 1970 risen to 40 per cent.[4] In individual industries, also, *Census of Production* data confirm that the dominant tendency was for the

TABLE 10.1   *Concentration in industry groups, 1957–69*

Shares of the largest five firms

Industry	1957 population (%)	1969 population (%)	Counter-factual 'merged' population (%)	Proportion of the increase due to mergers (%)
Food	41·3	52·7	49·9	75
Drink	32·7	69·5	68·9	98
Tobacco	96·5	100·0	100·0	100
Chemicals	71·0	73·7	74·5	130†
Metal manufacture*	45·7	59·5	63·9	132†
Non-electrical engineering	29·8	25·3	33·7	§
Electrical engineering	47·2	68·0	59·1	57
Shipbuilding	62·1	74·2	70·9	73
Vehicles	50·4	71·0	76·2	125†
Textiles	44·2	65·1	71·0	128†
Clothing and footwear	63·8	78·4	71·1	50
Building materials	53·1	51·1	53·1	§
Paper and publishing	47·5	63·2	65·1	112†

Share of the largest 100 firms

All manufacturing‡	60·1	74·9	75·3	103†

Notes:
* Excluding the nationalized British Steel Corporation and its constituents.
† A merger contribution above 100 per cent implies that, but for merger activity, concentration would have declined in this industry.
‡ Including the four industry groups – leather, timber, metal goods n.e.s. and miscellaneous – not separately listed in the table.
§ Concentration declined.
Source: Calculated from the data described in L. Hannah and J. A. Kay, *Concentration in Modern Industry: Theory, Measurement and the UK Experience* (1977).

largest firms to increase their market shares in all three of the inter-censal periods 1951–8, 1958–63 and 1963–8.[5] As in the earlier period of rapidly rising concentration, this more recent movement was associated with intensive waves of merger activity affecting a wide range of industries. Annual expenditure by manufacturing firms on mergers, which had been relatively low for almost three decades, had regained the high level of the 1920s (in real terms) by 1956, and reached new heights in the merger boom which peaked in 1968 (see Appendix 1). The significance of this merger wave in consolidating the population of firms can be measured in the listings of the larger (principally quoted) companies in UK manufacturing. The listings, compiled by the Board of Trade and its successors, include firms accounting for about two-thirds of manufacturing output.[6]

Table 10.1 shows the effects of mergers on concentration in thirteen major industry groups and for manufacturing overall between 1957 and 1969. These increases in concentration are less dramatic than those within the population of larger firms in the 1920s (see p. 98), but they confirm the picture of substantial further concentration of manufacturing assets into the leading firms. As in the 1920s, mergers were the major cause of increasing concentration quite generally; indeed in this period, in six industry groups and in manufacturing overall, the merger waves account for the whole of the increase in concentration. On the assumptions implicit in the counterfactual merged population,[7] concentration would have declined in the absence of merger – in five industry groups substantially and in manufacturing overall slightly.[8] Parallel to this movement towards larger enterprises, small firms continued their almost uninterrupted decline. Between 1958 and 1963, for example, the share in net output of manufacturing firms with less than 200 employees declined from 20 per cent of the total to only 16 per cent, and the demise of more than half of the small companies was reported to be due to acquisition by larger rivals.[9]

During these further substantial changes in industrial concentration the major industrial groups established in the interwar period remained at the core of corporate growth. There were of course new companies attaining a leading position, such as Glaxo, Plessey and International Computers, firms in rapidly expanding new industries. But the majority of the large companies of the 1960s could trace their origins as large enterprises to the earlier period of corporate growth,

and the corporations established between the wars showed a remarkable resilience. A study of the largest 100 companies in manufacturing and distribution of 1948, for example, found that, of the
forty-eight that had 'disappeared' by 1968, nine had been nationalized, twenty-seven had been acquired by other firms and only twelve
had actually regressed to a lower ranking.[10] Thus the majority of the
large companies were still among the 100 largest twenty years later,
whether in their own right, or as one of the partners in a large
amalgamated enterprise. There were, of course, significant changes
in ranking amongst the top 100 and there were newcomers to replace
those absorbed by merger and rationalization, but the suspicion of
Marshall, that 'vast joint stock companies . . . do not readily die',[11]
was borne out by the continued dominance of large firms of long
standing. Such firms had not by any means been standing still.
Imperial Chemical Industries and Unilever, which before the war
had been the largest manufacturing employers with around 50,000
employees, had not only been joined by around twenty-five other
manufacturing companies in that size category, but had themselves
grown to employ 143,000 and 80,000 people respectively by the early
1980s. Over the same period, GEC had grown from 24,000 employees to 188,000 and Courtaulds from 22,500 to 88,000.[12] Given
the trend of increased capital-intensiveness and improved labour
productivity, the output of these enterprises had, of course, expanded by considerably more than the increased employment figures
suggest.

The postwar movements towards higher concentration, based to a
large degree on established corporations, were in part the continua-
tion of processes that had provided the dynamic forces behind
concentration increases in earlier periods. Although, in view of
increasing public disquiet about monopolies, businessmen now less
readily admitted monopolization or the extension of their managerial
empires as a major motive of merger, these no doubt remained
fundamental attractions. Again, as in earlier periods of economic
expansion, the rising affluence and declining protectionism of the
postwar era created larger potential markets both at home and
abroad, and this opened up further opportunities for the division of
labour and generated further economies of scale. The existence of
such economies, which had previously been dismissed by sceptics,
was confirmed by new studies based on engineering data. Such
studies had, of course, been used by managers within large firms for

a long time, but by the 1960s it could no longer reasonably be doubted that in some industries there were substantial economies of scale which could not be achieved in the British market if there were more than a few producers.[13] In many industries in which the optimal scale of production was rising, fierce competition frequently ensued, with predictable results: the elimination of small companies, further mergers, and the progressive concentration of output under fewer producers. In the manufacture of television sets, for example, the number of firms in the UK market declined from sixty in 1954 to seven by 1969.[14] Of course, the scope for economies of scale was not confined to the operation of large plants, and though such economies were perhaps the most easily measured, they may not have been the most important ones in the minds of the managers of large companies: financial and marketing scale economies were also considered. More generally, the expansion of advertising (stimulated by commercial television as a new medium)[15] gave manufacturers an increased influence over consumer demand, and they sometimes used this to create a more uniform consumer taste. This was sometimes complementary to the achievement of scale-related economies on the production side. In the brewing industry, for example, the large-scale promotion of pasteurized keg beers (which could be transported and stored without deteriorating) effectively widened market areas and enabled the big brewers to phase out traditional draught beers (which need to be brewed locally) and to centralize production in fewer and larger breweries.[16] Scale economies in industrial research were also of increasing importance, and Britain, alone among Western nations, devoted as high a proportion of her resources as the United States to research and development.[17] As a result of the increasing pressure towards larger-scale enterprise, the vogue for 'restructuring', a term now widely used to denote mergers and the concentration of output in fewer firms, was popularized and was strongly reminiscent of the rationalization movement of the 1920s, both in the arguments used and in the oversimplifications to which its less intelligent advocates succumbed.

In addition to these factors – all of them in essence a development of tendencies inherent in earlier decades – there were also new features in the business environment of the postwar years which accelerated the rise in concentration. Some of the more important changes were political: the coming to power of the Labour Party (with its more critical attitude towards private monopolies) and the parallel change in the postwar Conservative Party. Already during the Second World War fears were expressed in government circles that monopolistic practices could endanger the postwar recovery, and this fear was embodied in the Labour legislation of 1948 which established the Monopolies and Restrictive Practices Commission.[18] Thereafter, stimulated by the reports of the Commission, the groundswell of opinion against restrictive business practices gathered force and a stronger deterrent, the Restrictive Practices Court, was established by the Conservative government in 1956. Whilst there were disagreements about the details, these antitrust initiatives received broad all-party support, and the Conservatives, who had once seen them as unwarrantable interferences with business autonomy, now espoused legislation, albeit somewhat uneasily, as a means of strengthening the case for private enterprise by increasing the competitive pressures within the capitalist system.[19] The Restrictive Trade Practices Act of 1956 was notable in assuming that restrictive practices were harmful unless they could be shown to be beneficial, and in the event the Court found that only 1 per cent of the agreements registered under the Act were consistent with the public interest. By 1966, 2100 registered agreements had been abandoned or terminated and there were no doubt many others which were abandoned or modified because of fears of the adverse publicity which registration might have brought.[20] Although some industries had a sufficiently oligopolistic structure for price leadership, informal agreements or secret collusion to be sufficient to maintain prices without formal restrictive agreements, the Act was successful in increasing competition in a significant number of industries.[21] At the same time, competitive forces were independently being intensified from other directions. Under the General Agreement on Tariffs and Trade (GATT), and later under the EFTA and EEC treaties, the level of tariff protection enjoyed by British industry since the 1930s was progressively reduced. With the further revival of major overseas competitors, British firms no longer faced the sellers' markets of the immediately postwar years but had to meet increasing competition both at home and abroad. Competition was also intensified by a further influx of foreign (principally American) capital into the British market, which stimulated rapid growth of (often technically and managerially superior) competitors for British firms.[22] There was a widespread desire to reduce such competitive pressures within the British market, and the merger waves of these years were undoubtedly in part a response to these feelings. Such compensating mergers need not imply that there was a net decrease in competition, but certainly the initial impact of the restrictive practices legislation and tariff reductions on the level of competition was in some degree neutralized by the increased level of concentration which followed them.[23]

The intensification of competitive pressures not only produced compensating merger movements to maintain monopoly and oligopoly positions, but also, by removing some of the restraints on the natural selection of firms by competitive attrition, strengthened the motivation to agree to merger as a means of gaining access to economies of scale. In the new, relatively unprotected environment, firms which attempted to remain at an inefficiently small scale could expect to encounter greater difficulties in maintaining their market position as competition intensified. At the same time another prewar restraint on the process of adjustment to optimal scale was removed by the rise of the takeover bid. Directors of firms which had slept on their assets in the 1930s and 1940s found that in the new postwar full employment conditions, takeover bidders could acquire their shares and make substantial profits by selling off assets at their higher current prices (or sometimes by operating them more efficiently themselves). Takeover bidding became more attractive and less risky as the proportion of family-dominated companies declined and as a combination of rising asset values, conservative accounting practices and dividend restraint depressed share values and improved the likely margin of profit on such a deal.[24] Government action also had its impact in this field; in particular the new accounting requirements of the 1948 Companies Act forced companies to disclose more about their true assets and profits, and this provided the information on which predators could by-pass the directors and make a bid directly to the shareholders.[25] The more aggressive takeover bidders – men like Mr Charles Clore in the 1950s and Mr Jim Slater in the 1960s – received most publicity, but the impact of takeover bidding extended more widely than this. While it is true that contested bids accounted for only a minority of actual takeovers,[26] it appears that the very threat of a bid was in many cases now sufficient to gain the compliance of a company's directors. As a result, the vulnerability of quoted companies to merger was considerably increased. In the fifteen years following 1948, for example, no less than a quarter of the companies quoted on the London stock exchange were acquired by other quoted companies, and in the ten years following 1957, when the pace of merger activity in general also quickened, 38 per cent of quoted firms were acquired by other quoted companies.[27] The impact of the divorce of ownership and control on creating a more fluid market in corporate control was thus belatedly, but forcefully, established as a major pressure on the directors of industrial firms.[28]

In the 1950s and 1960s, then, two important restraints on movements towards higher concentration – the absence of strong competitive forces and of takeover bids – were removed, in part as a result of government initiatives on restrictive practices, tariffs and company accounting. In addition to the stimulus to higher concentration caused, paradoxically, by competition policy, governments were also more directly active in the promotion of mergers; and, as with restrictive practices legislation, this policy was, despite differences of approach and emphasis, broadly bipartisan. Various factors induced governments to abandon the *laissez-faire* approach towards manufacturing mergers which they had adopted in the interwar years. In the first place the role of the government as a purchaser had greatly increased as military and welfare commitments expanded and as some major transport and energy industries were nationalized, so that an increasing number of firms depended on the government for orders and were thus obliged to respond to government pressures. In the aircraft industry, for example, where the armed forces' orders for military aircraft and the nationalized airlines' orders for civil aircraft dominated order books, the Conservative government was able in 1960 to persuade Vickers-Armstrong, English Electric, and Bristol Aeroplane to consolidate their airframe manufacturing interests into the British Aircraft Corporation.[29] This policy of intervention in private industry was considerably extended by the Labour government of 1964–70. The earlier fears of Labour leaders that mergers and rationalization created unemployment had now given way to a feeling that larger (and, it was hoped, more productive) units would in the long run be better for employment.[30] The newly created Ministry of Technology, Department of Economic Affairs, and Industrial Reorganization Corporation (established to 'promote or assist the reorganization or development of any industry')[31] were involved in promoting larger-scale units in computers, electrical engineering, motor-cars, ball bearings and scientific instruments.[32]

Some of the older industries also attracted the attention of government: the Shipbuilding Industry Board, for example, attempted to create viable enlarged shipbuilding groups by the merger of existing firms in private ownership.[33] More controversially, the British Steel Corporation in 1967 took into public ownership the fourteen largest steel makers, and planned large integrated steelworks, comparable to those appearing in Japan and the United States, which were intended eventually to replace the smaller and scattered plants which had been taken over from the private companies.[34] In the 1970s nationalization was extended to industries such as shipbuilding and aerospace, producing further concentration. Although industrialists in general opposed nationalization, there were important groups of businessmen who strongly supported the government's main initiatives in promoting concentration under private ownership, and others welcomed finance for their ailing firms.

Thus government involvement in creating large companies was more positive than that of the interwar years, when governments had been wary of entanglements involving government finance. However, in these merger waves, as in the past, the basic motivations in the majority of mergers remained those inherent in modern competitive enterprise: the classical desires to restrict competition and to achieve economies of scale. The government's favourable attitude was generally welcomed, and government finance was now sometimes used as a catalyst, but the prospects of enhanced private profits remained the major driving force. Managers were approaching the further growth of their firms with greater confidence than in the earlier period, in part it seems because they were now less inhibited by the managerial problems which had beset some of the earlier large companies. The progressive solution of these problems owed much to developments in technology. The computer and methods of operations research (both originally developed for wartime planning) made the administration of larger-scale enterprises more tractable, and the gradual build-up of experience of large-scale organization improved the capacity of large firms to undertake further growth. The professionalization of management, whose acceptability was symbolized by the foundation of the British Institute of Management in 1947, was given a further boost with the growth of management consultancy,[35] and by the belated development of business schools in Britain, notably the foundation of the London and Manchester Schools in the 1960s.

Perhaps the most significant and widespread postwar development in management was the adoption of the multidivisional organization structure which we saw in rudimentary form in the ICI of the 1930s. A study by Channon, which examined 100 large companies, found that by 1950 only 13 per cent of them had established a multidivisional structure, whereas by 1960 the proportion had risen to 30 per cent and by 1970 to 72 per cent.[36] British subsidiaries of American companies had been among the first to adopt this structure and British firms were often impressed by American methods and management consultants. Indeed McKinsey & Company, the US consultants, were an important force behind the introduction of the multidivisional structure in a number of British companies. These managerial improvements not only allowed large firms to grow within their own industries but also permitted a substantial programme of diversification. In Channon's sample of large companies, for example, only 25 per cent could be considered diversified in 1950, but by 1960 the proportion had risen to 45 per cent and by 1970 to 60 per cent.[37] Much of this diversification again appears to have been the result of corporate growth by merger: between 1957 and 1968, some 39 per cent of acquisitions by quoted firms were of firms in an industry other than that of the acquirer.[38] There was also a further expansion of the overseas subsidiaries of large British manufacturing firms: whereas only 29 per cent of large firms had extensive overseas manufacturing interests in 1950, the proportion had risen to 58 per cent by 1970.[39]

In the 1970s, as governments, businessmen and economists contemplated the radically changed structure of the corporate economy, it was natural that some misgivings should have been felt, as they had been after the earlier merger wave of the 1920s. Extrapolations of the concentration trends of the 1960s suggested that within several decades a few industrial giants would all but monopolize the manufacturing sector.[40] There were some commentators who warned against the alarmism of the more extreme predictions,[41] and their caution proved justified. In fact, the 1970s and early 1980s proved, like the 1930s and 1940s, to be a period of lull in the advance of the corporate economy. Merger activity remained relatively high in the early 1970s, but, after the oil crisis of 1973, and with a sluggish stock market, the number of mergers declined and they then accounted for a smaller proportion of total investment expenditure than for several decades.[42] The share of the largest 100 firms in the net output of the private manufacturing sector rose only slightly from its 1970 level of 40 per cent to 42 per cent in the mid-1970s before falling back again to 41 per cent in the later 1970s.[43] As after the previous merger wave of the 1920s, it seems, the potential benefits of merger and rapidly growing firms were being called into question, and this was limiting the development of expansionist strategies amongst the managers of large firms. At the same time, small firms appear to have been improving their performance in the 1970s,[44] though there is no clear sign of a reversal in concentration trends such as occurred in the 1930s and 1940s.

Some of the falling off of merger activity in the 1970s was due to disillusion with the exaggerated hopes of earlier merger strategies. There were, of course, some spectacular successes. GEC, for example, which had acquired its main rivals, AEI and English Electric, in 1967–8, successfully rationalized the group's manufacturing, and Lord Weinstock developed a highly personal and effective form of decentralized management. This structure succeeded in improving management incentives and profitability, so that by the later 1970s the group had become one of the most financially powerful electrical manufacturers in the world. Glaxo, ranked only 189th among British manufacturing companies in 1948, had acquired many of the smaller British pharmaceutical companies and developed a successful research and marketing strategy for the group, so that by 1982 it was among the largest dozen UK manufacturing firms.[45] At the other end of the spectrum of success was British Leyland, whose leading market position at the time of its major mergers of the 1960s was gradually whittled away by foreign car imports and more efficient (non-merging) domestic competitors like Ford. In other industries, too, the giants were by no means always the most successful. Courtaulds' market position in textiles, for example, collapsed after 1977 more markedly than the medium-sized companies in the industry.[46] A study of a large sample of mergers of the later 1960s found that (after careful standardization for industrial sectors, trade cycle factors, and accounting biases) the profit record of merging firms was disappointing, at least for the first seven years after the merger.[47] Both interview studies and econometric work suggested that much of the 1960s merger activity had not improved efficiency, but merely reduced competitive pressures on managers and enhanced their prestige and salaries, which were more closely related to the size of the firm than to its profitability.[48] The view – too often accepted by politicians and businessmen in the 1960s – that larger scale was a necessary or (still more naïvely) a sufficient condition for achieving economic efficiency was, moreover, called into question by evidence that countries with a less concentrated industrial structure than the USA and the UK could have a more impressive growth performance. This is not to say there were not British industries with uneconomically small plants, but it certainly raised doubts about casually advanced urgings to go for larger firms based on unsubstantiated assertions about scale economies.[49]

Evidence of this nature strengthened the hand of those within government who were not content to leave managerial disillusion with merger to do its own work, but insisted that the state should itself act to restrain merger activity. The Conservative government which followed Labour in 1970 soon abolished the Industrial Reorganization Corporation which had promoted mergers. Governments still in some cases[50] accepted mergers as conducive to employment stability or economic efficiency, but the unmistakable trend of policy had for some time been towards restraint. Already the first moves toward a hardening of government attitudes to mergers and large-scale enterprise could be seen in 1965, when Labour's Monopolies and Mergers Act strengthened the Monopolies Commission and conferred on the government powers to control mergers. By this Act, the Board of Trade (later the Department of (Trade and) Industry) could refer to the Monopolies Commission any merger in which the assets acquired exceeded £5 million, or where the combined company would have a monopoly. This was defined, for the purpose of the Act, as a situation in which one firm had a third of the market. Between 1965 and 1973 the government's mergers panel considered 833 mergers which came within these definitions and referred twenty of them to the Monopolies Commission for investigation. Of these, seven were abandoned voluntarily, seven were allowed to proceed, and the six which the Commission found to be against the public interest were duly prevented.[51] The Fair Trading Act of 1973 further reduced the statutory definition of a monopoly from a third to a quarter of the market, and added to the existing bureaucratic machinery of monopoly and merger surveillance an Office of Fair Trading which became an independent centre of initiative for investigations and referrals. This, together with the general change in the climate of opinion, resulted in more mergers being referred to the Monopolies and Mergers Commission than had been the case in its early years.[52] Despite the increased pressure to toughen antimerger policy,[53] many mergers in Britain were allowed through unexamined by the Commission which would have been prevented by the stronger US antitrust law, but most of the referred mergers were either abandoned on referral or, after investigation, were turned down by the Minister on the recommendation of the Commission.[54]

The greatest disincentive to merger in the 1970s was, however, the clear management difficulties and poor financial results of many of the earlier mergers. As in the 1930s and 1940s this led to a reappraisal of the desirability of merger and a more critical attitude to acquisition proposals both by the City and by industrial management. At the same time, some of the mismatching created by the previous merger wave was being sorted out. Demergers, involving the sale of subsidiaries between companies (which in the interwar merger waves had been a tiny proportion of total merger activity), by the 1970s amounted to a quarter of all mergers by number and more than 10 per cent by value.[55] The restructuring of industry was thus not, as one might have expected, inhibited by the proliferation and growth of large diversified enterprises. Indeed the active and fluid market in subsidiaries, less restricted than in the period when family ownership had been dominant, enabled some unwise conglomerate diversifications to be unscrambled, and generally enabled more rational (and perhaps more anti-competitive) horizontal matches to be made.[56] Another relatively new trend, gathering power in the later 1970s, was the growth of management 'buy-outs', the number of which exceeded a hundred a year by the early 1980s.[57] Large firms typically divested assets (which they had failed to operate profitably) to local management groups who, given the smaller scale and improved incentives in their newly independent situation, were, at least initially, able to turn in more acceptable results.

Since 1979 the Conservative government of Mrs Thatcher has placed increasing emphasis on deregulation, disengagement from intervention and enhanced competition as generators of efficiency. These changes, together with a deflationary macroeconomic policy and oil-boom induced sectoral shifts, have placed an unprecedentedly intense squeeze on the manufacturing sector, and led to a major corporate shake-up through bankruptcy, redundancies and reorganization. Both large and small firms have been squeezed in the depression, and substantial changes in the rankings of firms by output and employment have occurred. The aggregate effects of these changes have, however, yet to be seen in the concentration data, for the *Census of Production* figures for the post-1978 period have not at the time of writing (1982) been published. It is in principle possible for substantial degrees of concentration change to occur without intense merger activity in these circumstances,[58] but whether concentration has increased or decreased is not yet clear. Many large firms have, however, now come to terms with the problem of indigestion following the 1960s merger wave, and it cannot confidently be predicted that the 1980s will follow the pattern of the 1970s. Another substantial advance of merger-led expansion of large corporations, particularly if a stock exchange boom creates the financial conditions which have traditionally been conducive to merger waves, is a credible future possibility.

11

The upshot for welfare

The shoddy, greedy, profit grabbing, joint-stock company industrial
system we had allowed to dominate us, there was the real villain.

J. B. PRIESTLEY, *English Journey* (1934) p. 64.

Many people who are really objecting to Capitalism as a way of life, argue
as though they were objecting to it on the ground of its inefficiency
in attaining its own objects. . . . Capitalism, wisely managed, can
probably be made more efficient for attaining economic ends
than any alternative system yet in sight, but that in itself
is in many ways extremely objectionable. Our
problem is to work out a social organization
which shall be as efficient as possible
without offending our notions of a
satisfactory way of life.

J. M. KEYNES, 'The end of laissez-faire'
(1926, as reprinted in his *Essays in
Persuasion*, 1931), pp. 320–1.

୧୨୯

The rise and development of the corporate economy during the
present century raises important issues both for economic analysis
and for public policy. The benefits of large corporations – and their
disadvantages – have each been widely canvassed, and, though some
progress in understanding has been made as a result of this
long-standing debate, the issues raised at an early stage remain
central. In the 1920s, Sir Alfred Mond, ICI's first chairman, was
expressing the favourable view of rapidly advancing industrial
concentration when he argued that:

> Modern mergers are not created for the purposes of creating
> monopolies or for inflating prices. They are created for the
> purpose of realizing the best economic results which both capital
> and labour will share to the best advantage. They enable varieties
> of industries to form an insurance against fluctuations of markets
> and prices in individual products. . . . Amalgamations mean
> progress, economy, strength, prosperity.[1]

None the less, his case did not lack contemporary censure, and critics with equally simplistic recipes for economic welfare soon replied. The classic liberal economists' condemnation of monopoly power was the basis of Francis Hirst's unfavourable judgement:

> From the standpoint of general utility there is all the difference between the promoter of a real new enterprise and the promoter of a combination or amalgamation. The former is calculated to increase wealth; the latter is rather likely to diminish it. The former is good for employment, the latter is likely to reduce it. The former increases the good things of the world and multiplies the conveniences of life. The latter aims at restricting them and so increasing their cost. One is addition, the other subtraction. One enlarges the world's resources and enriches the consumer by giving him something new; the other exploits him by establishing a monopoly and so forcing him to pay higher prices or to pay the old prices for inferior articles.[2]

Apart from such narrowly economic considerations, there has also been a wide variety of views on the political and social consequences of the growth of big business. The alienation of workers – as measured by factors such as absenteeism or strike-proneness – is closely related to the size of the work unit, though unions have none the less often favoured large units because of the bargaining advantages they confer.[3] Politically, the corporate economy has led to a 'corporate bias' in which governments can, if they wish, attempt to influence business behaviour directly (as they did on prices in the early 1970s), though Mrs Thatcher has recently shown disdain for this method and demonstrated that the potential for consultation – whether with unions or with big business – is not one which governments are obliged to heed.[4] There have always been and there remain many elements on both the right and the left of British politics who see capitalistic competition as potentially damaging, and who welcome any move towards replacing it with more co-operative, altruistic or service-inspired modes of behaviour.[5] These broader questions pose interesting problems, and have generated a large, if not very clearly focused literature, but the analysis of them would require more attention than can be given here.[6]

Even if we confine the discussion to more narrowly economic considerations, however, the dilemma posed by Mond and Hirst has persisted, and it has been reflected in diverse policy prescriptions from economists concerned with industrial organization. In the

interwar years, for example, P. Sargent Florence, a leading industrial economist, pointed to the relatively small-scale family enterprises which characterized British industry as a major factor preventing her performing as well as Germany and America.[7] This perspective has been echoed in the postwar period too, though industrial
economists can now more commonly be heard to say precisely the
opposite: that Britain's industrial structure is excessively concentrated compared with that in America or Germany, that this is a
major explanation of Britain's relative economic decline, and that
restraints could with advantage be placed on the further advance of
large corporations.[8] The historian can record that at least one of their
premises is correct: Britain did once have an unconcentrated industrial structure by international standards, but now has a relatively
concentrated one, having seen a faster rate of change in the 1920s
and 1960s than the similar changes in America and Germany.
However, in the light of the clear evidence of Britain's consistently
poor growth performance relative to other industrial countries –
dating back to the last decades of the nineteenth century and
persisting with remarkable constancy even in the two periods of
drastic corporate reorganization[9] – the historian might be forgiven
for suspecting that, whatever the causes of Britain's weak performance, they may lie elsewhere than in the rise of the corporate
economy.

The diversity of views on the merits of large corporations derive
partly from the theoretical lacunae in the theory of markets and the
relative infancy of the theory of intra-firm organization.[10] Indeed,
one economic theorist has recently gone so far as to say, in relation to
the adequacy of the theory of markets for policy prescription, that
'we are quite uncertain of what really is the case. The pretence that it
is otherwise comes under the heading of religion or magic.'[11] There
is, moreover, sufficient disagreement on the nature of the potential
efficiency gains from competitive markets for attempts to quantify
the likely impact of reducing monopoly power to be rendered
nugatory.[12] Policy judgements in this area have, then, had a
powerful (if somewhat unappetizing) cocktail of ill-formed theory
and quantification from which to choose, and have really rested on
value judgements based on casual observation or wishful thinking
about the way their sponsors would wish the world to be. Even in
complicated areas – such as assessing the degree to which technical
progress will be helped or hindered by particular market structures –

this does not entirely prevent either useful rule-of-thumb policy conclusions or interesting theoretical developments.[13] It does, however, make it extremely difficult to generalize about broad historical movements with any confidence.

A further, serious problem is that it is far from obvious that the measured growth of large corporations and the high modern level of industrial concentration have led to a more monopolistic economy. Other things being equal, high concentration is likely to mean more monopoly, but for twentieth-century British manufacturing industry other things have been far from equal.[14] With more mature capital markets and the development of foreign multinationals, for example, barriers to new entry have been reduced. On the other hand, new barriers to entry, like the massive expansion of branding and advertising, may have neutralized this effect. At the beginning of the century the advertising industry was relatively small, but by the 1960s advertising expenditure had grown to almost 3 per cent of consumer expenditure. Similar developments occurred in branding: before the First World War some 95 per cent of dry grocery goods were taken from bulk and broken up into small lots by the retailer, while almost all are now pre-packaged and branded.[15] The counter-vailing power of the competitive (but highly concentrated) super-market chains may have done something to discipline this power,[16] but the net effect of these changes on the degree of monopoly or imperfect competition is difficult to gauge. The changing degree of competition from overseas producers is also difficult to quantify. In overseas markets and, increasingly since the 1950s, in the home market, British manufacturers have met growing foreign competition.[17] At a time (1982) when the share of imports in the sale of manufactured goods in the United Kingdom is approaching one third, and considerable further competition is only held back by various voluntary and government barriers, the proposition that large British corporations are powerful monopolies is, frankly, unsustainable in large areas of the manufacturing economy. The long-run trend of declining profit rates is, moreover, a clear warning against the simplistic conclusion that monopoly power has increased in the twentieth century commensurately with increasing concentration of output in the hands of fewer firms.[18]

This is not to deny the existence of clear examples of monopolists making exaggerated profits, or – equally damaging – taking their benefits in a quiet life instead, in sectors of the economy where monopoly has remained unthreatened by home competitors or importers. The writings of business historians and the reports of the Monopolies Commission contain numerous examples of the sleepiness of firms not subject to a competitive spur.[19] In some respects, however, the growth of large corporations may have improved the spirit of rivalry and emulation – a source of many of the dynamic gains from competition – by replicating some of the effects of competition *within* the firm. The rationalization movement of the 1920s, for example, emphasized emulation of the excellent and insisted on the need to develop greater comparability of results internally as a means of measuring and achieving that excellence. Large firms often attempted to recreate the competitive system of resource allocation internally:

> It is questionable [one enthusiast for rationalization wrote] whether the competitive system provides scope for such direct and fruitful competition as this pitting of experts one against the other in their own field. Costs and processes are kept top secret, and no direct comparison is possible between the costs and efficiency of rival firms. . . . Organized competition (i.e. within the firm) pits like with like and measures their comparative efficiency with precision; the free play of the competitive system (i.e. the market) confers its rewards and punishments indiscriminately. Organized competition and the encouragement of initiative and enterprise are essential to the success of large-scale organization.[20]

To the extent that the large multidivisional firms whose rise we have described were successful in developing this kind of constructive rivalry – and contemporary examples like GEC suggest that some have – part of the social benefits of 'competitiveness' will have been replicated internally within the firm.

None the less, external competitive spurs undoubtedly remain as the major stimulus to such firms. In the long run, as Alfred Chandler has pointed out in the context of the United States, it is principally those corporations which succeed in improving administrative co-ordination which will survive.[21] There can, in the interim, be considerable inefficiency bolstered by monopoly powers derived, for example, from patents, from control over unique resources or from government protection, but in manufacturing industry generally such monopolies have usually been short-lived.[22] New entry, whether from new firms perceiving the high profits, or from new products circumventing a particular mode of production by meeting a similar demand in a new way – synthetic fibres or chemicals substituting for the natural product, reinforced concrete or plastics for structural steel or wood – has consistently been an extremely potent discipline on the corporate economy. The visible hand of managerial hierarchies has certainly made enormous strides in the course of the twentieth century, but, for all its power, it still remains to a significant degree disciplined by the invisible hand of market competition. The discipline is, it is true, commonly underestimated by managers. The financial results of mergers seem quite generally to fall below the forecasts of their promoters or below the achievements of non-merging firms.[23] There is, then, a strong prima facie case for the view that managers have been subject to a kind of *deformation professionelle*, which has led them to believe that their own hierarchical management co-ordination of an enlarged enterprise will be more effective than in the event appears to be the case. The social consequences of these mistakes – in difficulties of reorganization and redundancy – may be damaging.

None the less, despite continuing evidence of this managerial miscalculation – the poor results of some firms participating in the 1960s merger wave mirror the same phenomenon in the 1920s – it is possible to discern, in the long-run review of the British corporate economy presented in the previous chapters, some cause for optimism about the capacity to learn from experience. The multi-firm mergers before the First World War generally developed insufficient central co-ordination and exhibited extreme managerial inefficiency.[24] That mode of growth was very largely abandoned by the interwar period and more effective managerial structures were then developed, but the large corporations created by merger in the 1920s none the less failed to hold their market share against new competitors in the 1930s and 1940s.[25] Even so, the majority of large firms created by 1930 remained among the largest firms for many decades thereafter,[26] and it seems reasonable to infer that they were, in general, able to come to terms with any managerial diseconomies of scale. The 1960s merger wave was not proof against disappointing financial results, but the evidence from the 1970s appears to be that the large firms were better able to maintain their market shares than they had been after earlier waves.[27] This pattern of gradual improvement in the staying power of large merged corporations in the twentieth century is paralleled by the gradually improving economic performance of Britain in the mid-century decades, at least relative to her abysmally low performance in the pre-First World War period.[28] The most recent analysts of that change suggest that the development of large corporations has been one among many factors in the trend improvement in growth performance,[29] and our story here of innovations in the corporate economy is compatible with that suggestion. The restructuring of the manufacturing capital stock into larger organizations was, however, arguably one of the easiest changes for British firms to make, given the highly developed and efficient capital market which existed. Complementary changes in social attitudes to business, in the educational system, in labour relations and in the quality of organization and management have been less easy to achieve. If Britain's corporate economy is generally to become as potent a force as that of the USA, Germany or other new industrial leaders, there remains much to be done by the current generation of managers.

Statistical appendices

The reason of the thing is not to be
enquired after, till you are sure the thing
itself be so. We commonly are at *what's
the reason of it?* before we are sure
of the thing.

JOHN SELDEN, *Table Talk* (1689), p. cxxi.

Appendix 1

Merger waves in United Kingdom manufacturing industry 1880–1981

 භය

Ideally merger statistics are compiled by a government agency with the aid of statutory merger disclosure requirements and an efficient financial press. Unfortunately for the historian of past merger movements, the late development of antitrust in this country leaves him with no reliable official statistics of acquisitions until the period from 1954 onwards. Moreover, in contrast to the position in the United States, where private enterprise was eager to fill this gap, British economists appear to have had only sporadic interest in mergers before they received the incentive of government policy criticism, which has since turned merger analysis into a flourishing academic industry. Between the excellent private enterprise study of the late Victorian merger waves by the Fabian civil servant Henry Macrosty,[1] and the assumption by the state of responsibility for the compilation of merger statistics, there is no very reliable tabulation of merger activity. J. M. Rees transcribes (sometimes inaccurately) the limited number of reports of the committees on trusts which were published between 1919 and 1921;[2] while P. Fitzgerald and and A. F. Lucas limit their coverage to a few of the major mergers of the interwar period and to price associations.[3] It was therefore necessary to construct an entirely new series for merger activity in Britain between 1880 and 1954. This task is described in detail elsewhere,[4] and readers are referred to these works for an account of the sources, assembly and classification of merger data for the years prior to 1940 and for fuller descriptions of the merger waves of these years, disaggregated by industry, by type, and by size categories. The purposes of this appendix are: first to summarize the main outlines of the methods of compilation used; and secondly, to link the series, in so far as is practicable, to the government statistics which begin in 1954 and which are more fully described in various government publications.[5]

Except where otherwise indicated, the term merger is taken to include both consolidations (in which a new holding company is formed to acquire the constituent companies) and acquisitions of one company by another. The treatment of both kinds of merger is standardized: if company A acquires company B, one 'firm disappearance' is recorded; if A and B merge to form a new company, C, one firm also disappears, the value of the smaller of A and B being taken in this case as the value of the 'disappearing' firm. Sales of subsidiaries between independent companies are also counted as 'firm disappearances' by merger. In general, only firms with significant assets in manufacturing industry and operating principally in the United Kingdom are included. A merger is defined as the acquisition by one company of more than 50 per cent of the voting power of another, and thus conforms to the criterion of control adopted in studies of concentration based on the *Census of Production*. Prior to 1954 the date of merger is taken to be the date of the decision (or of the announcement of intention) to merge, but in the official statistics it may be either the accounting year in which the merger took effect or (from 1969) the date of the announcement of the consummation of the merger.

The statistical series of merger activity presented in Table A.1 below is derived variously from business and industrial histories, year books, company accounts and reports in the financial press, and it would be rash to suppose that such heterogeneous sources had produced a series which was comparable in coverage at all points in time. An asterisk has been placed against points in the table where the major breaks in series occur and the reader is referred to the notes on subperiods below for an indication of the varying definitions and of the difficulty of effecting linkages. Broadly speaking, the modern data are probably the fuller and more reliable since they have been compiled in an environment created by the more stringent disclosure requirements of the postwar years and by greatly improved financial reporting services. The historical series, by contrast, relies variously for its raw data on mention in a less efficient financial press, on the commissioning of business histories by particular firms, on the interest of scholars studying particular industries in chronicling mergers, and on the historical investigations of the Monopolies Commission. It would be surprising if the mists of history had not obscured some past merger activity which under modern conditions would have been recorded. Even the current series, compiled in more advantageous contemporary circumstances, is by no means complete.[6] The merger activity shown in our table for any date is, then, only the tip of an iceberg, though, unlike the case of the iceberg, we cannot be sure of a constant relationship between the visible and submerged portions. A further problem of comparability arises where it has not been possible to maintain constant definitions of the population to which the statistics relate. Between 1954 and 1968, for example, the population includes acquisitions of foreign companies by UK quoted companies, but excludes some domestic acquisitions by non-quoted companies, whereas for 1880–1953 and from 1969 this position is reversed. It follows from this, and other changes in definitions noted below, that comparisons of the level of merger activity in widely separated years will be subject to potentially large margins of error. The series has been used in Chapters 7, 9 and 10 to establish a general presumption that the merger waves of 1919–30 were somewhat larger than those of the 1930s and 1940s (where the data would, if anything, probably be biased against this conclusion). It has also been taken to show that the merger-intensive 1920s were in some respects comparable to the 1950s and 1960s (where other evidence also suggests that the comparison is not wholly fanciful). Any attempt to use this imperfectly linked series for more precise analysis or for broader historical comparisons would, however, be hazardous, if it did not take account of the difficulties involved.

In the historical data, and to a lesser extent in recent data, the number series (column 1 in Table A.1) is likely to be more accurate than the value series (column 2), which rests on a mix of prices paid, market values and nominal values, and in the early years, on some arbitrary assumptions about unknown values. It is not immediately obvious whether numbers of firms disappearing by merger or their values (gross expenditure on acquisitions) are the more appropriate measure of the volume of merger activity. The preference for a value index to be seen in much of the recent merger literature derives from a feeling that the index should reflect a higher figure if two companies with a market valuation of millions of pounds merge than if the merging companies are valued at only a few thousand pounds. However, while this point has some force in studies of the effects of mergers on concentration or on the growth of large firms, where the sizes of the partners are important, it is not unambiguous even for that purpose. An example will serve to show this ambiguity. If there are three companies, X, Y and Z, with capitalizations respectively of £4 million, £2 million and £1 million, the value series will show discrepant results for very similar economic occurrences. For example, if X acquires first Y and then Z, £3 million will be shown as disappearing; while if Z first acquires Y and then X acquires $(Y + Z)$, £5 million in all will be shown as disappearing.

By contrast, the inadequacies of a number series can easily be overstated. If ten firms each worth £100,000 are acquired it is arguable that this should be reflected by a higher index number than the acquisition of one firm worth £1 million, for it does involve a correspondingly greater reduction in the number of independent decision-making units in the economy and a correspondingly greater number of decisions to merge. The number index also has the advantage of being in constant terms at different points in time, though the index of merger values at constant share prices (column 3 in Table A.1) compensates for this weakness in the value series.[7] (Share prices are a more appropriate deflator than retail prices since they reflect, in addition to the general change in the price level, the changing national stock of assets of which merging assets form a part. In comparing the 1920s with the 1960s, for example, we wish to take account of the fact that in the 1920s the capital stock in manufacturing industry was perhaps only two-fifths and retail prices only one third of their level in the 1960s: deflation by a share price index provides a rough approximation to this desired dual correction.) One advantage of using the value series is that, unlike the number series, it is not greatly altered by the addition of large numbers of small firms, and thus comparisons between widely separated years will be less hazardous for the value series since most large mergers (but a changing proportion of the smaller mergers) are included at all dates.

A further variant of the value series (again, however, subject to the same weaknesses as the raw value data) is shown in column 4 of the table. This indicates the proportional contribution of external growth (i.e. growth by merger) to the total growth, both internal and external, of manufacturing firms in each year. Using gross domestic fixed capital formation as an indicator of internal growth,[8] merger activity can be expressed as a proportion of 'total investment expenditure' (i.e. internal and external growth combined). The economic meaning which can be attached to this proportional measure is, of course, limited, since 'total investment expenditure' is an artefact of the financial data, not a fixed fund of real resources. While individual firms may have a choice between spending their surplus cash flow on the acquisition of existing firms and spending it on investment in new plant and buildings, the physical constraints on new investment in the economy as a whole differ from the constraints on the overall level of merger activity. For some purposes, however, the proportional contribution of merger activity to the growth of firms may be the more relevant measure.[9]

The following notes indicate the major characteristics of the various series in the six major subperiods between 1880 and 1973.

1880–1918

The only series in existence for this period, based on Macrosty, was found to be inadequate, and a new series (tripling Macrosty's coverage of mergers and extending the series from 1907 to 1918) was constructed, using business histories, industrial studies and contemporary reference works. A check in the investors' press suggested that the use of this as a further source would have improved coverage only slightly, at least until the later years of the period. The value series for this period is an extremely tenuous estimate: approximate figures for the price paid were available for only 44 per cent of the firm disappearances by merger, and the values of the remaining firm disappearances were arbitrarily assumed to average one quarter of the average known values of firm disappearances in the same decade.

1919–38

Two major series were constructed, one based on business and industrial histories, and the other on mergers reported in the *Investors Chronicle*. This method of compilation enabled corrections for omissions to be made, for although the probabilities of a merger occurring in each series were not known, the total finite population of mergers (of which the two series were independently drawn samples) could be estimated. The figures thus derived (some 41 per cent higher on average than the raw series of directly observed mergers) are only lower-bound estimates of the total numbers of mergers.[10] The values in column 2 for these years were grossed up from known values. The values of 63 per cent of the firm disappearances in the raw series were known, and the range of values presented in column 2 was estimated on the assumption that the unknown values were between one tenth and one quarter of the average known values of the same year.[11] The constant price value series in column 3 is also presented as a range. However, the proportion of total investment expenditure accounted for by mergers (column 4) appears as a single value, the middle of the estimated range of values being chosen for these purposes – implying, that is, an assumption that unknown values averaged one seventh of known values. In one year, 1926, the value series is, perhaps disproportionately, affected by the largest merger of the interwar years, the formation of Imperial Chemical Industries, in which three firms valued at £36 million (about one half of the total values estimated for 1926) disappeared.

1939–53

A series for these years has not previously been available, but it was possible to construct one by using a method akin to that used in the earlier series. In this case, however, statistics of mergers reported in the financial press have not been collected, and the method of correction for omissions using probability theory was thus not available. Instead the raw series derived from business histories and similar sources was grossed up by a multiple based on its relationship to the final estimate of merger activity for the interwar period. The series for this period is therefore somewhat less reliable than in the preceding or succeeding periods, since the year-to-year fluctuations are likely to be exaggerated by the narrower sample of mergers from which the figures are estimated. However, there is no reason to believe that the level of merger activity indicated for the period as a whole is misleading. A comparison both with the government statistics for 1954 onwards and with mergers reported in the financial press confirmed that the link at 1953–4 can be made without serious distortion of the level. The numbers of firm disappearances calculated for 1954, 1955 and 1956 by the method used for 1939–53 were 208, 190 and 198 respectively. The corresponding numbers reported in the official series were 197, 196 and 181. A supplementary check of merger activity reported in the financial press confirmed that, as this comparison indicates, the government figures for these years were slightly on the low side.

Because of the paucity of information on values in this period, total values were not estimated for 1940–8. The values for 1939 are calculated on the same basis as those for 1919–38. The values for 1949–53 are from an independent series based on company accounts[12] and, like the values for the later 1950s, they relate to a variety of accounting years and to acquisitions by quoted companies. Since these values are derived from a different source, we cannot be certain that they correspond directly to the numbers of firm disappearances shown in parallel in column 1.

1954–9

This series is from the government statistics produced by the Board of Trade in its analysis of company accounts. For a variety of reasons the figures for this period diverge most from the idealized definitions laid down in our preamble. The series is based on the accounts of companies whose financial years end within the twelve months to the 5 April following the year indicated. It thus relates to accounting, not calendar, years. It includes only acquisitions of independent companies by companies in the sample and transfers of subsidiaries between companies in the sample. Consolidations of independent companies (i.e. mergers in which a new holding company acquires two or more existing firms) are excluded. Two large consolidations, had they been included, would have increased the value index considerably: in the Yorkshire Imperial Metals merger of 1958 the smaller company (Yorkshire Copper Works) had net assets disappearing of £8 million, and in the Unigate merger of 1959 the smaller company (Cow & Gate) had net assets disappearing of £12.9 million. The series has a contrary tendency to overestimate the level of domestic merger activity by including acquisitions by UK quoted companies of foreign companies, which have been excluded in the years prior to 1949.

1960–8

The series is similar to that used for 1954–9 in that it is derived from company accounts, but there were two important changes in the procedure. First, from 1961 there was a net reduction of some 400 small companies (with assets of under £0·5 million or with income of £50,000 or below) in the Board of Trade's population. This probably reduced measured merger activity by 6·6 per cent relative to the earlier years, though the coverage was again widened somewhat in 1964 and 1968. Secondly, the improved treatment of consolidations, introduced in 1971 by the Department of Trade and Industry, has been applied retrospectively to these statistics: consolidations are therefore included, the large firm being considered the acquirer and the smaller the acquired, thus standardizing their treatment with that of acquisitions. Transfers of subsidiaries between companies, and acquisitions and consolidations of independent companies (including acquisitions by UK companies of foreign companies), are included.

The values recorded in 1968 were at a historically unprecedented level. Two large mergers in that year, British Leyland and GEC–English Electric, accounted for £732 million, or 44 per cent of the merger values recorded.

1969–81

The change in the basis of the official statistics in 1969 from company accounts to reports in the financial press enabled a number of improvements to be made. In particular, it was possible to date mergers by the calendar year in which the transaction was finalized rather than by the accounting year, to exclude acquisitions of foreign companies by UK quoted companies, and to widen coverage to include more non-quoted companies. Some quoted UK companies operating mainly overseas were also added to the population so that their UK acquisitions could now be included. Unfortunately, however, this change actually reduced coverage of manufacturing mergers considered as a whole, and this weakens the link between 1968 and 1969. We have figures for only one later year calculated on the same basis as the period 1960–8: in 1969, 621 firms valued at £724 million disappeared in mergers according to the earlier method, compared with the 481 firms valued at £722 million shown on the revised basis in our table. It might reasonably be inferred that a large number of small acquisitions, mentioned in company accounts but not in the financial press, were eliminated by the revision of method, and that the significance of the break in the value series is less than that in the number series.

TABLE A.1 *Merger activity in UK manufacturing industry, 1880–1981*

	Number of firm disappearances by merger	Values (at current prices) of firm disappearances (£ million)	Values (at 1961 share prices) of firm disappearances (£ million)	Merger values as a proportion of total investment expenditure (%)
1880	4	0·1	1	–
1	1	0	0	–
2	6	1·7	21	–
3	6	0·2	3	–
4	1	0	0	–
5	8	0·3	4	–
6	11	0·3	4	–
7	21	0·5	7	–
8	101	5·3	75	–
9	48	1·7	21	–
1890	92	8·9	111	–
1	35	0·8	10	–
2	24	0·7	9	–
3	11	0·2	3	–
4	17	0·4	5	–
5	32	0·9	10	–
6	69	5·8	53	–
7	83	4·3	36	–
8	151	8·3	70	–
9	255	11·5	94	–
1900	244	21·9	181	–
1	49	7·0	61	–
2	76	9·6	85	–
3	53	4·2	38	–
4	32	1·5	15	–
5	39	2·5	23	–
6	34	2·1	19	–
7	42	1·9	17	–
8	18	1·9	18	–
9	72	2·7	26	–
1910	38	9·9	89	–
1	63	8·1	69	–
2	58	5·5	47	–
3	31	3·2	28	–
4	32	2·9	26	–

TABLE A.1 (*continued*)

	Number of firm disappearances by merger	Values (at current prices) of firm disappearances (£ million)	Values (at 1961 share prices) of firm disappearances (£ million)	Merger values as a proportion of total investment expenditure (%)
1915	44	4·8	45	–
6	43	4·0	33	–
7	41	7·8	57	–
8	112★	26·2★	158★	–
9	228★	89–101	446–508★	–
1920	336	59–67	317–359	29
1	78	14–16	110–125	11
2	67	11–14	73–93	16
3	124	22–28	121–149	30
4	129	12–15	62–77	18
5	116	45–49	202–220	36
6	153	70–77	301–332	51
7	180	38–44	154–175	37
8	270	44–51	155–180	39
9	431	45–50	159–176	38
1930	158	28–31	120–136	30
1	101	16–19	88–105	25
2	86	9–10	49–57	16
3	92	14–17	67–82	23
4	121	16–18	66–75	18
5	187	18–20	67–75	20
6	274	30–37	98–124	26
7	174	19–23	63–75	14
8	127★	21–26	84–104	18
9	94★	13–17	57–74	–
1940	36	–	–	–
1	44	–	–	–
2	23	–	–	–
3	65	–	–	–
4	85	–	–	–
5	88	–	–	–
6	99	–	–	–
7	125	–	–	–
8	109	–	–	–
9	104	15	48	4

TABLE A.1 (*continued*)

	Number of firm disappearances by merger	Values (at current prices) of firm disappearances (£ million)	Values (at 1961 share prices) of firm disappearances (£ million)	Merger values as a proportion of total investment expenditure (%)
1950	49	10	31	2
1	78	4	10	1
2	185	9	28	1
3	122★	42★	125★	7★
4	197★	91★	203★	13★
5	196	67	127	8
6	181	120	247	12
7	223	109	210	10
8	251	100	206	9
9	385★	245★	320★	21★
1960	513★	313★	324★	22★
1	486	479	479	26
2	479	302	322	20
3	583	290	271	20
4	700	432	378	24
5	668	440	410	22
6	572	443	409	21
7	525	756	653	32
8	631★	1666★	1020★	49★
9	478★	716★	443★	26★
1970	426	668	467	23
1	424	372	220	14
2	576	1292	599	37
3	620	462	248	15
4	265	202	184	6
5	164	168	123	4
6	192	220	134	5
7	270	483	230	8
8	275	543	229	8
9	229	813	302	10
1980	215	559	195	7
1	235	530	163	7

TABLE A.1 (*continued*)

	Number of firm disappearances by merger	Values (at current prices) of firm disappearances (£ million)	Values (at 1961 share prices) of firm disappearances (£ million)	Merger values as a proportion of total investment expenditure (%)
	Summary of merger activity by decade[13]			
1880–9	207	10	136	–
1890–9	769	42	401	–
1900–9	659	55	483	–
1910–19	750	161–173	998–1060	–
1920–9	1884	360–411	1654–1886	32
1930–9	1414	184–218	759–907	21†
1940–9	778	–	–	–
1950–9	1867	797	1507	10
1960–9	5635	5837	4709	28
1970–9	3166	5223	2736	12

Notes:
– Data not available
* Major break in series
† 1930–8 only

Appendix 2

Industrial concentration in the United Kingdom 1907–78

ಬಿ

The measurement of industrial concentration poses many perplexing problems of both a theoretical and an empirical nature. The theoretical issues have been discussed in some detail elsewhere.[1] Hence the aim of this appendix is limited to placing some of the major empirical contributions in the existing literature on industrial concentration into perspective, by linking previous research and data collected in the course of the present study into a description of trends in concentration in the United Kingdom over the twentieth century as a whole. It is intended to amplify the statistical analysis of industrial concentration in Chapters 7, 9, and 10, and also introduces examples of indices of concentration which are more appealing technically than those employed there.

The simplest and most readily understood measure of concentration, and one we have used extensively in earlier chapters, is the concentration ratio: the share of the largest n firms in the total sales or output of an industry. Conventionally, when measuring concentration in manufacturing industry as a whole, n is taken as the top fifty or 100 firms. Since data on the sales or output of individual firms are not available for most years, such varied measures of size as profits, assets, market valuation of capital, and employment have also been used. Unfortunately, this diversity of approach vitiates direct comparisons between many studies of concentration, but it is none the less possible, by various methods of interpolation, using a range of assumptions, to construct a reasonably full statistical series of the share of the largest 100 firms in manufacturing net output over the period between 1907 and 1978. The full series is shown in Table A.2 below, and has also been plotted in graph form in Figure 7.1 (see p. 92 above).

TABLE A.2   *The share of the largest 100 firms in
manufacturing net output, 1907–70*

1907	15%	1948	22%
1919	17%	1953	26%
1924	21%	1958	33%
1930	26%	1963	38%
1935	23%	1970	40%
1939	23%	1978	41%

Source: See text.

The most reliable data in Table A.2 are for the years from 1958 onwards, which are taken directly from the *Census of Production*.[2] Two
alternative sets of interpolations already exist for the period prior to
that, both showing broadly similar trends over the century as a
whole, but with significant differences in specific years.[3] In addition,
information is now available on the share of the largest 100 firms in
employment in both 1907 and 1935.[4] On the assumption that the
ratio between employment shares and net output shares was as in
later years, approximate figures for the largest 100 firms' share in net
output in these years can be derived. The figures thus obtained for
1907 and 1935, shown in the table, are extremely approximate, but
are very close to those derived by alternative methods of extrapolat-
ing backwards by applying changes in the share of the largest 50
firms in profits, or by adjusting the incomplete data in the 1935
Census of Production, as modified by Leak and Maizels.[5] Figures for
1919, 1924, 1930, 1939 and 1948 are interpolations by the present
author;[6] the figure for 1953 is an estimate by S. J. Prais based on
changes in the share of the largest 100 firms in profits.[7] The
possibility of errors arising from the assumptions on which interpolations have been made renders comparisons between widely
separated years particularly hazardous since some errors may be
cumulative. Even in comparisons between adjacent years small
movements in concentration may be accounted for entirely by errors
in the data or by faulty assumptions in the interpolations. Until the
earlier *Census of Production* returns have been more carefully
analysed, however, it is unlikely to be possible to produce a more
acceptable description of changes in manufacturing industry as a
whole.[8]

Until 1968, the problem of defining the largest 100 corporate firms
in manufacturing industry is not compounded by nationalization,

which hardly affected manufacturing before that date. From that date onwards, the figures given in the Table A.2 are for the private sector only, since the mergers involved in large nationalizations of sectors such as steel, shipbuilding and aircraft have, in some respects at least, origins and effects different from those in the private corporate economy. None the less the inclusion of nationalized enterprises in both the numerator and denominator would probably not make a substantial difference. Around 1970, for example, the inclusion of the nationalized British Steel Corporation would raise the 100-firm concentration ratio by only one percentage point.[9] Further consolidations of large enterprises under nationalized corporations like British Shipbuilders and British Aerospace occurred in the 1970s, but in some cases their impact may well have been attenuated by their poor profit performance and large lay-offs of labour in recent years.[10]

A weakness of the approach exemplified in Table A.2 is that the choice of the share of the top 100 is a matter of computational convenience rather than of economic significance. It is possible that changes in concentration, as alternatively measured by, say, the share of the top ten or the top 1000 firms would be different, and, if this were so, it would be a matter of some interest. Ideally, then, what is required is a measure of the concentration ratio for all values of n, rather than for one of them: a measure of the whole distribution of firm sizes. Unfortunately it is difficult, especially in historical periods, to estimate the sizes of every firm in the economy, as such a measure would ideally require. Hence studies which have attempted a more generalized measure of concentration have usually been limited to quoted companies (and thus to the upper ranges of the size distribution of firms) for which estimates of size based on stock market valuations of capital can be made. P. E. Hart and S. J. Prais, for example, have estimated the sizes of quoted companies in manufacturing and distribution for the years 1907, 1924, 1939, 1950 and 1955.[11] However, there are difficulties in interpreting their conclusions on concentration since they used a measure of concentration – the variance of the logarithms of firms' sizes – which is inappropriate and potentially misleading.[12] None the less it proved possible to reconstruct their population of firms by calculating the sizes of the top dozen or so firms in each year from data published in the *Stock Exchange Daily Official List* and by using the midpoints of the size classes published by Hart and Prais for the smaller firms (in which deviations from the midpoints of size classes would not significantly affect the result). The results are shown on Table A.3. This uses a comprehensive numbers-equivalent measure of concentration which avoids the pitfalls of the variance of logarithms. This measure, K, which was originally suggested by J. A. Kay, is given by the expression

$$K = \left(\sum_i s_i^\alpha \right)^{\frac{1}{1-\alpha}}$$

where s_i is the market share of the ith firm and α is the elasticity of market power with respect to firm size.[13] The first column of Table A.3 indicates the range of values of α used. When α takes a low value (in practice $\alpha = 0.6$ is the lowest value used) changes among smaller firms in the lower part of the distribution will have a stronger impact on the index than when α takes a higher value. A high value of α (in practice $\alpha = 2.5$ is the highest used), on the other hand, will give great weight to the largest firms in the distributions.[14] The table thus supplies a more comprehensive measure than either a single concentration ratio or a single elasticity parameter.

The population of quoted firms (on which Table A.3 is based) accounts for a portion of manufacturing industry which rises over time, as more companies gain quotations. Thus it is important to compare constant samples of companies rather than the whole distributions for each year.[15] The appropriate pairwise comparisons of constant samples can be readily distinguished in the table since they lie between the vertical rules. From these comparisons it appears that, for all the relevant range of elasticities ($\alpha = 0.6$ to $\alpha = 2.5$), concentration within this population rose in 1907–24 and in 1924–39, declined in 1939–50 and began to rise again in 1950–5.[16] These results are consistent with the direction of change between the turning points indicated in the simpler measure of concentration employed in Table A.2. Since the sample of quoted firms, on which Table A.3 is based, accounts for a large portion of manufacturing industry (perhaps as much as half in the later years), the consonance of the results is reassuring.

Unfortunately the years for which Hart and Prais produced size distributions of firms do not give a full measure of the trend in those two decades – the 1920s and 1960s – in which, according to Table A.2, concentration was increasing most rapidly. This is, in the first

TABLE A.3 Concentration among quoted firms in the UK, 1907–55

Elasticity (α)	1907	1924 constant	1924	1939 constant	1939	1950 constant	1950	1955 constant
0	571	456	726	516	1712	1502	2103	1981
0·6	287	156	274	173	542	599	871	663
0·8	224	112	198	121	354	423	612	440
1·0	174	82	146	87	232	297	422	292
1·2	136	63	110	64	156	210	292	200
1·4	107	50	85	48	110	154	207	145
1·6	86	41	68	38	81	117	153	111
1·8	70	35	56	31	63	93	119	89
2·0	58	30	47	26	51	77	96	75
2·5	40	23	34	19	35	54	66	55

Note: The lower the index, the *higher* the concentration.
Source: See text.

place, because there is no estimate for any turning point between 1924 and 1939 (a period which probably includes an initial rise, followed by a fall in concentration); and, in the second place, because studies of later years (which share the major drawback of the earlier study by Hart and Prais) have not been reconstructed using a more appropriate index of concentration.[17] The study by J. A. Kay and the present author of the periods 1919–30 and 1957–68[18] does, however, confirm the picture of substantially rising overall concentration in those periods. That study also confirms the conclusion of Chapters 7, 9 and 10 that mergers, rather than the Gibrat effect favoured by Professor Prais, were the major source of these rises in concentration in the twentieth century overall, and that the 1930s and 1940s probably witnessed a decline in concentration.

Appendix 3

Historical listings of the largest UK firms

ໂຊ

For the post-Second World War period, numerous listings of the leading British firms are available, permitting a comprehensive ranking of the largest 100, 500 or even 1000 firms by a variety of measures.[1] Data on firm sizes for the earlier period are more difficult to obtain, but a number of broadly comparable lists exist. Christine Shaw for 1907 and Lewis Johnman for 1935 provide lists of firms which (though not certainly *the* largest 100 employers) include most of the top 100 manufacturing employers for these years.[2] Listings of the largest fifty or so firms ranked by *nominal* value of issued capital have also been compiled by Peter Payne for 1905 and Shin'ichi Yonekawa for 1929.[3] Listings of the largest 200 firms in manufacturing, ranked by the *market* value of their capital (a measure which reflects underlying profit-earning potential better than the nominal value of the capital) are available for 1919, 1930 and 1948.[4] Unfortunately, the varying definitions of industrial coverage and the different measures used make it difficult to utilize these lists in a comparative analysis of changes in the corporate UK manufacturing economy over the twentieth century as a whole. The purpose of this appendix is to provide lists of the largest fifty firms in manufacturing (as defined by Orders III–XIX of the Standard Industrial Classification) as closely as possible comparable to the list of the largest fifty manufacturing firms, ranked by the market value of their capital in 1930, reproduced on pp. 102–3 above. The aim has been to confine the lists to those firms which were throughout the period significantly engaged in domestic UK manufacturing production. Thus none of the lists include oil majors such as Shell or BP, since they were principally involved in overseas production and domestic marketing, and only developed a significant UK manufacturing presence in the postwar period. Similar considerations pointed to the exclusion of other leading British firms in areas such as meat importing (Union

Cold Storage) or overseas tobacco manufacture and sales (British-American Tobacco).

The lists should be seen as approximate indicators of the identity of the leading firms in the corporate manufacturing economy at the various dates, and not as precise indicators of relative size. Detailed examination of any industry by a variety of criteria illustrates the problem. Despite their exclusion from the two early tables, for example, there may have been car manufacturing establishments among the largest companies, either as subsidiaries of companies included (Vickers owned Wolseley in 1905, for example) or if rankings had been by an alternative criterion (e.g. by employment rather than size of capital in 1919). When car companies do enter the tables in 1930,[5] moreover, their ranking is not necessarily in an order familiar to historians of car manufacture. Ford, for example, appears as the largest firm by the market value of its capital (£21.2 million), nearly three times the size of the next largest car manufacturer, Morris (£7.6 million), and Austin does not appear at all. This is partly because Ford of Britain included a large number of continental European capital assets as well as the British assets, while Morris's unquoted capital has probably been undervalued in the estimate of its size in 1930. If the firms had been ranked by the number of cars produced or the gross value of final output, Morris would actually have led Ford, while if the rankings had been by the size of employment, Austin, which was more vertically integrated, would probaby have been the leader. Such detailed differences in composition and ranking of the leading fifty firms, dependent on variations in the quality of estimation and different criteria of size adopted, may be serious drawbacks of these lists for some purposes, but they provide useful order-of-magnitude estimates. For the limited purpose of identifying fifty of the leading manufacturing firms in the corporate economy, for which they have been used here, they serve their purpose well, and there is in fact a considerable degree of consonance between listings compiled on alternative bases.[6]

Table A.4 is a modification of Payne's 1905 list of the largest fifty-two industrial companies ranked by nominal value of issued capital to bring it more in line with the definitions of subsequent tables. Two companies inadvertently omitted by Payne, British Westinghouse and Ryland, have been added. Other companies listed by Payne have been omitted because it was thought they would not

TABLE A.4 *The fifty largest companies of 1905*

Rank	Industry	Name of company	Issued capital in 1905 (£ million)
1.	Tobacco	Imperial Tobacco	17·5
2.	Drink	Watney, Combe, Reid	15·0
3.	Textiles	J. & P. Coats	11·2
4.	Chemicals	United Alkali	8·5
5.	Textiles	Calico Printers Association	8·2
6.	Shipbuilding/engineering	Vickers	7·4
7.	Textiles	Fine Cotton Spinners and Doublers	7·3
8.	Building materials	APCM	7·1
9.	Textiles	Bleachers Association	6·8
10.	Drink	Arthur Guinness	6·0
11.	Shipbuilding	Armstrong-Whitworth	5·3
12.	Drink	Samuel Allsopp	5·1
13.	Drink	Whitbread	4·8
14.	Drink	Bass, Ratcliff & Gretton	4·6
15.	Metal manufacture	GKN	4·5
16.	Rubber	Dunlop	4·4
17.	Textiles	Bradford Dyers	4·3
18.	Drink	Barclay Perkins	4·3
19.	Electrical engineering	British Westinghouse (subsidiary of US Westinghouse)	4·3
20.	Metal manufacture	Bolckow Vaughan	4·2
21.	Drink	Cannon Brewery	4·2
22.	Paper	Wallpaper Manufacturers	4·1
23.	Drink	Charrington	4·0
24.	Food	Lever Bros	4·0
25.	Drink	Ind. Coope	3·7
26.	Drink	Truman, Hanbury & Buxton	3·5
27.	Drink	Mann Crossman & Paulin	3·3
28.	Textiles	English Sewing Cotton	3·1
29.	Drink	Peter Walker	3·0
30.	Shipbuilding	John Brown	2·9
31.	Textiles	Linen Thread	2·7
32.	Shipbuilding	Cammell Laird	2·6
33.	Textiles	Rylands & Sons	2·6
34.	Drink	Courage	2·5
35.	Metal manufacture	William Beardmore	2·5
36.	Food	Huntley & Palmers	2·4
37.	Chemicals	Brunner Mond	2·3
38.	Textiles	British Cotton & Wool Dyers Association	2·1

TABLE A.4 *(continued)*

Rank	Industry	Name of company	Issued capital in 1905 (£ million)
39.	Drink	Distillers	2·0
40.	Textiles	Yorkshire Woolcombers Assoc.	2·0
41.	Chemicals	Reckitt & Sons	2·0
42.	Textiles	Lister	2·0
43.	Food	J. & J. Colman	1·9
44.	Metal manufacture	Dorman Long	1·9
45.	Metal manufacture	Stewarts & Lloyds	1·8
46.	Vehicles	North British Locomotive	1·8
47.	Shipbuilding	Swan Hunter & Wigham Richardson	1·5
48.	Paper	Waterlow & Sons	1·4
49.	Textiles	Tootal, Broadhurst, Lee	1·3
50.	Chemicals	Nobel Explosives	1·3

Source: See text.

have qualified if their manufacturing interests alone had been included: United Collieries, Wigan Coal & Iron and the Salt Union were more heavily engaged in mining than in manufacturing. It was also thought that Maples, Waring & Gillow, and four breweries – Hoare, City of London, Threlfalls and Wilson – may not have qualified for inclusion if their retailing capital had been excluded. The resulting list contained forty-four manufacturing firms whose capital was known to qualify them for entry. Six firms were added to make the total fifty, by the expedient of calculating on a comparable basis the 1905 capital of all firms in Ms Shaw's list of 100 large employers of 1907 for which data were available,[7] and including the largest six of them as the final six firms in the list. Some private firms like Platt Bros (textile machinery) and Pilkingtons (glass) would almost certainly have qualified for inclusion had they published data on their capital, but they (and any public companies there may have been with issued capital of £1.3–£1.8 million but less than 3000 employees) are excluded from the 1905 list.

The coverage of Table A.5, which relates to 1919, is somewhat improved by the inclusion of some unquoted companies. The measure of company size in Table A.5 is also different from Table A.4: the market value of quoted capital and an estimate of the value

TABLE A.5   *The fifty largest companies of 1919*

Rank	Industry	Name of company	Estimated market value of capital (£ million)
1.	Textiles	J. & P. Coats	45·0
2.	Food	Lever Bros	24·3
3.	Tobacco	Imperial Tobacco	22·8
4.	Shipbuilding/engineering	Vickers	19·5
5.	Drink	Guinness	19·0
6.	Chemicals	Brunner Mond	18·7
7.	Chemicals	Nobel Industries	16·3
8.	Textiles (rayon)	Courtaulds	16·0
9.	Vehicles	Metropolitan Carriage Wagon and Finance	14·4
10.	Metal manufacture	United Steel	13·2
11.	Shipbuilding	Armstrong-Whitworth	12·2
12.	Textiles	Fine Spinners & Doublers	9·9
13.	Building materials	Associated Portland Cement	9·1
14.	Rubber	Dunlop Rubber	8·9
15.	Chemicals	Reckitt & Sons	8·8
16.	Metal manufacture	Guest Keen & Nettlefold	8·2
17.	Chemicals	Levinsteins (British Dyestuffs Corporation)	8·0
18.	Shipbuilding	John Brown	7·7
19.	Drink	Watney Combe Reid	6·9
20.	Textiles	Bleachers Association	6·7
21.	Metal manufacture	Consett Iron	6·6
22.	Engineering	Babcock & Wilcox	6·5
23.	Metal manufacture	Dorman Long	6·5
24.	Textiles	Calico Printers Association	6·4
25.	Food	Maypole Dairy	6·2
26.	Metal manufacture	Richard Thomas	6·2
27.	Textiles	Bradford Dyers Association	6·1
28.	Chemicals	United Alkali	6·1
29.	Publishing	E. Hulton	6·0
30.	Metal manufacture	Mond Nickel	5·6
31.	Drink	Bass Ratcliffe & Gretton	5·3
32.	Engineering	Hadfields	5·3
33.	Drink	Buchanan-Dewar	5·2
34.	Chemicals	Boots Pure Drug	5·0
35.	Textiles	English Sewing Cotton	5·0
36.	Metal manufacture	Stewarts & Lloyds	5·0
37.	Shipbuilding	Cammell Laird	4·8
38.	Engineering	Birmingham Small Arms	4·6
39.	Textiles	Horrockses Crewdson	4·5

TABLE A.5 *(continued)*

Rank	Industry	Name of company	Estimated market value of capital (£ million)
40.	Chemicals	Borax Consolidated	4·4
41.	Textiles	Linen Thread	4·4
42.	Drink	Distillers	4·3
43.	Food	Liebigs Extract of Meat	4·3
44.	Food	J. Lyons	4·3
45.	Publishing	Amalgamated Press	4·2
46.	Publishing	Associated Newspapers – Daily Mail Trust	4·2
47.	Metal manufacture	Ebbw Vale	4·1
48.	Engineering	Platt Bros	4·0
49.	Metal manufacture	John Lysaght	3·9
50.	Electrical engineering	English Electric	3·8

Source: See text.

of unquoted capital (based on nominal values, dividend yields, etc.) for both quoted companies and a selection of large unquoted companies is taken, rather than the nominal value of issued capital. This arguably produces a better estimate of the sustainable market share of the company. The 1919 list is compiled in precisely the same way as the 1930 list on pp. 102–3 above, and can be directly compared to it.[8] However, because of differences in the sources and measures

TABLE A.6   *The fifty largest companies of 1948*

Rank	Industry	Name of company	Estimated market value of capital (£ million)
1.	Tobacco	Imperial Tobacco	257·8
2.	Chemicals	Imperial Chemical Industries	197·5
3.	Food	Unilever	185·6
4.	Drink	Distillers	127·6
5.	Drink	Guinness	67·0
6.	Textiles	Courtaulds	57·1
7.	Rubber	Dunlop Rubber	55·9
8.	Textiles (rayon)	J. & P. Coats	55·9
9.	Shipbuilding/engineering	Vickers	39·3
10.	Metal	Guest Keen & Nettlefold	35·3
11.	Chemicals	Reckitt & Colman	33·6

TABLE A.6 *(continued)*

Rank	Industry	Name of company	Estimated market value of capital (£ million)
12.	Metal manufacture	Stewarts & Lloyds	31·9
13.	Paper and publishing	Kemsley Newspapers	31·8
14.	Food	Tate & Lyle	29·8
15.	Electrical engineering	Associated Electrical Industries	28·9
16.	Food	J. Lyons & Co.	28·0
17.	Electrical engineering	General Electric	28·0
18.	Building materials	APCM	28·0
19.	Metal manufacture	Richard Thomas & Baldwins	27·7
20.	Drink	Bass Ratcliffe & Gretton	27·3
21.	Building materials	Turner & Newall	25·9
22.	Tobacco	Carreras	25·6
23.	Paper and Publishing	Bowater Paper	24·9
24.	Vehicles	Morris Motors	24·8
25.	Drink	Watney Combe Reid	24·5
26.	Chemicals	Boots	23·7
27.	Metal manufacture	Tube Investments	23·4
28.	Vehicles	Ford Motor	23·3
29.	Textiles	British Celanese	23·3
30.	Metal manufacture	Steel Co. of Wales	22·5
31.	Chemicals	Beechams	22·4
32.	Electrical engineering	British Insulated Callenders Cables	21·2
33.	Chemicals	British Oxygen	21·2
34.	Metal manufacture	United Steel	21·0
35.	Films	Gaumont–British	20·3
36.	Matches	British Match	18·6
37.	Food	Ranks	18·3
38.	Mechanical engineering	British United Shoe Machinery	17·3
39.	Drink	Walker Cain	17·3
40.	Drink	Mitchell & Butlers	17·3
41.	Food	United Dairies	16·9
42.	Tobacco	Gallaher	16·4
43.	Mechanical engineering	Babcock & Wilcox	16·3
44.	Drink	Charrington	15·7
45.	Metal manufacture	Stavely Coal & Iron	15·1
46.	Clothing	Montague Burton	15·0
47.	Paper and publishing	Daily Mail Trust	14·8
48.	Metal manufacture	British Aluminium	14·7
49.	Food	Spillers	14·7
50.	Metal manufacture	John Summers	14·5

used, the changes in composition or of size between the 1905 and 1919 lists should be interpreted with extreme caution.[9] A case could be made, for example, for omitting from the 1919 list Maypole, Boots and Lyons, as primarily engaged in retailing, and of Borax Consolidated and Liebigs, as principally engaged in overseas production. However the 1948 list in Table A.6 is compiled on a similar basis to Table A.5 and can be compared directly with it.[10]

Select bibliography

ကည

This bibliography is intended as a brief guide to the literature on the history and economics of the corporate economy. It does not attempt to list all the sources used in the writing of the present work, since this bibliographical requirement has been largely catered for in the note references themselves. In order to minimize the necessary search time, full references, including place and date of publication, have been included in the first mention of each book or article *in the notes to each chapter*. Except where otherwise stated, the place of publication of items mentioned is London.

There are a number of texts covering the historical background to the British economy in this period. D. H. Aldcroft and H. W. Richardson, *The British Economy 1870–1939* (1969), contains a useful survey of research, and reprints a number of the authors' articles on the new industries and economic expansion between the wars. The 'new' economic history school is variously represented in R. Floud and D. McCloskey (eds), *The Economic History of Britain since 1700*, vol. 2, *1860 to the 1970s* (Cambridge, 1981). The dimensions of modern economic growth are authoritatively covered in R. C. O. Matthews, C. H. Feinstein and J. C. Odling-Smee, *British Economic Growth 1856–1973* (Oxford, 1982). Peter Payne provides a masterly survey of 'Industrial entrepreneurship and management in Great Britain' in his chapter of P. Mathias and M. M. Postan (eds), *The Cambridge Economic History of Europe*, vol. 7 (Cambridge, 1978). The evidence of retardation in Britain's growth before 1914 is discussed in D. H. Aldcroft (ed.), *The Development of British Industry and Foreign Competition 1875–1914* (1968), and A. L. Levine, *Industrial Retardation in Britain 1880–1914* (1967); though some commentators take a more favourable view of this period. W. Ashworth, *An Economic History of England 1870–1939* (1960), for example, defends the performance of the British economy before 1914. S. Pollard, *The Development of the British Economy 1914–1967* (1969), provides a useful coverage of the later period, and D. Landes, *The Unbound Prometheus* (Cambridge, 1970), sets the whole subject in an international context. The economist C. P. Kindleberger reflects on some key historical issues in his *Economic Growth in France and Britain 1851–1950* (1964). Marxist interpretations may be found in M. Dobb, *Studies in the Development of Capitalism* (1946), and E. J. Hobsbawm, *Industry and Empire* (1968). C. L. Mowat, *Britain between the Wars 1919–1940* (1955), and A. Marwick, *Britain in the Century of Total War 1900–1967* (1968), provide useful accounts of the political and social background. The best surveys of social attitudes and the British business climate are G. C. Allen, *The British Disease* (Hobart Paper no. 67, 1979) and M. J. Wiener, *English Culture and the Decline of the Industrial Spirit 1850–1980* (Cambridge, 1981).

Economists have written much on the subject of industrial structure, though their writing usually lacks a sense of historical context and much of it is policy orientated. Perhaps the best textbook of industrial organization is F. M. Scherer, *Industrial Market Structure and Economic Performance* (Chicago, 1980), though the majority of his examples are American, as are those of G. J. Stigler's useful collection of essays, *The Organisation of Industry* (Homewood, Illinois, 1968). The best British competitor is D. A. Hay and D. J. Morris, *Industrial Economics: Theory and Evidence* (Oxford, 1979). A Marshall, *Industry and Trade* (1919), and E. A. G. Robinson, *The Structure of Industry* (1931), are evergreens, much reprinted; and a number of empirical studies by British economists are of abiding interest for the economic historian, notably P. S. Florence, *The Logic of Industrial Organisation* (1933), and its successor *The Logic of British and American Industry* (rev. edn 1961). Two interesting, but neglected, theoretical contributions to the study of industrial organization may be found in R. H. Coase, 'The nature of the firm', *Economica*, vol. 4 (1937), reprinted in American Economic Association (ed.), *Readings in Price Theory* (1953), and G. B. Richardson, 'The organisation of industry', *Economic Journal*, vol. 82 (1972). R. Marris, *The Economic Theory of 'Managerial' Capitalism* (1964), is an attempt to modify traditional theories of the firm to take account of institutional changes, and this, and other revisions of economic models, are discussed in R. Marris and A. Wood (eds), *The Corporate Economy* (1971). A wider view is taken in some more speculative and readable volumes on large British and American corporations, written from a variety of viewpoints. P. A. Baran and P. M. Sweezy, *Monopoly Capital* (Harmondsworth, 1968), is a Marxist essay on the American social and economic order, while

J. K. Galbraith, *The New Industrial State* (1967), and J. A. Schumpter, *Capitalism, Socialism and Democracy* (1943), have a meliorist outlook. E. T. Penrose, *The Theory of the Growth of the Firm* (Oxford, 1959), is a pioneering attempt to study the limits to the size of the firm in a dynamic context, and G. B. Richardson, *Information and Investment* (1960), provides a suggestive treatment of the relationship between industrial structure and the efficiency of investment decisions.

On the historical front, there is nothing to match A. D. Chandler's classic descriptions of the evolution of enterprise structure in the United States, *Strategy and Structure, Chapters in the History of Industrial Enterprise* (Cambridge, Mass., 1962) and *The Visible Hand: The Managerial Revolution in American Business* (Cambridge, Mass., 1977). But there are a number of studies in the history of management and of individual businesses which make the darkness less than total. D. F. Channon, *The Strategy and Structure of British Enterprise* (1973), is confined to post-1950 developments; and G. Turner, *Business in Britain* (1969), also covers this period well, as do the various case studies included in R. S. Edwards and H. Townsend, *Business Enterprise* (1958), and in their companion volume *Studies in Business Organisation* (1961). For the earlier period the best sources are the many histories of individual businesses, though these differ tremendously in quality, from the adulatory public relations exercises to the serious and critical scholarly studies. Among the most important of the latter are: W. J. Reader, *Bowater: A History* (Cambridge, 1981); D. C. Coleman, *Courtaulds, An Economic and Social History* (3 vols, Oxford, 1969 and 1980); C. Wilson, *The History of Unilever* (2 vols, Oxford, 1954), and its sequel *Unilever 1945–1965* (1968); W. J. Reader, *Imperial Chemical Industries, A History* (2 vols, 1970 and 1975); P. L. Payne, *Colvilles and the Scottish Steel Industry* (Oxford, 1979); P. Mathias, *Retailing Revolution* (1967); and B. W. E. Alford, *W. D. & H. O. Wills and the Development of the UK Tobacco Industry 1786–1965* (1973). A good 'sampler' of these and other works is provided in a volume of essays specially commissioned by the Economic History Society: B. Supple (ed.), *Essays in British Business History* (Oxford, 1977). Written more obviously from the perspective of the present, but none the less historically illuminating, are G. Turner, *The Leyland Papers* (1970), and R. Jones and O. Marriott, *Anatomy of a Merger, A History of GEC, AEI and English Electric* (1970). All of these studies have much to say on the role of individual entrepreneurs in the growth of firms, a theme which is more explicitly treated in P. W. S. Andrews and E. Brunner, *The Life of Lord Nuffield* (Oxford, 1955), and in the series edited by Neil McKendrick which includes R. A. Church's biography of *Herbert Austin* (1979) and many other entrepreneurial biographies. The forthcoming many-volumed *Dictionary of Business Biography*, edited by D. J. Jeremy, also throws light on this topic. R. A. Church, *Kenricks in Hardware, A Family Business* (Newton Abbot, 1969), is a scholarly treatment of a medium-sized business providing us with some insight into the kind of firm about which much is said but little is known. Studies of individual industries can also be helpful and they are almost as common as business histories. Amongst the more interesting may be listed: W. Minchinton, *The British Tinplate Industry* (Oxford, 1957); H. R. Edwards, *Competition and Monopoly in the British Soap Industry* (Oxford, 1962); G. Maxcy and A. Silberston, *The Motor Industry* (1959); J. E. Vaizey, *The Brewing Industry 1886–1951* (1960); and J. C. Carr and W. Taplin, *A History of the British Steel Industry* (Oxford, 1962). Various collections of papers also include useful studies of individual industries, including P. L. Cook and R. Cohen, *The Effects of Mergers* (1958), and D. L. Burn (ed.), *The Structure of British Industry* (2 vols, Cambridge, 1958).

The historical experience of merger activity is still most fully described in contemporary works. The files of the *Economist* and the *Investors Chronicle* are perhaps the most useful among periodicals. H. Macrosty, *The Trust Movement in British Industry* (1907), has comprehensive coverage of the earlier period, while P. Fitzgerald, *Industrial Combination in England* (1927), and A. F. Lucas, *Industrial Reconstruction and the Control of Competition* (1937), are sketchier. On the more recent period, there are G. D. Newbould, *Management and Merger Activity* (Liverpool, 1970), and M. A. Utton, 'Mergers and the growth of large firms', *Bulletin of the Oxford University Institute of Statistics*, vol. 34 (1972). Other recent publications which survey the historical experience of mergers and concentration are: M. A. Utton, 'Some features of the early merger movements in British manufacturing industry', *Business History*, vol. 14 (1972); P. L. Payne, 'The emergence of the large-scale company in Great Britain, 1870–1914', *Economic History Review*, vol. 20 (1967); L. Hannah, 'Mergers in British manufacturing industry 1880–1918', *Oxford Economic Papers*, vol. 26 (1974); P. E. Hart, 'Business concentration in the United Kingdom', – *Journal of the Royal Statistical Society*, series A, vol. 123 (1960); L. Hannah and J. A. Kay, *Concentration in Modern Industry: Theory, Measurement and the UK Experience* (1977); K. Cowling *et al.*, *Mergers and Economic Performance* (Cambridge, 1980), and S. J. Prais, *The Evolution of Giant Firms in Britain* (Cambridge, 1976). The reasons for the early absence of takeover bids in Britain are discussed in L. Hannah, 'Takeover bids in Britain before 1950', *Business History*, vol. 16 (1974); while A. Singh, *Takeovers, Their Relevance to the Stock Market and the Theory of the Firm* (Cambridge, 1971), provides an econometric analysis of later takeover activity. The role of capital market imperfections in inducing more rapid industrial concentration in the United States is discussed in L. Davis, 'The capital markets and industrial concentration: the US and the UK, a comparative study', *Economic History Review*, vol. 19 (1966), though this is self-confessedly only a very partial explanation of the differences in the experience of the two countries.

Other aspects of corporate behaviour continue to attract the attention both of economists and historians. J. Jewkes, D. Sawers and R. Stillerman, *The Sources of Invention* (1958), go further than their evidence justifies to belittle the achievement of large corporations in the field of research and development; while M. Sanderson, 'Research and the firm in British industry, 1919–1939', *Science Studies*, vol. 2 (1972), perhaps overcompensates. M. J. Peck, 'Science and technology', in R. E. Caves (ed.), *Britain's Economic Prospects* (1968), is a critical review of more recent British research efforts. A. Silberston surveys the modern evidence on 'Economies of scale in theory and practice', in *Economic Journal*, vol. 82, supp. (1972), though for the historical evidence on this subject one has to turn to studies in individual businesses and particular industries. The various *Reports* of the Monopolies Commission (1950, continuing) provide a useful survey of scale economies and monopolistic practices, though more recently the Commission has curtailed its historical enquiries and focused its attention more closely on the recent practices of the firms investigated. Much recent evidence is brought together in the green paper *A Review of Monopolies and Mergers Policy* (Cmd. 7198, 1978). Useful comparisons with the United States and Germany are presented in S. J. Prais, *Productivity and Industrial Structure* (Cambridge, 1981); in D. C. Mueller (ed.), *The Determinants and Effects of Mergers: An International Comparison*

(Cambridge, Mass., 1980); and in A. D. Chandler and H. Daems (eds), *Managerial Hierarchies* (Cambridge, Mass., 1980).

The bare facts of government intervention in industry are chronicled in J. W. Grove, *Government and Industry in Britain* (1962), but a more interesting approach can be found in the writings of the politicians themselves, the classics being the Liberal Industrial Inquiry's report *Britain's Industrial Future* (1928) and C. A. R. Crosland's *The Future of Socialism* (1957). The Conservatives have produced no work of similar quality on the political implications of the growth of corporations, though A. Marwick, 'Middle opinion in the thirties, planning, progress and political agreement', *English Historical Review*, vol. 79 (1964), and N. Harris, *Competition and the Corporate Society: British Conservatives, the State and Industry 1945–64* (1972), suggest that some Conservatives were also developing new ideas in response to contemporary economic changes. K. Middlemas, *Politics in Industrial Society: the Experience of the British System since 1911* (1979) is a pioneering attempt to explore the interaction of corporatism and politics, more successful on industrialists' attitude to labour than to broader economic questions. M. A. Utton, *The Political Economy of Big Business* (Oxford, 1982), is a useful survey of economic writing on the implications of large corporations. The development of ministerial views on relations with industry can now be followed in the files of the Cabinet and of the Board of Trade at the Public Record Office, for the period up to the early 1950s. The *Reports* of the (Macmillan) Committee on Finance and Industry (Cmd. 3897, 1931) and of the (Balfour) Committee on Industry and Trade (Cmd. 3282, 1929) should be read together with the earlier and fuller research reports of the latter Committee: *Overseas Markets* (1925); *Industrial Relations* (1926); *Factors in Industrial and Commercial Efficiency* (1927); *Survey of Metal Industries* (1928); *Survey of Textile Industries* (1928); and *Further Factors in Industrial and Commercial Efficiency* (1928).

Readers requiring further guidance in the technical literature should consult the Board of Trade's *Competition, Monopoly and Restrictive Practices, a Select Bibliography* (1970), or, for more recent literature, R. Marris and D. C. Mueller, 'The corporation, competition and the invisible hand', and R. E. Caves 'Industrial organisation, corporate strategy and structure', both in *Journal of Economic Literature*, vol. 18 (1980).

Notes and references

ౠ

Except where otherwise stated, the place of publication is London.

CHAPTER 1

1. This book mainly confines itself to trends in manufacturing industry, though similar trends have occurred in most other sectors of the economy.
2. (Bolton) Committee of Inquiry on Small Firms, *Report* (Cmd. 4811, 1971), pp. 59–60.
3. R. H. Coase, 'The nature of the firm', *Economica*, vol. 4 (1937), as reprinted in American Economic Association (ed.), *Readings in Price Theory* (1953), p. 334. See also O. E. Williamson, *Markets and Hierarchies* (New York, 1975), for a development of the theory, and, for indications of the problems raised by applying a straight dichotomy between market and firm, cf. Ken-ichi Imai and Hiroyuki Itami, 'The firm and market in Japan: mutual penetration of the market principle and organisation principle', Hitotsubashi University, *Discussion Paper no. 104* (Tokyo, 1981).
4. J. K. Galbraith, *The New Industrial State* (1967).
5. C. Wilson, *History of Unilever*, vol. 1 (1954), p. ix.
6. D. C. Coleman, *Courtaulds, An Economic and Social History* (3 vols, Oxford, 1969 and 1980). W. J. Reader, *Imperial Chemical Industries: A History*, vol. 1 (1970), vol. 2 (1975). Useful selections from company histories can be found in B. Supple (ed.), *Essays in British Business History* (Oxford, 1977) and K. A. Tucker (ed.), *Business History: Selected Readings* (1977).
7. But not in the United States, where Professor A. D. Chandler has made two classic studies of the American corporate economy in his *Strategy and Structure, Chapters in the History of Industrial Enterprise* (Cambridge, Mass., 1962), and *The Visible Hand: the Managerial Revolution in American Business* (Cambridge, Mass., 1977). See also his presidential address to the American Economic History Association, 'Decision making and modern institutional change', *Journal of Economic History*, vol. 33 (1973).

8. E. T. Penrose, *The Theory of the Growth of the Firm* (Oxford, 1959), p. 3. See also Scott Moss, *An Economic Theory of Business Strategy* (Oxford, 1981).

9. The British government operates a 'thirty-year rule', so that the official records of departments such as the Board of Trade are (with some absurd anomalies such as the withholding of *Census of Production* returns) available. For a discussion of current policy see *Report of the (Wilson) Committee on Modern Public Records: Selection and Access* (Cmd. 8204, 1981). Some large corporations operate a similar 'thirty-year' rule, though most have no official policy of allowing access to archives. Details of their current policy may be found in the companies index at the National Register of Archives, Historical Manuscripts Commission, Quality Court, Chancery Lane, London WC2.

10. Because of factors such as this it may be more correct to see increasing concentration as a change in the kind of monopoly, rather than in the degree of monopoly power exercised. This issue is more fully discussed in Chapter 11 below and in L. Hannah, 'Mergers, cartels and concentration: legal factors in the US and European experience', in N. Horn and J. Kocka (eds), *Recht und Entwicklung der Grossunternehmen im 19. und Frühen 20. Jahrhundert* (Göttingen, 1979).

11. A. Marshall, *Industry and Trade* (1st edn 1919), p. 316, quoted in S. J. Prais, 'A new look at the growth of industrial concentration', *Oxford Economic Papers*, vol. 26 (1974).

12. R. Gibrat, *Les Inégalités Economiques* (Paris, 1931). Prais, 'A new look at the growth of industrial concentration'.

13. The same might be true of, say, the distribution of wealth, and in this case there would be a progressive concentration of wealth in fewer hands, even if there were no inherent advantages to large rather than small wealth holdings. However, in the case of wealth, increases in concentration do not in fact occur because regressive tendencies (the term is used in the Galtonian sense of regression towards the mean, see Prais, 'A new look at the growth of industrial concentration'), such as partible inheritance and estate duties, operate to neutralize it. Of course regressive tendencies may in some periods neutralize the Gibrat effect's power to increase concentration among firms also (see Chapter 9).

14. S. J. Prais, *The Evolution of Giant Firms in Britain: A Study of*

the Growth of Concentration in Manufacturing Industry in Britain 1909–70 (Cambridge, 1976), ch. 2.

15. L. Hannah and J. A. Kay, *Concentration in Modern Industry: Theory, Measurement and the UK Experience* (1977), pp. 98–110.

CHAPTER 2

1. For an original and stimulating discussion of the biggest of them, see K. N. Chaudhuri, *The Trading World of Asia and the English East India Company, 1660–1760* (Cambridge, 1978).

2. See generally, S. D. Chapman, *The Cotton Industry in the Industrial Revolution* (1972).

3. S. D. Chapman and S. Chassagne, *European Textile Printers in the Eighteenth Century: A Study of Peel and Oberkaupf* (1981). Chapman, *The Cotton Industry*, p. 26. H. Perkin, *The Origins of Modern English Society 1780–1880* (1969), p. 109. S. Pollard, *The Genesis of Modern Management* (Harmondsworth, 1968), pp. 44–7.

4. B. R. Mitchell and P. Deane, *Abstract of British Historical Statistics* (Cambridge, 1962), pp. 177–9.

5. A. Marshall, *Principles of Economics* (8th edn 1920), pp. 221, 237–9, 378–80.

6. Chapman, *The Cotton Industry* p. 70. Because of multiple ownership the increase in the number of firms was probably below that in the number of factories, but not significantly so. See also V. A. C. Gatrell, 'Labour, power and the size of firms in Lancashire cotton in the second quarter of the nineteenth century', *Economic History Review*, vol. 30 (1977); R. Lloyd-Jones and A. A. Le Roux, 'Marshall and the birth and death of firms', *Business History*, vol. 24 (1982).

7. For thorough surveys of the contemporary evidence, see: Pollard, *The Genesis of Modern Management*, pp. 78 ff.; Perkin, *The Origins of Modern English Society*, pp. 107 ff.; J. H. Clapham, *An Economic History of Modern Britain*, vol. 1 (Cambridge, 1926), pp. 143 ff.

8. Though for some precursors, albeit ones employing hundreds, rather than the thousands of later mechanical engineering companies, see, e.g., A. E. Musson, 'Joseph Whitworth and the growth of mass-production engineering', *Business History*, vol.

17 (1975); idem, 'British origins', in O. Mayr and R. C. Post (eds), *Yankee Enterprise: The Rise of the American System of Manufactures* (Washington DC, 1981).

9. On mid-Victorian competition, generally, see R. Church, *The Dynamics of Victorian Business: Problems and Perspectives to the 1870s* (1980).

10. E.g. D. C. Coleman, 'Combination of capital and of labour in the English paper industry, 1789–1825', *Economica*, vol. 21 (1954); S. R. H. Jones, 'Price associations and competition in the British pin industry 1814–1840', *Economic History Review*, vol. 26 (1973).

11. Adam Smith, *The Wealth of Nations* (1776), E. Cannan (ed.) (6th edn 1950), vol. 1, p. 75.

12. P. Mathias, *The First Industrial Nation* (1969), pp. 293–5.

13. G. Channon, 'A nineteenth century investment decision: the Midland Railway's London extension', *Economic History Review*, vol. 25 (1972). M. Zinkin, 'Galbraith and consumer sovereignty', *Journal of Industrial Economics*, vol. 16 (1967), pp. 3–4. For a more sceptical view of the similarities, see G. Hawke, *Railways and Economic Growth in England and Wales 1840–1870* (Oxford, 1970), pp. 384–92. Cf. p. 79 above.

14. H. Parris, *Government and the Railways in Nineteenth Century Britain* (1965).

15. E.g. P. L. Payne, *Rubber and Railways in the Nineteenth Century* (Liverpool, 1961), pp. 95–113.

16. P. Deane ('New estimates of gross national product for the United Kingdom 1830–1914', *The Review of Income and Wealth*, vol. 14 (1968), p. 96) suggests that GNP grew at 2.4 per cent per annum between the 1840s and the 1870s, but at only 1.9 per cent per annum between the 1870s and 1914. See also S. Nicholas, 'Total factor productivity growth and the revision of post-1870 British economic history', *Economic History Review*, vol. 35 (1982).

17. Smith, *Wealth of Nations*, Cannan (ed.), vol. 1, p. 21. See also: A. Young, 'Increasing returns and economic progress', *Economic Journal*, vol. 38 (1928); G. B. Richardson, 'Adam Smith on competition and increasing returns', in A. S. Skinner and T. Wilson (eds), *Essays on Adam Smith* (Oxford, 1975).

18. Smith, *Wealth of Nations*, Cannan (ed.), vol. 2, pp. 271–2.

19. See Richardson, 'Adam Smith on competition and increasing

returns', for a fuller consideration of the possible explanations.
20. For a fuller account see B. W. E. Alford, *W.D. & H. O. Wills and the Development of the United Kingdom Tobacco Industry 1786–1965* (1973), pp. 139–57, 223, 225–33, 302.
21. Examples are numerous in the reports of the Monopolies Commission and in business histories, though curiously the phenomenon has been generally ignored by economic historians. It would repay more systematic investigation, for, like the patent system on which it is sometimes based, its effect may be either beneficial (in encouraging invention) or harmful (in suppressing innovation).
22. A. F. Weber, *The Growth of Cities in the Nineteenth Century* (New York, 1899, reprinted 1965), pp. 40–64.
23. H. W. Macrosty, *The Trust Movement in British Industry* (1907).
24. J. Vaizey, 'The brewing industry', in P. L. Cook and R. Cohen (eds), *The Effects of Mergers* (1958), pp. 400–11.
25. W. Ashworth, *An Economic History of England 1870–1939* (1960), pp. 91–102. J. S. Jeans, *Trusts, Pools and Corners* (1894), pp. 3–4. H. W. Macrosty, 'The grain milling industry', *Economic Journal*, vol. 12 (1903).
26. Chapman, *The Cotton Industry*, pp. 29, 32. Alford, *Wills and the Development of the UK Tobacco Industry*, p. 73.
27. Chapman, *The Cotton Industry*, pp. 38–9. D. Landes, *The Unbound Prometheus* (Cambridge, 1969), pp. 72–3.
28. The paragraphs which follow are based on: H. A. Shannon, 'The coming of general limited liability', *Economic History*, vol. 2 (1931); H. A. Shannon, 'The first 5000 limited companies and their duration', *Economic History*, vol. 2 (1932); H. A. Shannon, 'The limited companies of 1866–1883', *Economic History Review*, vol. 4 (1933); G. Todd, 'Some aspects of joint stock companies 1844–1900', *Economic History Review*, vol. 4 (1932); J. B. Jefferys, 'The denomination and character of shares 1855–1885', *Economic History Review*, vol. 16 (1946); J. B. Jefferys, 'Trends in Business Organisation in Great Britain 1856–1914' (PhD thesis, London, 1938, reprinted New York, 1977); (Balfour) Committee on Industry and Trade, *Factors in Industrial and Commercial Efficiency* (1927), pp. 125–7; Clapham, *An Economic History of Modern Britain*, vol. 1, pp. 201–91. See also R. H. Campbell, 'The law and the joint stock company in Scotland', in P. L. Payne (ed.), *Studies in Scottish*

Business History (1967); P. L. Payne, *The Early Scottish Limited Companies, 1856–1895* (Edinburgh, 1980).

29. Smith, *Wealth of Nations*, Cannan (ed.), vol. 2, pp. 264–5.
30. *Parliamentary Papers* (1816), III, *S.C. on Children Employed in the Manufactories of Great Britain*, p. 136, quoted in Perkin, *Origins of Modern English Society*, p. 114.
31. A reference to the practice of recruiting 'guinea pig' directors to lend lustre to a company prospectus.
32. W. S. Gilbert, *Utopia Limited*, in *Original Plays*, third series (1895 edn), p. 434.
33. P. E. Hart and S. J. Prais, 'The analysis of business concentration: a statistical approach', *Journal of the Royal Statistical Society*, series A, vol. 119 (1956), p. 154.
34. Quoted from G. H. Phillips, *Phillips' Investors Annual* (1887), in Jefferys, *Trends in Business Organisation*, p. 340.
35. F. Lavington, *The English Capital Market* (1921), p. 219.
36. L. Hannah, 'Mergers in British manufacturing industry 1880–1918', *Oxford Economic Papers*, vol. 26 (1974).
37. F. Harris, *My Life and Loves* (1966 edn), p. 827.
38. Hannah, 'Mergers in British manufacturing industry 1880–1918', p. 9 using data for 1880–1918, records an $\bar{R}^2$ of 0·62 in correlating share prices and merger activity.
39. Macrosty, *The Trust Movement in British Industry*.
40. The account of the merger waves which follows draws substantially on: Hannah, 'Mergers in British manufacturing industry 1880–1918'; Macrosty, *The Trust Movement in British Industry*; and P. L. Payne, 'The emergence of the large-scale company in Great Britain, 1870–1914', *Economic History Review*, vol. 20 (1967).
41. Acquisitions of foreign or non-manufacturing companies are excluded from the figures in this paragraph, so that the total number of firms involved in these mergers was in some cases even larger than indicated. For a fuller listing, see M. A. Utton, 'Some features of the early merger movements in British manufacturing industry', *Business History*, vol. 14 (1972), p. 53.
42. L. Davis, 'The capital markets and industrial concentration: the US and the UK, a comparative study', *Economic History Review*, vol. 19 (1966).
43. J. Moody, *The Truth about Trusts* (New York, 1904), pp. 137, 151–2.

44. C. Shaw, '100 large employers of 1907', *Business History*, vol. 25 (1983).
45. R. L. Nelson, *Merger Movements in American Industry 1895–1956* (Princeton, 1959), pp. 139–53. There are some difficulties in making such direct international comparisons, but they are unlikely by themselves to account for such a large discrepancy.
46. Hannah, 'Mergers in British manufacturing industry 1880–1918', pp. 10–12.
47. J. S. Jeans (ed.), *American Industrial Conditions and Competition* (1902), pp. 74–85, and see pp. 86–8 above.
48. Davis, 'The capital markets and industrial concentration'.
49. Payne, 'Emergence of the large-scale company', pp. 532–7, 533, 536–9.
50. For a list of the fifty largest manufacturing firms, see Appendix 3.
51. (Balfour) Committee, *Factors in Industrial and Commercial Efficiency*, p. 125.
52. The *Stock Exchange Year Book* for 1913 shows that thirty-two out of the fifty-one directors of these companies bore the names of their founding family firms. Other rapidly growing firms such as Lever Brothers were controlled by individual entrepreneurs like William Lever rather than by professional corporate managers. See, generally, Payne, 'Emergence of the large-scale company', pp. 530–6.
53. Compare the list in Payne, 'Emergence of the large-scale company', pp. 539–40, with the list on pp. 102–3. However, contrasting measures of size in the two studies make precise comparison hazardous. See also Appendix 3.
54. Payne, 'Emergence of the large-scale company', p. 539–40. Cf. pp. 186–8 above.
55. All three firms were eventually to join Imperial Chemical Industries.
56. G. Maxcy and A. Silberston, *The Motor Industry* (1959), p. 12, I. C. R. Byatt, 'Electrical products', in D. H. Aldcroft (ed.), *The Development of British Industry and Foreign Competition 1875–1914* (1968), pp. 244–73.
57. See e.g.: E. H. Phelps Brown and Margaret H. Browne, *A Century of Pay* (1968), pp. 174–95; R. C. O. Matthews, C. H. Feinstein and J. C. Odling-Smee, *British Economic Growth 1856–1973* (Oxford, 1982).

CHAPTER 3

1. See, generally, A. S. Milward, *The Economic Effects of the World Wars on Britain* (1970).
2. E.g. H. W. Macrosty, *The Trust Movement in British Industry* (1907), p. 334; A. L. Levine, *Industrial Retardation in Britain 1880–1914* (1967), pp. 44–54.
3. Speech at the Guildhall, Nov. 1914.
4. E. M. H. Lloyd, *Experiments in State Control* (Oxford, 1924). J. M. Rees, *Trusts in British Industry 1914–1921. A Study of Recent Developments in Business Organisation* (1922). S. Pollard, *The Development of the British Economy 1914–1950* (1962), pp. 42–62, 76–87. J. M. Winter (ed.), *War and Economic Development* (Cambridge, 1975).
5. Quoted, from Caillard's pamphlet *Industry and Production*, by A. Wright, 'The new phase in industry', *Financial Review of Reviews*, vol. 22 (1929), pp. 42–9.
6. R. H. Tawney, 'The postwar abandonment of economic controls 1919–1921', *Economic History Review*, vol. 13 (1943); R. Lowe, 'The Erosion of State Intervention in Britain 1917–24', *Economic History Review*, vol. 31 (1978).
7. See, e.g., Board of Trade Committee on the Electrical Trades after the War, *Report* (Cmd. 9072, 1918).
8. Industrial Reconstruction Council, *Reconstruction Handbook* (1918), p. 2.
9. B. R. Mitchell and P. Deane, *Abstract of British Historical Statistics* (Cambridge, 1962), pp. 65, 67.
10. *Economist* (7 Dec. 1929), p. 1073. For examples of the ragbag of ideas associated with the movement, see: W. T. Davies, *The Rationalization of Industry* (n.d. 1928?); L. F. Urwick, *The Meaning of Rationalization* (1929); J. A. Bowie, *Rationalization* (1931); L. J. Barley, *The Riddle of Rationalization* (1932); A. C. Pigou, chairman, 'Problems of rationalization' (discussion), *Economic Journal*, vol. 40 (1930); International Management Institute, *Interim Report on Management Terminology* (Geneva, 1930).
11. E.g. British Electrical and Allied Manufacturers' Association, *The Electrical Industry in Great Britain* (1929), p. 193; (Macmillan) Committee on Finance and Industry, *Minutes of Evidence* (2 vols, 1931), qq. 3881–3, 7908 (subsequent references to this source are abbreviated to *Macmillan Evidence*).

12. Attributed to Professor Gregory in W. Meakin, *The New Industrial Revolution* (1928), p. 131, and A. Watson, 'How far can rationalization go?', *Business* (Aug. 1931), p. 55.
13. D. H. MacGregor, *Enterprise, Purpose and Profit* (Oxford, 1934), p. v. See also E. A. G. Robinson, *The Structure of Competitive Industry* (1931 edn), ch. 12 ('Rationalization').
14. Urwick, *Meaning of Rationalization*, p. 134 (present author's italics). For Urwick's other writings on rationalization, see his 'The pure theory of organization with special reference to business enterprise' (British Association, 1930, typescript); *The Management of Tomorrow* (1933); and 'Rationalization', *British Management Review*, vol. 3 (1938). Urwick was the director of the International Management Institute at Geneva, and, on its demise in the 1930s, became a successful management consultant.
15. L. Urwick, 'The international position', speech at the meeting of the British Association, 1931, reprinted in R. J. Mackay (ed.), *Business and Science* (1931). International Management Institute, *Rationalization and Prosperity* (Geneva, 1933).
16. R. Brady, *The Rationalization Movement in German Industry* (Berkeley, 1933); R. R. Locke, *The End of the Practical Man* (1983, forthcoming).
17. MacGregor, *Enterprise, Purpose and Profit*, pp. 125, 127.
18. Urwick, 'International position', p. 3.
19. ibid., p. 22.
20. Barley, *Riddle of Rationalization*, p. 62.
21. H. Macmillan, 'The place and functions of large-scale manufacturers in a planned economy', typescript, read to Management Research Group No. 1 (7 Mar. 1934), p. 3. These papers, and many others relating to the early history of management, were collected by Mr Harry Ward and are now held in the Business History Unit Library, London School of Economics, see S. P. Keeble, 'Management Research Groups', *Business Archives*, no. 47 (1981).
22. Urwick, *Meaning of Rationalization*, p. 27.
23. Quoted, with approval, in 'The case for rationalization', *Economist* (12 Oct. 1929), pp. 652–3.
24. The etymology of the word is obscure, but the implication of rationality clearly gained its acceptance.
25. For a parallel, see R. Graves and A. Hodge, *The Long Week-End* (1941), p. 260.

26. J. Stamp, *The Science of Social Adjustment* (1937).
27. Urwick, 'Pure theory of organization', p. 10.
28. E.g. Urwick, *Meaning of Rationalization*, p. 27; Pigou, chairman, 'Problems of rationalization', p. 366; S. Myers, *Business Rationalization* (1932), p. 50.
29. 'S.R.', 'Advantages and disadvantages of rationalization', *Manchester Guardian Commerical* (18 Oct. 1928).
30. Urwick, 'Pure theory of organization', p. 10.
31. Sir Alfred Mond, 'The rationalization of industry', in his *Industry and Politics* (1927). Barley, *Riddle of Rationalisation*, ch. 11. Sir William Seager, 'British industry must nationalize or rationalize', *Business* (May 1932), pp. 9–10.
32. H. Bolitho, *Alfred Mond, First Lord Melchett* (1933), p. 313.
33. On the conciliatory aspects of business opinion, generally, see H. A. Clegg, 'Some consequences of the general strike', *Manchester Statistical Society Transactions* (Jan. 1954), p. 25.
34. Urwick, *Meaning of Rationalization*, p. 127.
35. Mr Roundway, criticizing Professor Florence in Pigou, chairman, 'Problems of rationalisation', p. 365.
36. Proposals of the National Confederation of Employers' Associations on the Depression, dated 10 Feb. 1926, *Baldwin Papers*, vol. 28, pp. 183–95 (the *Baldwin Papers* are deposited in the University Library, Cambridge). See also F. Lee, 'A manufacturer's pointer for British industry', *Ashridge Journal* (Mar. 1932).
37. Seager, 'British industry must nationalize or rationalize', pp. 9–10.
38. P. S. Florence, *The Logic of Industrial Organization* (1933), p. 48.
39. A. D. Chandler, *The Visible Hand: The Managerial Revolution in American Business* (Cambridge, Mass., 1977).
40. E.g. A. Marshall, *Industry and Trade* (4th edn 1923), p. 82; Urwick, *Management of Tomorrow*, p. 70; 'To amalgamate or not to amalgamate', *Business* (Jan. 1928), pp. 14–15.
41. Committee of the Privy Council for Scientific and Industrial Research, *Report for the Year 1915–16* (Cmd. 8336, 1916), p. 42. See also: Dyestuffs Industry Development Committee, *Third Report* (Cmd. 4191, 1932), p. 8; Management Research Group Minutes (Feb. 1935), p. 20.
42. S. Brooks, 'A British captain of industry', *Sperling's Journal* (Nov. 1921), p. 19.

43. E.g. Andrew Stewart, *British and German Industrial Conditions* (1916); Sir Philip Dawson, *Germany's Industrial Revival* (1926); W. Meakin, *The New Industrial Revolution* (1928); H. Quigley, 'The large-scale organisation of production', *Manchester Guardian Commercial* (28 Oct. 1926); D. Warriner, *Combines and Rationalization in Germany* (1931); B. Austin and W. F. Lloyd, *The Secret of High Wages* (1926); *Macmillan Evidence*, qq. 3883–92, 3895–6, 8326–7, and vol. 2, pp. 147 ff.

44. 'Report of the Subcommittee on the Advantages and Disadvantages of Competition', appendix A to Federation of British Industries, *Report of the Committee on Commercial Efficiency* (privately reprinted with amendments, 1935).

45. W. J. Reader, *Imperial Chemical Industries. A History*, vol. 1 (1970), p. 455. British Electrical and Allied Manufacturers' Association, *Combines and Trusts in the Electrical Industry* (1927).

46. Marshall, *Industry and Trade*, p. 579.

47. ibid., p. 580.

48. P. L. Payne, *British Entrepreneurship in the Nineteenth Century* (1974), p. 55. Sir Hugo Hirst, 'The manufacturer and the state' (address at the annual dinner of GEC Ltd, 1910). Sir Alfred Mond, *Industry and Politics* (1927). B. H. Tripp, *Renold Chain, a History of the Company and the Rise of the Precision Chain Industry* (1956). R. Jones and O. Marriott, *Anatomy of a Merger, a History of GEC, AEI, and English Electric* (1970), pp. 72–5, 77.

49. B. W. E. Alford, *W. D. & H. O. Wills and the Development of the UK Tobacco Industry 1786–1965* (1973), pp. 251–77. See also S. B. Saul, 'The American impact on British industry 1895–1914', *Business History*, vol. 2 (1960).

50. Reader, *Imperial Chemical Industries*, vol. 1, pp. 439–66.

51. One banking enterprise which aimed to provide American capital for the rationalization of British industry was the Finance Corporation of Great Britain and America, set up in 1928 by the US Chase Bank and ICI jointly.

52. Among leading companies which refused American takeover bids were Huntley & Palmer, GEC, Morris and Austin. A number of firms attempted to change their articles of association in order to bar the possibility of American control. On the general background to American direct investment see J. H. Dunning, *American Investment in British Manufacturing Industry* (1958); M. Wilkins, *The Maturing of Multinational Enterprise:*

American Business Abroad from 1914 to 1970 (Cambridge, Mass., 1974).

53. A. A. Baumann, 'An attack [on rationalization]', *Business* (Mar. 1928).

CHAPTER 4

1. *Economist* (9 Feb. 1924), p. 241.
2. C. Wilson, *The History of Unilever*, vol. 1 (1954), pp. 73–88.
3. P. M. Williams, 'Public opinion and the railway rates question in 1886', *English Historical Review*, vol. 67 (1952). Departmental Committee on Railway Agreements and Amalgamations, *Report* (Cmd. 5631, 1911). Sir Alfred Mond, *Questions of Today and Tomorrow* (1912), pp. 141–7.
4. N. W. Salt *v.* Electrolytic Alkali Co., A.C. 461, 469, quoted in R. B. Stevens and B. S. Yamey, *The Restrictive Practices Court* (1965), p. 31.
5. Cf. W. J. Reader, *Imperial Chemical Industries: A History*, vol. 1 (1970), p. 447.
6. Quoted in W. D. Esslemont, 'Some legal aspects of trade combinations', *Scottish Law Review*, vol. 44 (1928).
7. ibid.
8. Committee on Trusts, *Report* (Cmd. 9236, 1918). Committee on Commercial and Industrial Policy after the War, *Final Report* (Cmd. 9035, 1918).
9. Quoted, from the *Report of the War Cabinet* (1918), in A. C. Pigou, *Aspects of British Economic History 1918–25* (1947), p. 121.
10. ibid., pp. 129–30.
11. As a subcommittee of the Central Committee established at the Board of Trade under the Profiteering Act.
12. BT/55/55, Minutes, 6 Oct. 1919.
13. W. H. Beveridge, *British Food Control* (1928), pp. 287–9.
14. For a review of the weaknesses of the Committee, based on its published reports, see J. M. Rees, *Trusts in British Industry* (1922), ch. 11. The surviving minutes of the Committee (BT/55/55) confirm the gradual ebbing away of the political support and power of the Committee.
15. *Special Report of the Select Committee on High Prices and Profits, with the Evidence* (Cmd. 166, 1919). PRO/CAB/23/11 (8 Aug. 1919, discussion of Profiteering Bill).

16. CAB/23/21 (20 Apr. 1920).
17. CAB/23/15 (quoted in A. Marwick, *Britain in the Century of Total War* (1968), p. 147).
18. BT/55/55, Minutes of the 68th, 69th and 71st meetings (Apr.–May 1921).
19. E.g. Royal Commission on Food Prices, *First Report* (Cmd. 2390, 1925), paras 342–4.
20. Sir Philip Lloyd-Greame, 139 *H. C. Deb.*, 5s., cols 602–3. He did, however, promise legislation on trusts in a future session, but no legislation was in fact introduced though he remained at the Board of Trade for most of the next decade. The view that his assurance was not honoured because he fell from power with the Lloyd George coalition in October 1922 (see Political and Economic Planning, *Industrial Trade Associations* (1957), p. 19) misses the point. It is Lloyd-Greame's espousal of rationalization, not a change of regime, that explains this policy development.
21. H. G. Williams, *Politics and Economics* (1926), p. 159. Williams later became a junior minister at the Board of Trade.
22. There were residual price surveillance powers in dyes and explosives, and the prices of buildings and food were reviewed periodically, but these initiatives were of little significance.
23. (Balfour) Committee on Industry and Trade, *Final Report* (Cmd. 3282, 1929), 'Memorandum accompanying Terms of Reference', p. iii.
24. ibid., pp. 191–2. However, the Committee did suggest that an investigating tribunal might be valuable, and two minority reports stressed the need for more positive action. Neither of these suggestions was adopted by the government.
25. S. Haxey, *Tory MP* (1939), J. M. McEwen, 'Conservative and Unionist MPs 1914–1939' (unpublished PhD thesis, London, 1959), ch. 2.
26. P. Mathias, *History of the FBI* (forthcoming).
27. *Baldwin Papers*, vol. 32, p. 179. Lord Swinton, *I Remember* (n.d. 1948?), p. 27.
28. T. H. Ryland, minority report, in Royal Commission on Food Prices, *First Report* (Cmd. 2390, 1925), p. 173.
29. L. F. Urwick, *The Meaning of Rationalization* (1929), p. 124.
30. Committee on Industry and Trade, *Final Report*, p. 189. See also British Electrical and Allied Manufacturers' Association, *Combines and Trusts in the Electrical Industry* (1927), p. 21.

31. As is witnessed by a failure of the Labour government's Consumers' Council Bill of 1931, which would have created a council of seven to investigate restrictions of competition and endowed the Board of Trade with price-fixing powers, see *Economist* (4 Apr. 1931), p. 720, 253 *H. C. Deb.*, 5s., cols 2105–200. For the co-operative viewpoint, see (Macmillan) Committee on Finance and Industry, *Minutes of Evidence* (2 vols, 1931), qq. 6334–6.

32. E.g. *Economist* (7 June 1919), pp. 1040–1; (12 Feb. 1921), p. 273; (26 Mar. 1921), p. 644; (2 May 1936), pp. 248–9.

33. However, even when strongly condemning trusts, the *Economist* opposed US style antitrust laws with all their 'difficulties and complications'; see 'The cartelisation of England', *Economist* (18 Mar. 1939), p. 552.

34. D. H. MacGregor, 'Rationalization of industry', *Economic Journal*, vol. 37 (1927), p. 319. See also *Economist* (22 Dec.1928), p. 1150.

35. J. Robinson, *The Economics of Imperfect Competition* (1933), p. 327. A. C. Pigou, *The Economics of Welfare* (1924), pp. 306–13. For a strident, and somewhat inflated, condemnation of economists for their silence on the issue, see W. H. Hutt, *Economists and the Public: A Study of Competition and Opinion* (1936).

36. L. Robbins, *The Economic Basis of Class Conflict* (1939), p. 45.

37. Quoted, with approval, in R. Boothby *et al.*, *Industry and the State: A Conservative View* (1927), p. 47.

38. Cf. W. Letwin, 'The past and future of the American business-man', *Daedalus*, vol. 97 (1969).

39. Reader, *Imperial Chemical Industries*, vol. 1, pp. 258–81.

40. Eg. the Post Office speeded the rationalization of the cable industry in this way; see Monopolies and Restrictive Practices Commission, *Report on the Supply of Insulated Electric Wires and Cables* (1952), p. 40. But, for the failure of government to adopt such a policy elsewhere, cf. P. Fearon, 'The British airframe industry and the state, 1918–35', *Economic History Review*, vol. 27 (1974).

41. Boothby *et al.*, *Industry and the State*. Economic Advisory Council, *Report on the Cotton Industry* (Cmd. 3615, 1930).

42. Sir Arthur Steel-Maitland, Minister of Labour 1924–9; see *Baldwin Papers*, vol. 30, pp. 9–17.

43. W. H. Coates, 'Memorandum', dated 5 December 1933, criti-

cizing a National Confederation of Employers' Organizations report because it had 'assumed that the economic factor of management and organization in British industry needs no comment' (ICI archives).

44. *Baldwin Papers*, vol. 30, pp. 41–3 (memorandum dated Feb. 1929).
45. E.g. letter from Sir W. J. Larke to Sir P. Cunliffe-Lister, dated 3 Dec. 1925 (*Baldwin Papers*, vol. 27, p. 232).
46. BT/55/49, Sir P. Cunliffe-Lister, memorandum of 1927, p. 18.
47. Finance Act, 1927, section 55. P. F. Simonson, *The Law Relating to the Reconstruction and Amalgamation of Joint Stock Companies* (3rd edn 1919), ch. 5. A. Mond, 'National Savings, profits and double taxation', in his *Industry and Politics* (1927). The concession was very rigidly circumscribed and some mergers still failed to qualify; see R. W. Moon, *Amalgamations and Takeover Bids* (2nd edn 1960), ch. 4.
48. *Macmillan Evidence*, q. 4111. A. F. Lucas, *Industrial Reconstruction and the Control of Competition* (1937), p. 139.
49. Lord Chandos, *Memoirs* (1962), p. 125. Reader, *Imperial Chemical Industries*, vol. 1, pp. 251, 247. A. G. Whyte, *Forty Years of Electrical Progress* (1930), p. 93.
50. *Economist* (16 Jan. 1932), p. 107.
51. E.g., for Churchill's refusal to finance the Vickers-Armstrong merger, see J. D. Scott, *Vickers: A History* (1962), p. 165. The merger proceeded none the less.
52. A file of J. H. Thomas, who inherited this policy in 1929 (BT/56/14, CIA/621), states that his predecessors 'had in mind an adaptation of the Trade Facilities Acts to stimulate amalgamation and reorganization'. It cannot have advanced very far. The Trade Facilities Act lapsed in 1927. For examples of the opposition to renewal, see *Baldwin Papers*, vol. 30, p. 18. And on Norman's views see Sir Henry Clay, *Lord Norman* (1957), ch. 8.
53. 227 *H.C.Deb.*, 5s., col. 58.
54. *Macmillan Evidence*, qq. 7961–6 (Ernest Bevin). G. D. H. Cole (ed.), *Studies in Capital and Investment* (1935), p. 42. *Economist* (23 May 1931), p. 1090.
55. T. E. Gregory, 'Rationalization and unemployment', *Economic Journal*, vol. 40 (1930). J. A. Hobson, *Rationalization and Unemployment* (1930). *Macmillan Evidence*, qq. 4886, 4951–7,

5003. But cf. L. F. Urwick, 'Rationalization does *not* lead to unemployment: a reply to Professor Gregory' (typescript in Management Research Group papers, 1930).

56. BT/56/37, Board of Trade comments on the Mosley Memorandum.

57. BT/56/14. BT/56/37. BT/56/43.

58. *Economist* (25 Apr. 1931), p. 885.

59. Lucas, *Industrial Reconstruction*, p. 331. Sir Herbert Hutchinson, *Tariff Making and Industrial Reconstruction* (1965).

60. Hutchinson, *Tariff Making and Industrial Reconstruction*, p. 78.

61. ibid., pp. 125–30. They did, however, by threatening withdrawal of duty gain the adoption of a price agreement.

62. Sir Horace Wilson (interview, 28 July 1969) confirmed that he and Sir Leonard Brewitt continued to visit industrialists to draw their attention to the facilities offered by banks, and liaised weekly with Charles Bruce-Gardner of the BIDC.

63. Speech (9 May 1934) reported in *The Times* (10 May 1934), p. 16.

64. S. H. Beer, *Modern British Politics* (1965), pp. 293–7.

65. There was only one case of a legislatively backed merger in manufacturing industry in the 1930s: the unification of six beet sugar processing companies to form the British Sugar Corporation. The government was heavily involved financially in subsidies to beet growers, and this motivated the exceptional intervention of the Sugar Industry (Reorganization) Act, 1936.

66. Reported in the *Financial News* (7 Jan. 1929), p. 7.

67. L. Robbins, *The Great Depression* (1934); and his *Economic Basis of Class Conflict*, pp. 50–1.

68. Compare the adverse comments on Baldwin's extreme *laissez-faire* in 1929 (*Economist*, 12 Jan. 1929, p. 47) with the articles on 'The new feudalism' (*Economist*, 2 Apr. 1938, pp. 2–3) and 'The cartelisation of England' (*Economist*, 8 Mar. 1939, p. 552).

69. E.g. N. E. H. Davenport, *Vested Interests or Common Pool* (1942), p. 54.

70. E. J. Hobsbawm, *Industry and Empire* (1968), p. 181.

71. See e.g. L. Hannah, *Electricity before Nationalisation* (1979); G. G. Jones, *The State and the Emergence of the British Oil Industry* (1980).

72. Robbins, *Economic Basis of Class Conflict*, pp. 59, 62.

73. *Economist* (8 March 1939), p. 552.

74. However, for the government's more positive support of restrictive business practices, see pp. 135–6.

75. The major exceptions were grants under the Trade Facilities Acts in the 1920s and under the special areas legislation in the 1930s. In both cases, the sums going to manufacturing industry from the Treasury were tiny, and they were not in general conditional on mergers.

CHAPTER 5

1. W. D. Rubinstein found in the probate registers only six people leaving more than £3.2 million in Britain in 1880–1909, none of them British manufacturers, see his *Men of Property: The Very Wealthy in Britain Since the Industrial Revolution* (1981), p. 44.
2. J. Revell, 'Changes in the social distribution of property in Britain during the twentieth century', *Transactions of the Third International Congress of Economic History*, vol. 1 (Munich, 1965), p. 379. Of course this figure reflects the concentration of other forms of asset holdings as well as of manufacturing wealth.
3. Liberal Industrial Inquiry, *Britain's Industrial Future*, p. 74. This figure includes, for example, capital raised by privately owned electricity undertakings possessing a statutory monopoly.
4. P. W. S. Andrews and E. Brunner, *The Life of Lord Nuffield* (Oxford, 1955). R. J. Overy, *William Morris, Viscount Nuffield* (1976).
5. E.g. R. H. Tawney, *The Acquisitive Society* (1921).
6. (Balfour) Committee on Industry and Trade, *Factors in Industrial and Commercial Efficiency* (1927), p. 128.
7. P. Sargant Florence, *Ownership Control and Success of Large Companies 1936–51* (1961). W. H. Coates, 'Administration and capital', *British Management Review*, vol. 3 (1938), p. 62. 'Shareholders and control', *Economist* (30 Mar. 1929), p. 691.
8. In 1968–9 the chairmen of the largest 100 industrial companies in Britain on average controlled 2½ per cent of their companies' equity and the whole boards of directors only 7½ per cent; see A. Lumsden, 'Wealth and power in Britain's top boardrooms', *The Times* (9 Sept. 1969). Cf. S. Nyman and A. Silberston, 'The ownership and control of industry', *Oxford Economic Papers*, vol. 30 (1978), for the continuing importance of owner-control.

9. Revell, 'Changes in the social distribution of property', p. 379. It could, however, more plausibly be argued that, because of the nationalization of some industries and the spread to less wealthy groups of insurance and pension funds, the benefit of the profits, if not of the power of control, of industrial capital are now spread more widely.

10. Of course, some fortunes had been made and others had been lost, so that neither the wealthy families of 1960, nor the assets which made up their wealth, were the same as those of 1911. However, inheritance and the sluggish growth of the British economy has ensured that there has been remarkable stability in this sense also.

11. This is an oversimplified view of what actually happened: the holdings of wealthy families were often already diversified in the nineteenth century and their later portfolios often included a range of investments other than quoted companies. However, contemporary wills and the private financial papers of business-men indicate that a diversifying movement of this kind was occurring within such broader movements. The absurd practice of the Registrar-General in barring access to English and Welsh probate inventories for 125 years inhibits research in this subject, but no such bar exists in Scotland and the researches of Dr W. P. Kennedy on the Scottish inventories will enable future historians to speak with more precision on this subject.

12. See Chapter 2. Of course, families could also liquidate their holdings more gradually be reinvesting their profits in stock market securities (rather than in the family firm itself, as they had in the past). The effect is similar.

13. (Colwyn) Committee on National Debt and Taxation, *Report* (Cmd. 2800, 1927), appendix 20.

14. J. R. Allen (ed.), *Crombies of Grandholm and Cothal 1805–1960* (Aberdeen, 1961), p. 122. B. Newman, *100 Years of a Good Company* (1957), pp. 95–7. (Macmillan) Committee on Finance and Industry, *Minutes of Evidence* (2 vols, 1931), q. 3704.

15. The 1922 Finance Act closed a loophole which had also allowed *past* profits to be retained by closely held companies and subsequently capitalized by sale, but the capitalization of future profits by sale remained possible; see L. H. Seltzer, *The Nature and Tax Treatment of Capital Gains and Losses* (New York,

1951), p. 260. Cf. J. K. Butters, J. Lintner and W. L. Cary, *Effects of Taxation: Corporate Mergers* (Boston, 1951); R. Lacks, 'Income tax on capital profits', *Modern Law Review*, vol. 6 (1943); (Cohen) Committee on Company Law Reform, *Minutes of Evidence* (1943), p. 126.

16. J. M. Keynes, *The General Theory of Employment, Interest and Money* (1936), p. 159.

17. N. J. Grieser, 'The British investor and his sources of information' (MSc thesis, London, 1940). Departmental Committee on Share Pushing, *Report* (Cmd. 5539, 1937).

18. H. O. O'Hagan, *Leaves from My Life* (1929). F. Lavington, *The English Capital Market* (1921), pp. 213–14. A. Marshall, *Industry and Trade* (4th edn 1923), pp. 330–4.

19. G. D. H. Cole, *Studies in Capital and Investment* (1935), pp. 124–5. But cf. A. T. K. Grant, *A Study of the Postwar Capital Market* (1937), pp. 130–2, 159–61; R. F. Henderson, *The New Issue Market* (1951), pp. 24–6.

20. This can be seen by comparing the merger statistics in Appendix 1, below, with the share price index. Various econometric estimates of the interwar relationship are calculated in L. Hannah, 'The political economy of mergers in manufacturing industry in Britain between the wars' (unpublished D.Phil thesis, Oxford, 1972). Such a correlation is commonly found in other periods and other countries, see e.g. R. Tilly, 'Mergers, external growth and finance in the development of large-scale enterprise in Germany, 1880–1913', *Journal of Economic History*, vol. 42 (1982), p. 651.

21. E.g. E. V. Morgan and W. A. Thomas, *The Stock Exchange* (1962), p. 106; E. T. Hooley, *Hooley's Confessions* (n.d. 1925?), pp. 303–6; E. V. Morgan, *Studies in British Financial Policy 1914–25* (1952), pp. 64, 77, 264–6; A. Vallance, *Very Private Enterprise* (1955); 'Amalgamations and new issues', *Economist* (25 Dec. 1926), p. 1120; Grant, *Postwar Capital Market*, pp. 143–5, 155.

22. *Economist* (6 Dec. 1919), pp. 1029–30.

23. P. W. S. Andrews and E. Brunner, *Capital Development in Steel* (Oxford, 1951), pp. 159–61. H. Levy, *The New Industrial System* (1936), p. 203. Morgan and Thomas, *The Stock Exchange*, pp. 206–7.

24. Collin Brooks (ed.), *The Royal Mail Case* (1933), pp. xvii–xviii.

25. Lord Aberconway, *The Basic Industries of Great Britain* (1927), pp. 202, 231. *Economist* (28 Sep. 1929), pp. 576–7. J. R. Parkinson, *The Economics of Shipbuilding* (1960), pp. 34–5. *Sperling's Journal* (1919–21).

26. 'The results of the 1928 new issue boom', *Economic Journal*, vol. 41 (1931). R. E. Harris, 'A re-analysis of the 1928 new issue boom', *Economic Journal*, vol. 43 (1933). *Economist* (15 Feb. 1930), pp. 363–4. *Economist* (26 July 1930), p. 182. This performance was worse than the average for all quoted companies during the world slump.

27. If management divorced from ownership was less efficient, or pursued goals different from those of the shareholders, the wealth holders' returns on their investments might, however, be prejudiced.

28. P. E. Hart and S. J. Prais, 'The analysis of business concentration: a statistical approach', *Journal of the Royal Statistical Society*, series A, vol. 119 (1956), p. 154.

29. Calculated from the stock exchange *Daily Official List*. The price level increased between 1907 and 1939, but, since it less than doubled, the rise is not mainly due to price inflation.

30. Colwyn Committee, *Minutes of Evidence*, qq. 8550–1. National Institute of Economic and Social Research, *Company Income and Finance 1949–53* (privately printed, 1956), pp. 7–8.

31. The next richest man on the probate registers was Edward Guinness, first Earl of Iveagh, who left £13.5 millions in 1927, see Rubinstein, *Men of Property*, p. 44, and his entry on Sir John Ellerman in D. J. Jeremy (ed.), *Dictionary of Business Biography* (forthcoming). Probably William Morris (who died after the war) was also worth something around the Ellerman level in the 1930s, together with others whose fortunes were in family trusts or other devices to escape estate duty.

32. See Appendix 3. The change is a real one, and not the effect of inflation, for there was no firm in 1919 which approached the size of J. & P. Coats and share prices rose by only 15 per cent between 1919 and 1930.

33. G. Maxcy and A. Silberston, *The Motor Industry* (1959), p. 162. See also E. Nevin, *The Mechanism of Cheap Money* (Cardiff, 1955), pp. 246–8.

34. P. E. Hart, *Studies in Profit, Business Saving and Investment in the United Kingdom, 1920–1962*, vol. 1 (1965), pp. 119–20.

35. H. Clay, 'The financing of industrial enterprise', *Transactions of the Manchester Statistical Society* (1931–2), pp. 213–15. The estimate, which is based on W. H. Coates's evidence to the Colwyn Committee, is only a very approximate indicator. H. W. Richardson's stronger assertion (*Economic Recovery in Britain 1932–39* (1967), p. 149, but cf. p. 201), that in the interwar years new issues were a more important source of funds than either before or since, is problematical, for the historical data on the flow of funds are obscure.

36. *Macmillan Evidence*, qq. 1537, 8746–52. *Investors Chronicle* (24 Apr. 1937), p. 1184.

37. Grant, *Postwar Capital Market*, pp. 196–7. W. J. Reader, *Imperial Chemical Industries: A History*, vol. 1 (1970), pp. 384, 421. 'Rationalizing the investment portfolio', *Economist* (5 Apr. 1930), pp. 779–80.

38. Monopolies Commission, *Report on the Supply of Electrical Equipment for Mechanically Propelled Land Vehicles* (1963), p. 26.

39. Committee on Scientific Research of the Economic Advisory Council, 'First Report' (1937) (typescript in the *G. D. H. Cole Papers*, Nuffield College Library, Oxford). Grant, *Postwar Capital Market*, p. 279.

40. These generalizations are based on the author's examination of the files of the commercial, technical and development departments of a number of large companies. A fuller and quantitative study of the relative efficiency of large firms, the stock market and individual investors in financing the innovative process would be required to establish the point convincingly.

41. D. Finnie, *Finding Capital for Business* (1931). 'How new industries grow', *Planning*, no. 68 (Feb. 1936).

42. *Macmillan Evidence*, q. 3700; see also qq. 7976–9. Andrews and Brunner, *Capital Development in Steel*, pp. 349–60.

43. *Macmillan Evidence*, qq. 1869–74, 1950, 1977, 2203, though cf. qq. 2388–9. For a complaint by Steel-Maitland of the timidity of bankers and particularly of McKenna of the Midland, see *Baldwin Papers*, vol. 29, pp. 54–63.

44. J. C. Carr and W. Taplin, *A History of the British Steel Industry* (Oxford, 1962), p. 449.

45. Sir Henry Clay, *Lord Norman* (1957), ch. 8. A. F. Lucas, 'The Bankers' Industrial Development Company', *Harvard Business Review* (1930), pp. 270–79. R. S. Sayers, *The Bank of England*

1891–1944 (Cambridge, 1976), ch. 14. S. Tolliday, 'Industry, finance and the state: an analysis of the British steel industry in the interwar years' (unpublished PhD thesis, Cambridge, 1980).

46. Clay, *Lord Norman*, p. 358. PRO/BT/56/14.

47. It was seen in the City as an essentially temporary expedient and it was hoped that the financial burden which the banks had shouldered would eventually be floated off to the public when conditions were favourable; see *Macmillan Evidence*, qq. 828–59, 9146. The company was known in the City as B.I.D.: 'Brought in Dead'.

48. See the debate on the 'Hammersley Scheme' for the cotton industry, which violated this principle and therefore failed to gain support, in *Lloyds Bank Monthly Review* (Oct. 1930, Feb. and Mar. 1931).

49. Lancashire Cotton Corporation Archives, Annual Reports and Reports of Extraordinary General Meetings, 1929–33 (Courtaulds, Northern Spinning Division). The more generally quoted figure of 140 is incorrect: it refers to projected acquisitions and to *mills* not firms.

50. *Macmillan Evidence*, qq. 1511–25. *The Times* (30 Feb. 1930), p. 13. Lancashire Cotton Corporation Board Minutes 1929–30.

51. R. Robson, *The Cotton Industry in Britain* (1957), pp. 158–9.

52. Carr and Taplin, *History of the British Steel Industry*, pp. 441, 444–7, 536. Tolliday, 'Industry finance and the state'.

53. There is a growing body of evidence from modern studies of mergers that financial economies of scale have received less attention in the literature than they merit; see, e.g., J. Kitching, 'Why do mergers miscarry?', *Harvard Business Review*, vol. 45 (1967).

54. (Macmillan) Committee on Finance and Industry, *Report* (Cmd. 3897, 1931), pp. 173–4.

55. Lavington, *English Capital Market*, pp. 168–9, 223. T. Balogh, *Studies in Financial Organisation* (1947), pp. 294–7.

56. Henderson, *New Issue Market*, pp. 106–13. *Macmillan Evidence*, qq. 1526–7, 3950.

57. J. Stamp, *The Relation of Finance to Rationalization* (1926), p. 5. Grant, *Postwar Capital Market*, pp. 186–9. Balogh, *Financial Organisation*, p. 79. A. E. Musson, *Enterprise in Soap and Chemicals: Joseph Crosfield and Sons Limited 1815–1965* (Manchester, 1965), p. 297.

58. Stamp, *The Relation of Finance to Rationalization*, p. 25.
59. E. R. Lewis, *No C in C* (1956), pp. 15–19.
60. C. Wilson, *The History of Unilever*, vol. 1 (1954), p. 247. *Investors Chronicle* (27 Mar. 1920), pp. 196, 306.
61. L. Hannah, 'Takeover bids in Britain before 1950', *Business History*, vol. 16 (1974), p. 72.
62. C. Erickson, *British Industrialists. Steel and Hosiery 1850–1950* (Cambridge, 1959), pp. 48, 188–203; D. J. Jeremy (ed.), *Dictionary of Business Biography* (forthcoming).
63. Liberal Industrial Inquiry, *Britain's Industrial Future*, p. 90.
64. Of course, high profits may be necessary both to enable the firm to grow and to reward shareholders, so the objectives of shareholders and managers may in practice coalesce.
65. Liberal Industrial Inquiry, *Britain's Industrial Future*, pp. 90–1.

CHAPTER 6

1. This chapter draws on and expands an earlier article by the author on 'Managerial innovation and the rise of the large-scale company in interwar Britain', *Economic History Review*, vol. 27 (1974).
2. (Macmillan) Committee on Finance and Industry, *Minutes of Evidence* (2 vols, 1931), q. 2356.
3. Quoted in *Business* (Aug. 1931), p. 55. See also E. A. G. Robinson, 'The problem of management and the size of firms', *Economic Journal*, vol. 44 (1934).
4. Cf. the remark attributed to Henry Ford in *Business* (Sep. 1928), p. 129, that 'time given to the study of competition is time lost for one's own business'.
5. 'The trust movement in Great Britain', *Economist* (9 Feb. 1924), pp. 240–1.
6. F. D. Klingender, *The Condition of Clerical Labour in Britain* (1935), p. 61.
7. An increase in this proportion could, of course, be interpreted as the consequence of a less rapid growth in administrative than in operative productivity, but in fact it is more likely to reflect an increasing proportion of explicit administrative work being undertaken by managers when previously it was done by the market (or by operative workers themselves).

8. Although precise figures for 1907 are only available for all census industries, rather than manufacturing alone, the latter figure would have been only slightly higher than the figure shown in Table 6.1. See S. Melman, *Dynamic Factors in Industrial Productivity* (Oxford, 1956), especially p. 77.

9. Quoted in D. C. Coleman, *Courtaulds: An Economic and Social History*, vol. 2 (Oxford, 1969), p. 238.

10. PRO/BT/56/37, Office of the Chief Industrial Adviser, 'Industrial reorganisation', p. 27.

11. Management Research Group Minutes (27 Feb. 1935), pp. 12–13.

12. Quoted in R. Wilson, *Scotch, The Formative Years* (1970), p. 396.

13. E. T. Penrose, *The Theory of the Growth of the Firm* (Oxford, 1959). G. B. Richardson, 'The limits to a firm's rate of growth', *Oxford Economic Papers*, vol. 16 (1964).

14. P. S. Florence, 'Reply', *Economic Journal*, vol. 44 (1934).

15. H. W. Macrosty, *The Trust Movement in British Industry* (1907). P. L. Payne, 'The emergence of the large-scale company in Great Britain, 1870–1914', *Economic History Review*, vol. 20 (1967).

16. Only two of the large multi-firm consolidations of the turn of the century – Bradford Dyers, and Fine Spinners – are singled out by Payne ('The emergence of the large-scale company', p. 530) as having efficient management. Others, which involved fewer firms and started with a more promising managerial core firm (e.g. J. & P. Coats, and Imperial Tobacco), were also relatively successful.

17. Forty-eight out of the seventy multi-firm mergers between 1919 and 1939 involved only five, six or seven firms, and the great majority of these had a combined capital of under £500,000.

18. See pp. 64–5 above. The account of the Lancashire Cotton Corporation which follows is based on the archives of the company (now held by Courtaulds' Northern Spinning Division) and of the Bank of England.

19. Letter, 7 Dec. 1931, from Sir Eric Geddes to E. R. Peacock (Bank of England Archives, Securities Management Trust File).

20. For a review of this literature, see O. E. Williamson, 'Managerial discretion, organisational form and the multi-division hypothesis', in R. Marris and A. Wood (eds), *The Corporate Economy* (1971), pp. 343–86.

21. Six was often suggested as the optimum, though the complexity of the decision situation will, of course, permit a higher number (or dictate a lower number) in particular circumstances, and managerial theorists are now less willing than their predecessors to formulate rules on this. See L. Urwick, *Scientific Principles and Organisation* (American Management Association, Institute of Management Series no. 19, 1933), p. 8. Cf. J. Child, *Organisation: A Guide to Problems and Practice* (1977).
22. A. Marshall, *Industry and Trade* (4th edn 1923), pp. 229, 363, n. 2. *Textile Recorder* (15 May 1919), p. 29.
23. Hannah, 'Managerial innovation and the rise of the large-scale company', p. 257.
24. Quoted from *Stewarts and Lloyds Limited 1903–1953* (1953), p. 15, in Payne, 'The emergence of the large-scale company in Great Britain 1870–1914', pp. 534–5.
25. Advertisement, *Business* (Oct. 1930), p. 152.
26. L. R. Dicksee, *Office Machinery and Appliances* (1928), p. 177. 'How Holleriths came to Britain', *Tabacus* (1957). 'Machinery in the office', *Economist* (26 Feb. 1938), pp. 431–2. C. H. Costello, 'A quarter century's progress in management method and business equipment', *Business* (Jan. 1933), pp. 31–3, 44, 47. A. P. Hodges, 'Development in office machinery and equipment', in R. Pugh (ed.), *British Management Year Book* (1939). A. E. Musson, *Enterprise in Soap and Chemicals: Joseph Crosfield and Sons Limited* 1815–1965 (Manchester, 1965), p. 293.
27. Management Research Group Minutes (10 Nov. 1937), p. 3.
28. H. Whitehead, 'The changing environment of management', *British Management Review*, vol. 6 (1947).
29. A. M. Carr-Saunders and P. A. Wilson, *The Professions* (Oxford, 1933), pp. 278 ff.
30. Management Research Group Papers, Business History Unit, London. The companies included ICI, AEC, Standard Telephones & Cables, Metal Box, and Dunlop.
31. J. M. Clark, *Overhead Costs* (1923), pp. 119–23, 141. D. H. Robertson, *The Control of Industry* (1928), pp. 22–6. *Economist* (16 Aug. 1930), pp. 329–30.
32. For criticisms that business did not succeed in attracting the ablest men, see, e.g.: H. J. Habakkuk, *American and British Technology in the Nineteenth Century* (Cambridge, 1962), p. 191; Liberal Industrial Inquiry, *Britain's Industrial Future* (1928), pp. 130–1; and p. 88 above.

33. R. Jones and O. Marriott, *Anatomy of a Merger: A History of GEC, AEI and English Electric* (1970), pp. 147–8. M. R. Bonavia, *Railway Policy between the Wars* (Manchester, 1981), p. 35.

34. J. H. Jones, *Josiah Stamp: Public Servant: The Life of the First Baron Stamp of Shortlands* (1964), pp. 179–86, 281–91. Cf. J. Stamp, 'Administration of business and public affairs', *Journal of the Institute of Public Administration*, vol. 1 (1923).

35. Cf. F. Lee, *Manufacturer* (1938), p. 102. General Sir Ian Hamilton, *The Soul and Body of an Army* (1921), pp. 230, 239.

36. *Macmillan Evidence*, q. 4128.

37. N. McKendrick, 'Josiah Wedgewood and cost accounting in the industrial revolution', *Economic History Review*, vol. 23 (1970).

38. L. R. Dicksee, *Business Methods and the War* (1915), pp. 42–3.

39. J. Stamp, *Some Economic Factors in Modern Life* (1929), p. 159. See on accounting generally: N. A. H. Stacey, *English Accountancy, 1800–1954: A Study in Economic and Social History* (1954); R. H. Parker, *Management Accounting, An Historical Perspective* (1969); F. R. M. de Paula, *Developments in Accountancy* (1948); E. Jones, *Accountancy and the British Economy 1840–1980: The Evolution of Ernst & Whinney* (1981).

40. Stacey, *English Accountancy*, p. 215. De Paula, *Developments in Accountancy*, p. 207.

41. Dicksee, *Business Methods and the War*, p. 43.

42. 'The role of finance and accountancy in the management of large business combines' (1933), reprinted as ch. 13 in de Paula, *Developments in Accountancy*, and Management Research Group Minutes (12 Mar. 1934), 'Budgetary control practice', discussion.

43. C. Wilson, *The History of Unilever* (1954), vol. 1, pp. 273, 297–310; vol. 2, pp. 309–13.

44. P. S. Florence, *The Logic of British and American Industry* (1961), p. 211.

45. Quoted in *Economist* (3 May 1930), p. 988.

46. *Economist* (30 Oct. 1926), p. 721.

47. The analysis of the managerial structure at Nobel and ICI which follows is based on various published and unpublished sources, listed in Hannah, 'Managerial innovation and the rise of the large-scale company in interwar Britain', p. 260, n. 4.

48. Anon., *ICI Ltd and its Founding Companies*, vol. 1 (1938), p. 240.

49. It appears to have been the view of the Nobel directors that such a cycle of decentralization was necessary in a merger, centralization initially providing unified accounting and personnel policies and being followed by decentralization to encourage local managerial initiative and efficiency; see, e.g., J. Stamp, 'The management and direction of industry', 1930 broadcast reprinted in his *Criticism and Other Essays* (1931).
50. Cf. L. F. Haber, *The Chemical Industry 1900–1930* (1970), p. 341.
51. L. Hannah, 'Strategy and structure in the manufacturing sector', in L. Hannah (ed.), *Management Strategy and Business Development: An Historical and Comparative Study* (1976), pp. 186, 189–91.
52. This was the first historical work to develop the multidivision hypothesis systematically; see A. D. Chandler, *Strategy and Structure, Chapters in the History of Industrial Enterprise* (Cambridge, Mass., 1962).
53. D. F. Channon, *The Strategy and Structure of British Enterprise* (1973) suggests that only a dozen British firms had multidivisional structures by 1950, most of them subsidiaries of US firms.
54. Melman, *Dynamic Factors in Industrial Productivity*, p. 131; US Department of Commerce, Bureau of the Census, *Historical Statistics of the United States from Colonial Times to 1970* (Washington DC, 1975), p. 666.
55. E.g. de Paula, 'The role of finance and accountancy in the management of large business combines'.
56. E.g. A. Plant, 'Centralize or decentralize' in his *Some Modern Business Problems* (1937); L. Urwick, T. G. Rose and K. G. Fenelon, 'Discussion on problems of amalgamation and decentralisation', British Association Meeting, Norwich (1935).
57. J. J. Raskob, 'Management policies that built General Motors', *Business* (Oct. 1928). A. Sloan, 'What I have found most important in management', *Business* (June 1930).
58. Especially through the Management Research Groups, one of which (no. 1) was reserved for large companies.
59. 'How far should managers be managed? How we work from head office by the chief executives of 19 firms', *Business* (Feb. 1930), pp. 72–4.
60. W. G. Hiscock, 'Centralisation or decentralisation', *British Management Review*, vol. 4 (1940), pp. 136–9. Sir Gilbert Garnsey and T. B. Robson, *Holding Companies* (3rd edn 1936), pp. 18–24.

61. G. Walker, 'Development and organisation of AEI Ltd.', in R. S. Edwards and H. Townsend, *Business Enterprise* (1958), pp. 309–13. Jones and Marriott, *Anatomy of a Merger*, p. 150.

62. Edwards and Townsend, *Business Enterprise*, pp. 66, 220–7, 293. G. Turner, *Business in Britain* (1969), pp. 52, 352. B. W. E. Alford, *W. D. & H. O. Wills and the Development of the UK Tobacco Industry, 1786–1965* (1973), pp. 309–18, 331–3, 365–70, 445–6. *Economist* (31 Oct. 1931), p. 825. Unilever, especially under William Lever in the early 1920s, was also run as a loose confederation, see Wilson, *History of Unilever*, vol. 1, pp. 267–96.

63. For a similar point, see O. E. Williamson, *Markets and Hierarchies: Analysis and Antitrust Implications* (New York, 1975), pp. 143–4.

64. Quoted in P. Fitzgerald, *Industrial Combination in England* (1927), pp. 193–4.

65. A. D. Chandler, 'The development of modern management structure in the US and UK', in L. Hannah (ed.), *Management Strategy and Business Development: An Historical and Comparative Study* (1976); idem, 'The transnational industrial firm in the United States and the United Kingdom: a comparative analysis', *Economic History Review*, vol. 33 (1980).

66. Family firms were not *necessarily* backward. Indeed there is evidence of some of the best of them defining 'family' sufficiently widely to create an extremely efficient management structure (e.g. T. C. Barker, *The Glassmakers: Pilkington: The Rise of an International Company 1826–1976* (1977), chs 19 and 22) and, more recently, of owner-managed firms having a superior performance to professionally managed ones (S. Nyman and A. Silberston, 'The ownership and control of industry', *Oxford Economic Papers*, vol. 30 (1978)). But there can be no doubt of the conservatism of many later generations of family owners in the 1920s and 1930s; see pp. 128–32 above.

67. D. C. Coleman, 'Gentlemen and players', *Economic History Review*, vol. 26 (1973).

68. S. Keeble, unpublished manuscript, Business History Unit, London School of Economics (1983).

69. M. J. Wiener, *English Culture and Decline of the Industrial Spirit 1850–1980* (Cambridge, 1981). While it is possible to take issue with the implicit view of Professor Wiener that English cultural attitudes changed after 1850, the evidence he presents of the deep social, cultural and educational roots of low prestige for

industry is impressive. See also W. D. Rubinstein, 'Wealth, elites and the class structure of modern Britain', *Past and Present*, no. 76 (1977), p. 116.

70. G. H. Copeman, *Leaders of British Industry* (1955), p. 76. D. P. Barritt, 'The stated qualifications of directors of larger public companies', *Journal of Industrial Economics*, vol. 5 (1957). R. Locke, *The End of the Practical Man* (forthcoming). J. Hirschmeier and T. Yui, *The Development of Japanese Business 1600–1980* (1981), pp. 145 ff.

71. Political and Economic Planning, *Report on the British Cotton Industry* (1934), p. 108.

CHAPTER 7

1. See Appendix 2 for a fuller discussion of changes in aggregate concentration over time.

2. For fuller discussion of the downward trend of concentration in the 1930s and 1940s, see Chapter 9.

3. S. J. Prais, *The Evolution of Giant Firms in Britain* (Cambridge, 1970), p. 213, estimates the share of the largest 100 firms in net output in the USA as 22 per cent in 1909 and 25 per cent in 1929. More disaggregated evidence for 1935 is also consistent with the view that on average British industries were about as concentrated as US industries in 1935. For a discussion of the methodological issues and the statistics, see: P. S. Florence, *The Logic of British and American Industry* (2nd edn 1961), pp. 132–5; G. Rosenbluth, 'Measures of concentration', in Conference of the Universities – National Bureau Committee for Economic Research, *Business Concentration and Price Policy* (Princeton, 1955), pp. 70–7; W. G. Shepherd, 'A comparison of industrial concentration in the United States and Britain', *Review of Economics and Statistics*, vol. 43 (1961); J. S. Bain, *International Differences in Industrial Structure* (New Haven, 1966), pp. 76–81; B. P. Pashigian, 'Market concentration in the United States and Great Britain', *Journal of Law and Economics*, vol. 11 (1968). The leading firms were, however, still larger in the USA than in Britain, but now because of the relatively larger size of the American economy, rather than, as before the First World War, because of higher concentration levels in the USA.

4. Some element of subjective judgement enters into the choice of the decade of the major merger: e.g. when a choice has to be made between a founding merger and a subsequent period of

substantial growth by acquisition. For an indication of the methods adopted in such cases, see L. Hannah, 'The political economy of mergers in manufacturing industry in Britain between the wars' (unpublished D.Phil thesis, Oxford, 1972), pp. 143–4, 272–8. The companies of 1948 are the largest manufacturing companies (ranked by net assets) in the National Institute of Economic and Social Research list for that year. The companies of 1970 are the largest (ranked by sales) in the *Times 1000* list.

5. The results for the large firms of 1948 are of course also different from those of 1970 because of a change in the identity of large firms between those dates; see G. Whittington, 'Changes in the top 100 quoted companies in the United Kingdom 1948 to 1968', *Journal of Industrial Economics*, vol. 21 (1972).

6. R. L. Nelson, *Merger Movements in American Industry 1895–1956* (Princeton, 1959), p. 4. Thirty-seven of Nelson's 100 corporations had no important mergers, the others registering eleven before 1895, twenty in 1895–1904, seven in 1905–14, five in 1915–24, eleven in 1925–34, none in 1935–44, and nine in 1945–55.

7. There were, of course, also significant mergers in other sectors beyond our present concern, e.g. the regrouping of the railways, and further consolidation of road, electricity generation, cinema chains, petrol distribution, and the financial and retail sectors.

8. Because of the differences in the coverage of the sample and the bias towards larger and quoted companies (which may be more or less representative of firms in particular industries), the data in Table 7.2 should be used only to compare changes in the level of concentration within individual industries between 1919 and 1930. It is not an adequate indicator of differences between the levels of concentration in the various industries at any one date.

9. L. Hannah and J. A. Kay, *Concentration in Modern Industry* (1977), pp. 64–5.

10. For a persuasive argument to this effect, see G. J. Stigler, 'The statistics of monopoly and merger', *Journal of Political Economy*, vol. 64 (1956).

11. An earlier study by P. E. Hart and S. J. Prais 'The analysis of business concentration: a statistical approach', *Journal of the Royal Statistical Society*, series A, vol. 119 (1956)) reached the contrary conclusion that mergers were quite unimportant as a source of increasing concentration in a very similar sample of firms between 1885 and 1950; but their results are invalidated both by the use of inappropriate measures of concentration and by the omission from

their study of 99 per cent of merger activity, including four-fifths of the largest mergers of the interwar period. For an unconvincing attempt to defend their results, see P. E. Hart, 'On bias and concentration', *Journal of Industrial Economics*, vol. 27 (1979) and S. J. Prais, 'The contribution of mergers to industrial concentration: what do we know?', *Journal of Industrial Economics*, vol. 29 (1981). The estimate in the text may well be an underestimate because of the omission of many small mergers by the firms in the sample.

12. In vehicles, the limited importance of merger was due to the rapid expansion of output through new investment by the leading producers; much the same may have been true of the clothing and footwear industry about which less is known. In the case of textiles, mergers were not very important in increasing the share of the leading five firms like Courtaulds, then investing significantly in expanding the rayon sector. Further down the same distribution, however, mergers such as Combined Egyptian Mills and the Lancashire Cotton Corporation were the major cause of increasing concentration. For a more sophisticated measure of concentration, which captures changes in the whole size distribution, see Hannah and Kay, *Concentration in Modern Industry*.

13. Disaggregation to '3-digit' industry levels of industrial products or trades rather than to the '2-digit' or industry group level of Table 7.2 is only possible for 1935 onwards. Following the pioneering work of H. Leak and A. Maizels, 'The structure of British industry', *Journal of the Royal Statistical Society*, series A, vol. 108 (1945) on the 1935 Census data, the *Census of Production* statistics have regularly provided data at this level of disaggregation.

14. R. C. O. Matthews, C. H. Feinstein, and J. C. Odling-Smee, *British Economic Growth 1856–1973* (Oxford, 1982).

15. H. W. Richardson, 'The new industries between the wars', *Oxford Economic Papers*, vol. 13 (1961).

CHAPTER 8

1. For a list of the largest fifty firms of 1919 see Appendix 3.

2. Share prices in December 1930 were only 15 per cent higher than in January 1919, while the total values of the top fifty were 125 per cent higher in 1930, so the change is a real one, not merely the consequence of inflated capital values.

3. C. Shaw, 'The large manufacturing employers of 1907', *Business History*, vol. 25 (1983). L. Johnman, unpublished manuscript, Business History Unit, LSE, for 1935.

4. See Chapter 2 above.
5. In December 1930 their average market value was only two-thirds of the 1919 level, despite a 15 per cent rise in the general level of stock exchange prices.
6. See Appendix 3.
7. The reduction in the number of large companies in the staple industries among the largest fifty of 1930 is perhaps exaggerated by this factor: their share in manufacturing output was still in 1930 somewhat higher than their share in market values on which Table 8.1. is based.
8. D. H. Aldcroft, *The Interwar Economy: Britain, 1919–1939* (1970), pp. 121, 137–76.
9. B. H. Tripp, *Grand Alliance, a Chapter of Industrial History* (1951). B. H. Tripp, *Renold Chain, a History of the Company and the Rise of the Precision Chain Industry* (1956). C. G. Renold, 'Rationalization of the management of companies under a merger', in Sixth International Congress of Scientific Management, *Development Section Papers* (1936). *Economist* (12 Jan. 1924), pp. 47–8. Board of Trade Working Party, *Report on the Jute Industry* (1948), p. 25.
10. S. R. Dennison, 'Vertical integration in the iron and steel industry', *Economic Journal*, vol. 49 (1939).
11. Sir Frederick Scopes, *The Development of Corby Works* (1968), p. 65.
12. (Balfour) Commitee on Industry and Trade, *Final Report* (Md. 3282), p. 179.
13. The following section is based on an examination of the archives of the Lancashire Cotton Corporation. For other examples of industries in which exit was hastened by mergers, see P. L. Cook and R. Cohen, *The Effects of Mergers* (1958).
14. S. Yonekawa, 'The growth of cotton spinning firms: a comparative study', in A. Okochi and S. Yonekawa (eds), *The Textile Industry and its Business Climate* (Tokyo, 1982). W. Lazonick, 'Production relations, Labour productivity and choice of technique: British and US cotton spinning', *Journal of Economic History*, vol. 41 (1981).
15. Neil K. Buxton, 'Economic growth in Scotland between the wars: the role of production structure and rationalization', *Economic History Review*, vol. 33 (1980). Idem, 'Efficiency and organisation in the Scottish iron and steel industry during the interwar period', *Economic History Review*, vol. 29 (1976).

16. J. D. Scott, *Vickers: A History* (1962), pp. 137–40.
17. *Investors Chronicle* (22 Dec. 1928), p. 1358.
18. (Macmillan) Committee on Finance and Industry, *Minutes of Evidence* (2 vols, 1931), qq. 3616, 3621.
19. High concentration industries had, in fact, been growing faster than low concentration industries. In 1935, for example, the seven industrial groups which had the highest average three-firm concentration ratios accounted for 56 per cent of UK industrial output, whereas in 1907 they had accounted for only 46 per cent (calculated from information in H. Leak and A. Maizels, 'The structure of British industry', *Journal of The Royal Statistical Society*, series A, vol. 108 (1945), p. 157; B. R. Mitchell and P. Deane, *Abstract of British Historical Statistics* (Cambridge, 1962), p. 270).
20. See, generally: H. W. Richardson, 'Overcommitment in Britain before 1930', *Oxford Economic Papers*, vol. 17 (1965), reprinted in D. H. Aldcroft and H. W. Richardson, *The British Economy 1870–1939* (1969); W. P. Kennedy, 'Foreign investment, trade and growth in the United Kingdom, 1870–1913, *Explorations in Economic History*, vol. 11 (1974); W. P. Kennedy, *Economic Maturity in Historical Perspective: A Critique of British Economic Performance, 1870–1914* (Cambridge, forthcoming).
21. H. Tyszynski, 'World trade in manufactured commodities, 1899–1950', *Manchester School*, vol. 19 (1951). D. H. Aldcroft, 'Economic progress in Britain in the 1920s', *Scottish Journal of Political Economy*, vol. 13 (1966), reprinted in Aldcroft and Richardson, *The British Economy 1870–1839*.
22. P. W. S. Andrews and E. Brunner, *The Life of Lord Nuffield* (Oxford, 1955), p. 112. G. Maxcy and A. Silberston, *The Motor Industry* (1959), pp. 13–16.
23. J. Harrop, 'The growth of the rayon industry between the wars', *Yorkshire Bulletin of Economic and Social Research*, vol. 20 (1968). D. C. Coleman, *Courtaulds, an Economic and Social History*, vol. 2 (Oxford, 1969), pp. 171–204.
24. Aldcroft, *The Interwar Economy*, pp. 184, 189.
25. The comments on ICI which follow are based on an examination of the company's archives, now held by the ICI parent company. The files of the technical department and the development department were particularly useful. See also: W. J. Reader, *Imperial Chemical Industries: A History*, vol. 1 (1970), pp. 249–466; vol. 2 (1975); J. Stamp, 'Amalgamations', in his *Some*

Economic Factors in Modern Life (1929).
26. L. J. Barley, 'Memorandum on development policy', dated 27 Apr. 1926 (Nobel archives).
27. The three leading electrical engineering companies' histories are described in R. Jones and O. Marriott, *Anatomy of a Merger: A History of GEC, AEI, and English Electric* (1970), on which the following two paragraphs draw substantially. See also: Monopolies and Restrictive Practices Commission, *Report on the Supply of Electric Lamps* (1951), and *Report on the Supply and Exports of Electrical and Allied Machinery and Plant* (1957).
28. The company was American-controlled until 1934 when British shareholders regained majority control; see Jones and Marriott, *Anatomy of Merger*, p. 108; cf. Monopolies and Restrictive Practices Commission, *Report on the Supply and Exports of Electrical and Allied Machinery and Plant*, p. 102
29. PRO/BT/55/49. P. Cunliffe-Lister, memorandum dated 22 Nov. 1927, p. 2. Cf. G. B. Richardson, *The Future of the Heavy Electrical Plant Industry* (1969).
30. Though this did not show up in the productivity record of the industry, which was among the worst of the new industries, perhaps because the manufacture of large generating plant to individual specifications did not allow much scope for mass production techniques; see K. S. Lomax, 'Growth and productivity in the United Kingdom', *Productivity Measurement Review*, vol. 38 (1964), p. 21.
31. T. A. B. Corley, *Domestic Electrical Appliances* (1966), pp. 36–48.
32. But cf. pp. 125–6 for some indication that in the 1930s and 1940s the growth of large firms was relatively unimpressive.
33. See, generally, G. B. Richardson, 'The organisation of industry', *Economic Journal*, vol. 82 (1972), for a formal treatment of the reason for the specialization of firms by capabilities. See also pp. 63–4 above for the advantages of a core of technical expertise in appraising investment projects.
34. P. Jennings, *Dunlopera* (privately published, 1961), pp. 131–2. Monopolies and Restrictive Practices Commission, *Report on the Supply and Export of Pneumatic Tyres* (1955) and *Report on the Supply of Certain Rubber Footwear* (1956).
35. Monopolies Commission, *Report on the Supply of Asbestos and Certain Asbestos Products* (1973). N. A. Morling, 'History of

Turner Brothers Asbestos Co. Ltd', *Rochdale Literary and Scientific Society Transaction*, vol. 24 (1961).

36. The paragraphs which follow draw extensively on: M. Sanderson, 'Research and the firm in British Industry 1919–1939', *Science Studies*, vol. 2 (1972); L. F. Haber, 'The British chemical industry between the wars' (unpublished, 1972); L. Hannah, 'Applied science and research expenditure in twentieth century Britain' (unpublished, 1972).

37. Reader, *Imperial Chemical Industries*, vol. 1, p. 414.

38. *Economist* (15 Apr. 1933), p. 830.

39. Department of Scientific and Industrial Research, *Report of the Year ending 31 March 1936* (Cmd. 5350, 1937), p. 15.

40. J. Jewkes, D. Sawers and R. Stillerman, *The Sources of Invention* (1958), p. 105. Their case studies of major inventions show a trend towards corporate invention and innovation similar to that in the patent statistics, though the authors are, somewhat perversely, concerned to emphasize that the individual inventor remains important (which is true) rather than that a major shift has occurred (which is striking).

41. R. S. Sayers, 'The springs of technical progress in Britain 1919–39', *Economic Journal*, vol. 60 (1950).

42. C. Wilson, *The History of Unilever*, vol. 2 (1954), pp. 301–99. P. Mathias, *Retailing Revolution* (1967), pp. 258–97. W. J. Reader, *Hard Roads and Highways, S.P.D. Ltd. 1918–1968* (1969).

43. E.g. there would be the problem of assessing the extent to which, by increasing barriers to entry and artificially differentiating products, their increased advertising expenditure produced welfare losses.

44. Royal Commission on the Press, *Report* (Cmd. 7700, 1949), p. 193.

45. Monopolies Commission, *Report on the Supply of Metal Containers* (1970). R. Evely and I. M. D. Little, *Concentration in British Industry* (Cambridge, 1960), pp. 249–50. Monopolies Commission, *Report on the Supply of Electrical Equipment for Mechanically Propelled Land Vehicles* (1963). Monopolies Commission, *Report on the Supply of Chemical Fertilisers* (1959).

46. Evely and Little, *Concentration in British Industry*, pp. 189–90.

47. See p. 102 above.

48. J. H. Dunning, *American Investment in British Manufacturing Industry* (1958), pp. 36–57. See also M. Wilkins, *American*

Business Abroad from 1914–1970 (Cambridge, Mass., 1974).

49. Reader, *Imperial Chemical Industries*, vol. 2 (1975).
50. Jones and Marriott, *Anatomy of a Merger*, pp. 140–1. PRO/BT/ 56/44, Chief Industrial Adviser, file 1884/7. Andrews and Brunner, *The Life of Lord Nuffield*, pp. 131–4.
51. Research on postwar direct investment has suggested that there is a critical size below which a firm cannot envisage overseas expansion; for a contemporary business statement of the same view by Josiah Stamp, see *Macmillan Evidence*, qq. 3921, 3944–5. Cf. P. L. Payne, *British Entrepreneurship in the Nineteenth Century* (1974), p. 54.
52. An unpublished study (worksheets in Business History Unit, LSE) of overseas acquisitions by British firms reported in business histories and the financial press, suggests that they made more overseas acquisitions in 1920–9 than in the whole of the previous four decades, though there may be a bias in this data because of better financial press coverage in the 1920s.
53. J. M. Stopford, 'The origins of British-based multinational manufacturing enterprise', *Business History Review*, vol. 48 (1974). G. G. Jones, 'The expansion of British multinational manufacturing 1890–1939', in T. Inoue and A. Okochi, *Overseas Business Activities: Proceedings of the Ninth Fuji Conference* (Tokyo, 1983). Wilkins, *American Business Abroad from 1914 to 1970*. Wilkins, 'Modern European economic history and the multinationals', *Journal of European Economic History*, vol. 6 (1977).
54. Reader, *Imperial Chemical Industries*, vol. 1, p. 464. See also Lord Melchett, 'Internationalism and big business', *Ashridge Journal* (Sep. 1932).
55. This was sometimes under pressure from European governments wishing to develop indigenous manufacturing and substitute for imports from the UK, see e.g. R. F. Holland, 'The Federation of British Industries and the international economy', *Economic History Review*, vol. 34 (1981), p. 294.
56. US Department of Commerce, *Foreign Investments in the US* (Washington, 1937), p. 17.
57. Jones, 'Expansion of British multinational manufacturing'.
58. *Sunday Times* (3 July 1927), quoted in G. M. Colman, *Capitalist Combines* (1927), p. 28.
59. Andrews and Brunner, *Life of Lord Nuffield*, pp. 159–60.

60. (Macmillan) Committee on Finance and Industry, *Report* (Cmd. 3897, 1931), p. 165.
61. Reader, *Imperial Chemical Industries*, vol. 1, pp. 116, 147.
62. C. Wilson, 'Economy and society in later Victorian Britain', *Economic History Review*, vol. 18 (1965).
63. H. Macrosty, *The Trust Movement in British Industry* (1907), p. 128.
64. Maxcy and Silberston, *The Motor Industry*, pp. 12–15.
65. L. Hannah, 'Mergers in British manufacturing industry, 1880–1918', *Oxford Economic Papers*, vol. 26 (1974), p. 11. L. Hannah, 'Political economy of mergers in manufacturing industry in Britain between the wars' (unpublished D.Phil thesis, Oxford, 1972), p. 154.
66. Sanderson, 'Research and the firm in British industry', pp. 112, 124.
67. See also the listings for 1905 in Appendix 3 and compare with the listing for 1919, though in that case the samples are less clearly comparable.
68. Cf. R. C. Edwards, 'Stages in corporate stability and the risks of corporate failure', *Journal of Economic History*, vol. 35 (1975). In the USA the stability emerged in the early 1920s, rather longer after the major merger wave of the 1890s than was the case with Britain's wave of the 1920s.
69. Aldcroft, *The Interwar Economy*, p. 173.
70. Maxcy and Silberston, *The Motor Industry*, p. 15. Aldcroft, *The Interwar Economy*, pp. 184.
71. Coleman, *Courtaulds: An Economic and Social History*, vol. 2, pp. 242–3.
72. (Balfour) Committee on Industry and Trade, *Final Report*, p. 218.
73. Though, in so far as concentration led to increased monopoly power and restricted output, the *a priori* considerations would suggest a very different view.

CHAPTER 9

1. E.g. P. E. Hart, 'Business concentration in the United Kingdom', *Journal of the Royal Statistical Society*, series A, vol. 123 (1960), pp. 51–2.

2. The level of concentration shown in Table 9.1 for 1930 cannot be directly compared with that for the same year in Table 7.2 (p. 98 above), because the coverage of the 1930–48 sample population was improved. The *caveats* in note 8 of Chapter 7 also apply to this table. For similar findings for the period 1939–50, derived by adjusting the Hart and Prais data, see p. 183.

3. R. Evely and I. M. D. Little, *Concentration in British Industry 1935–51* (Cambridge, 1960). For many industries, definitional changes made comparison between the two years difficult. However, where comparisons were possible, concentration rose in twenty-seven and declined in fourteen industries.

4. W. J. Reader, *Bowater: A History* (Cambridge, 1981).

5. P. L. Payne, *Colvilles and the Scottish Steel Industry* (Oxford, 1979).

6. (Bolton) Committee of Inquiry on Small Firms, *Report* (Cmd. 4811, 1971), p. 59.

7. The complexity of these changes can only be captured by a more sophisticated range of concentration measures than those employed here. For a further discussion, see L. Hannah and J. A. Kay, *Concentration in Modern Industry* (1977), pp. 72–81.

8. R. A. Church, *Kenricks in Hardware* (Newton Abbott, 1969), p. 213; see also pp. 216–17, 247–8, 321, 329. R. E. Wilson, *200 Precious Metal Years: A History of the Sheffield Smelting Company Limited, 1760–1960* (1960), pp. 207–18.

9. A. E. Cutforth, *Methods of Amalgamation* (1926), p. 17. See also: J. Ryan in 'Problems of rationalization', *Economic Journal*, vol. 40 (1930), p. 365; Mr and Mrs F. H. Crittall, *Fifty Years of Work and Play* (1934), p. 162.

10. P. S. Florence in 'Problems of rationalization', p. 365.

11. (Macmillan) Committee on Finance and Industry, *Minutes of Evidence* (2 vols, 1931). q. 5995; see also qq. 859, 2800, 7497. M. Webster Jenkinson, 'Memorandum on the steel trade', PRO/BT/56/2.

12. Viscount Inchcape, 'Shipowners and shipbuilders', in *Transactions of the First World Power Conference*, vol. 1 (1924), p. 1115.

13. (Balfour) Committee on Industry and Trade, *Factors in Industrial and Commercial Efficiency* (1927), pp. 266–98.

14. Lord Camrose (W. E. Berry), *British Newspapers and Their Controllers* (1947), p. 17. Royal Commission on the Press,

Report (Cmd. 7700, 1949), pp. 67–9. See also Monopolies and Restrictive Practices Commission, *Report on the Supply of Certain Industrial and Medical Gases* (1956), pp. 21–2, 92.

15. L. Hannah, 'Takeover bids in Britain before 1950', *Business History*, vol. 16 (1974).

16. Cutforth, *Methods of Amalgamation*, p. 37.

17. Quoted in Hannah, 'Takeover bids in Britain before 1950', p. 72.

18. P. E. Hart and S. J. Prais, 'The analysis of business concentration: a statistical approach', *Journal of the Royal Statistical Society*, series A, vol. 119 (1956), p. 169.

19. The exceptionally low contribution of mergers to concentration increase in the vehicle industry in Table 7.2 (p. 98 above) is no doubt partly due to this factor.

20. A similar remark was made by the chairman of Stewarts & Lloyds, that 'concentration of production could not take place without concentration of demand' (Annual General Meeting, 18 May 1938). Cf. F. M. Scherer, *Industrial Market Structure and Economic Performance* (Chicago, 1970), pp. 116–18.

21. M. A. Adelman, 'The measurement of industrial concentration', *Review of Economics and Statistics*, vol. 33 (1951).

22. W. J. Reader, *ICI: A History*, vol. 2 (Oxford, 1975), pp. 170–82. R. Church and M. Miller, 'The big three: competition, management and marketing in British motor industry, 1922–1939', in B. Supple (ed.), *Essays in British Business History* (Oxford, 1977), pp. 170–3.

23. E.g. PRO/BT/55/49; P. W. S. Andrews and E. Brunner, *Capital Development in Steel* (Oxford, 1951), p. 172. The suspicion remains, however, that in many such cases the anticipated market was not sufficiently large because of market imperfections, and an unwillingness to overcome them through merger, rather than because of an overall deficiency in demand.

24. A. T. K. Grant, *A Study of the Postwar Capital Market* (1937), pp. 189–96.

25. W. Piercy, 'The financing of small business', *British Management Review*, vol. 3 (1938). R. Frost, 'The Macmillan gap 1931–1953', *Oxford Economic Papers*, vol. 6 (1954).

26. H. F. Heath and A. H. Hetherington, *Industrial Research and Development in the United Kingdom* (1946).

27. I. F. Grant, 'The small unit in industry', *Economic Journal*, vol.

32 (1922). Anon., 'Why we did not join the amalgamation', *Business* (Jan. 1928), p. 15. J. Jewkes, 'A statistical study of the economies of large-scale production', *Transactions of the Manchester Statistical Society* (1931–2). But cf. L. Rostas, *Productivity Prices and Distribution in Selected British Industries* (Cambridge, 1948), pp. 28–30, for evidence of increasing returns over a wide field of industry in 1935.

28. L. Hannah, *Electricity Before Nationalisation* (1979).

29. C. Wilson, *The History of Unilever*, vol. 1 (1954), p. 298. J. D. Scott, *Vickers: A History* (1962), pp. 167–8. A study of large companies between 1919 and 1939 showed that for every seventeen subsidiaries which they acquired, one subsidiary was demerged; see L. Hannah, 'The political economy of mergers in British manufacturing industry between the wars' (unpublished D.Phil thesis, Oxford, 1972), p. 270.

30. L. Hannah, 'Managerial innovation and the rise of the large-scale company in interwar Britain', *Economic History Review*, vol. 27 (1974), pp. 267–9.

31. ibid., p. 269.

32. See, generally: A. F. Lucas, *Industrial Reconstruction and the Control of Competition* (1937); Monopolies and Restrictive Practices Commission, *Collective Discrimination* (Cmd. 9504, 1955); Political and Economic Planning, *Industrial Trade Associations* (1957). L. Hannah, 'Mergers, cartels and concentration: legal factors in the US and European experience', in N. Horn and J. Kocka (eds), *Recht und Entwicklung der Grossunternehmen im 19. und Früher 20. Jahrhundert* (Göttingen, 1979).

33. W. Friedmann, 'The Harris tweed case and freedom of trade', *Modern Law Review*, vol. 6 (1942), p. 13. A. L. Haslam, *The Law Relating to Trade Combination*, (1931).

34. Lucas, *Industrial Reconstruction and the Control of Competition* pp. 55–6. H. Macmillan, *Winds of Change 1914–1939* (1966), pp. 370–2. A. Marwick, 'Middle opinion in the thirties, planning, progress and political agreement', *English Historical Review*, vol. 79 (1964). L. P. Carpenter, 'Corporatism in Britain 1930–1945', *Journal of Contemporary History*, vol. 11 (1956). For a useful theoretical discussion of cartels, see O. E. Williamson, *Markets and Hierarchies* (New York, 1975), pp. 238 ff.

35. Minutes of Cabinet meeting of 27 Mar. 1935, CAB 23/81. Similar proposals in the postwar period were also rejected, this time by industrialists fearing the Labour government's interven-

tion in their affairs through such state-backed cartels.

36. Finance Act 1935, s. 25.

37. Lucas, *Industrial Reconstruction*, pp. 55–6.

38. The Cotton Industry (Reorganization) Act 1936. A further Act in 1939 envisaged price restriction in the cotton industry but was never fully implemented.

39. Sir Herbert Hutchinson, *Tariff Making and Industrial Reconstruction* (Oxford, 1965).

40. D. H. Aldcroft, 'Government control and the origin of restrictive trade practices in Britain', *Accountants Magazine*, vol. 66 (1962).

41. P. J. D. Wiles, 'Pre-war and wartime controls', in G. D. N. Worswick and P. H. Ady (eds), *The British Economy 1945–1950* (Oxford, 1952), p. 151. See also: G. C. Allen, 'The concentration of production policy', in D. N. Chester (ed.), *Lessons of the British War Economy* (Cambridge, 1951), pp. 167–81; Evely and Little, *Concentration in British Industry*, pp. 178–80.

42. Cf. (Balfour) Committee, *Factors in Industrial and Commercial Efficiency*, p. 70.

43. Lucas, *Industrial Reconstruction and the Control of Competition*, p. 176. G. J. Stigler, 'A theory of oligopoly', *Journal of Political Economy*, vol. 72 (1964).

44. L. F. Urwick, *The Meaning of Rationalization* (1926), pp. 39, 86–9. L. Barley, *The Riddle of Rationalization* (1932), ch. 9.

45. R. Jones and O. Marriott, *Anatomy of a Merger, A History of GEC, AEI, and English Electric* (1970), p. 124. For similar views on other industries, see: Church, *Kenricks in Hardware*, p. 161; F. Lee, 'Will the big business last?', *Ashridge Journal* (Sep. 1933).

46. Though in some industries problems of overcapacity actually intensified competition.

47. There appears to be no clear relationship between productivity performance and levels of concentration in industries during this period; see, e.g., C. F. Carter and B. R. Williams, *Industry and Technical Progress* (1957), p. 121.

48. Cf. G. C. Allen, 'An aspect of industrial reorganization', *Economic Journal*, vol. 55 (1945).

49. Jones and Marriott, *Anatomy of a Merger*, pp. 130, 138. 'New management raises profits £200,000', *Business* (Apr. 1932), pp. 7–8.

50. J. Jewkes, D. Sawers and R. Stillerman, *The Sources of Invention*

(Oxford, 1958), pp. 339–42, 387–8.

51. A. Armstrong and A. Silberston, 'Size of plant, size of enterprise, and concentration in British manufacturing industry 1935–58', *Journal of the Royal Statistical Society*, series A, vol. 28 (1965). (Bolton) Committee, *Report*, p. 59.

52. See pp. 65–7 above. Mergers may also facilitate investments on a larger scale by reducing uncertainty in investment planning; see G. B. Richardson, *Information and Investment* (Oxford, 1960).

53. (Bolton) Committee, *Report*, p. 59.

54. Armstrong and Silberston, 'Size of plant, size of enterprise, and concentration in British manufacturing industry 1935–58', pp. 398, 408, suggest that most of the corresponding increase in the share of output came from plants with 1000 or more employees. Of course not all of these were built by the largest firms; some would have grown from a smaller size and still be owned by relatively small firms. See also Evely and Little, *Concentration in British Industry*, pp. 165–75, 181–3.

55. K. S. Lomax, 'Growth and productivity in the United Kingdom', *Productivity Measurement Review*, vol. 38 (1964). W. E. G. Salter, *Productivity and Technical Change* (Cambridge, 1966). R. C. O. Matthews, C. H. Feinstein, and J. C. Odling-Smee, *British Economic Growth 1856–1973* (Oxford, 1982).

56. Between 1935 and 1951 the increase in output was met by an increase of 18 per cent in the number of plants; but between 1951 and 1958, when output again rose, the number of plants actually declined; see Armstrong and Silberston, 'Size of plant, size of enterprise, and concentration in British manufacturing industry 1935–58', p. 408. Of course, it could be argued that there were just fewer scale economies available in the earlier period. Cf. J. Jewkes, 'The size of the factory', *Economic Journal*, vol. 62 (1952).

57. A number of Monopolies Commission reports ascribe the failure to rationalize in these years to monopolistic practices and the absence of competitive pressure. On firms which were loose confederations of subsidiaries, see pp. 86–7 above.

58. N. Leyland, 'Productivity', in G. D. N. Worswick and P. H. Ady (eds), *The British Economy 1945–1950* (Oxford, 1952), pp. 381–98. L. Rostas, *Comparative Productivity in British and American Industry* (Cambridge, 1948), pp. 60–3. Cf. S. J. Prais, *Productivity and Industrial Structure* (Cambridge, 1981), p. 291.

CHAPTER 10

1. C. A. R. Crosland, *The Future of Socialism* (1956). A. Shonfield, *Modern Capitalism* (1965). S. Holland (ed.), *Beyond Capitalist Planning* (Oxford, 1978). J. Tomlinson, *The Unequal Struggle? British Socialism and the Capitalist Enterprise* (1982).
2. R. Marris, *The Economic Theory of 'Managerial Capitalism'* (1964).
3. D. F. Channon, *The Strategy and Structure of British Enterprise* (1973). K. Cowling *et al.*, *Mergers and Economic Performance* (Cambridge, 1980). K. D. George, *Industrial Organisation: Growth and Structural Change in Britain* (1971). P. E. Hart, M. A. Utton and G. Walshe, *Mergers and Concentration in British Industry* (Cambridge, 1973). D. A. Hay and D. J. Morris, *Industrial Economics: Theory and Evidence* (Oxford, 1979). G. Meeks, *Disappointing Marriage: A Study of the Gains from Merger* (Cambridge, 1977). G. D. Newbould, *Management and Merger Activity* (Liverpool, 1970). S. J. Prais, *The Evolution of Giant Firms in Britain* (Cambridge, 1976). A. Singh and G. Whittington, *Growth Profitability and Valuation: A Study of United Kingdom Quoted Companies* (Cambridge, 1968). A. Singh, *Takeovers: Their Relevance to the Stock Market and the Theory of the Firm* (Cambridge, 1971). M. A. Utton, 'Mergers and the growth of large firms', in *Bulletin of the Oxford University Institute of Statistics*, vol. 34 (1972).
4. See Appendix 2.
5. K. D. George, 'Changes in British industrial concentration 1951–8', *Journal of Industrial Economics*, vol. 15 (1967). M. C. Sawyer, 'Concentration in British manufacturing industry', *Oxford Economic Papers*, vol. 23 (1971). P. E. Hart and R. Clarke, *Concentration in British Industry 1935–1975* (Cambridge, 1980).
6. The level of concentration in industry groups in Table 10.1 cannot be compared with the levels shown in Table 9.1 because the measure of company size used is different (net assets rather than market values) and the sample of firms is also constructed on a different basis.
7. Calculated according to the procedure described on pp. 97–9 above. The 1957 population was hypothetically 'merged' according to the mergers which actually happened in 1957–69 and that level of concentration compared with the actual level in

1969. This may understate or overstate the contribution of merger, depending on what would have happened to the market shares of the merging firms in the absence of merger.

8. Other studies, usually over shorter periods or using less reliable measures, have concluded that mergers were a major force in concentration change, but less important than these results indicate. For surveys see *A Review of Monopolies and Merger Policy: A Consultative Document* (Cmd. 7198, 1978), appendix D; Hay and Morris, *Industrial Economics*, ch. 15. The results for the five-firm concentration ratios are confirmed by the more comprehensive measures of concentration employed in L. Hannah and J. A. Kay, *Concentration in Modern Industry* (1976), ch. 6. They are consistent with the findings of Hart and Clarke, *Concentration in British Industry, 1935–1975*, ch. 5.

9. (Bolton) Committee of Inquiry into Small Firms, *Report* (Cmd. 4811, 1971), pp. 10–11, 59.

10. G. Whittington, 'Changes in the top 100 quoted manufacturing companies in the United Kingdom, 1948 to 1968', *Journal of Industrial Economics*, vol. 21 (1972).

11. A. Marshall, *Principles of Economics*, vol. 1 (9th edn, C. W. Guillebaud (ed.), 1961), p. 316.

12. 1935 data from an unpublished paper by Lewis Johnman, Business History Unit, London; includes UK employees only. Early 1980s figures from individual company reports.

13. R. M. Dean and C. F. Pratten, *The Economies of Large-Scale Production in British Industry* (Cambridge, 1965). C. F. Pratten, *Economies of Scale in Manufacturing Industry* (Cambridge, 1971). A. Silberston, 'Economies of scale in theory and practice', *Economic Journal*, vol. 82, supp. (1972).

14. Monopolies Commission, *Report on the Proposed Merger of Thorn Electrical Industries Limited and Radio Rentals* (1968), p. 4.

15. B. Sendall, *Independent Television in Britain*, vol. 1, *Origin and Foundation, 1946–62* (London, 1982).

16. Channon, *Strategy and Structure*, p. 94. Campaign for Real Ale, *Good Beer Guide* (Leeds, 1974), pp. 1, 96–7.

17. M. J. Peck, 'Science and technology', in R. E. Caves (ed.), *Britain's Economic Prospects* (1968), pp. 448–84.

18. W. H. Beveridge, *Full Employment in a Free Society* (1944), pp. 203–4. H. Dalton, *Memoirs 1931–1945* (1957), p. 447. W. T. Morgan, 'Britain's election: a debate on nationalization and

cartels', *Political Science Quarterly*, vol. 61 (1946). G. C. Allen, *Monopoly and Restrictive Practices* (1968), pp. 61–4.

19. N. Harris, *Competition and the Corporate Society: British Conservatives, the State and Industry 1945–64* (1972), pp. 221–7.

20. Registrar of Restrictive Trading Agreements, *Report* (Cmd. 3188, 1967), p. 8. See also R. B. Stevens and B. S. Yamey, *The Restrictive Practices Court, A Study of the Judicial Process and Economic Policy* (1965).

21. Monopolies Commission, *Parallel Pricing* (Cmd. 5330, 1973). D. Swann, D. P. O'Brien, W. P. J. Maunder and W. S. Howe, *Competition in British Industry: Restrictive Practices Legislation in Theory and Practice* (1974), pp. 144–214.

22. J. H. Dunning, *The Role of American Investment in the British Economy* (PEP Broadsheet no. 507, 1969).

23. Allen, *Monopoly and Restrictive Practices*, p. 98. Swann *et al.*, *Competition in British Industry*, pp. 172–8. *Economist* (11 Feb. 1961), p. 580. Cf. J. B. Heath, 'Restrictive practices and after', *Manchester School*, vol. 29 (1961), pp. 185–7. See also pp. 135–8 above.

24. See, generally: G. Bull and A. Vice, *Bid for Power* (1958); R. W. Moon, *Business Mergers and Takeover Bids* (1959); J. F. Wright, 'The capital market and the finance of industry', in G. D. N. Worswick and P. H. Ady (eds), *The British Economy in the Nineteen-Fifties* (Oxford, 1962), pp. 464–73; J. Slater, *Return to Go: My Autobiography* (1977).

25. L. Hannah, 'Takeover bids in Britain before 1950', *Business History*, vol. 16 (1974), p. 75.

26. Less than 20 per cent. See e.g.: The Panel on Takeovers and Mergers, *Report on the Year ended 31 March 1971* (1971), p. 5; H. B. Rose and G. D. Newbould, 'The 1967 takeover boom', *Moorgate and Wall Street* (Autumn 1967), pp. 9–10. For examples, see Slater, *Return to Go*.

27. R. L. Marris, 'Incomes policy and the rate of profit in industry', *Transactions of the Manchester Statistical Society* (1964), p. 18. Department of Trade and Industry, *Survey of Mergers 1958–68* (1970), p. 19.

28. For an interesting case study of this process within a firm, see D. C. Coleman, *Courtaulds – An Economic and Social History*, vol. 3, *Crisis and Change 1940–1965* (Oxford, 1980), ch. 10. Econometric evidence has cast doubts on the efficiency of this

disciplining force, see e.g. D. Kuehn, *Takeovers and the Theory of the Firm* (1975); A. Singh, *Takeovers* (Cambridge, 1971); but cf. Hannah and Kay, *Concentration in Modern Industry*, pp. 124–5 for a contrary interpretation of their results.

29. Channon, *Strategy and Structure*, pp. 110–11.
30. It was, of course, recognized that there would be unemployment problems following mergers, but these were now felt to be problems of a transitional phase. The social costs faced by unemployed workers were also more broadly shared as a result of the redundancy payments scheme initiated by Labour.
31. Industrial Reorganization Corporation Act 1966, s. 2.1.
32. A. Graham, 'Industrial policy', in W. Beckerman (ed.), *The Labour Government's Economic Record 1964–1970* (1972), pp. 189–91.
33. ibid., p. 197.
34. Channon, *Strategy and Structure*, pp. 119–20.
35. On the effectiveness of consultants see J. Johnston, 'The productivity of management consultants', *Journal of the Royal Statistical Society*, series A, vol. 126 (1963).
36. Channon, *Strategy and Structure*, p. 67.
37. ibid., pp. 24, 45, 60.
38. Department of Trade and Industry, *Survey of Mergers 1958– 1968*, p. 5.
39. Channon, *Strategy and Structure*, p. 78.
40. Prais, *Evolution of Giant Firms in Britain*. G. Newbould and A. Jackson, *The Receding Ideal* (Liverpool, 1972).
41. E.g. J. Jewkes, *Delusions of Dominance* (Institute of Economic Affairs, Hobart Paper no. 76, 1977). Jewkes made some telling debating points, though his general argument about the long-run trends to increasing concentration is quite unsupported by the evidence, cf. Appendix 2.
42. See Appendix 1.
43. See Appendix 2 and the annual Business Statistics Office tabulations prepared from the *Census of Production*. The aggregate figures are for the private sector only, and are distorted by the nationalization of industries such as shipbuilding and aerospace. None the less, the signs of slackening concentration change can also be seen in individual industries, see Hart and Clarke, *Concentration in British Industry 1935–75*.
44. Between the *Censuses of Production* of 1973 and 1978 the share of

employment of firms employing less than 200 employees rose.
45. Rankings by market value of quoted capital. 1948 ranking from unpublished study by the author; 1982 ranking from *The Financial Times European 500* (21 Oct. 1982), p. 1.
46. J. A. Blackburn, 'The vanishing UK cotton industry', *National Westminster Bank Quarterly Review* (Nov. 1982).
47. Meeks, *Disappointing Marriage*. For a survey of this and some other work on the effects of mergers, see *A Review of Monopolies and Mergers Policy* (Cmd. 7198, 1978), pp. 100 ff.
48. Meeks, *Disappointing Marriage*. Newbould, *Management and Merger Activity*, pp. 126–42. *Economist* (18 Sep. 1982), pp. 75–7.
49. S. J. Prais, *Productivity and Industrial Structure* (Cambridge, 1981). G. Bannock, *The Juggernauts* (1971). J. S. Bain, *International Differences in Industrial Structure* (New Haven, 1966). Confederation of British Industry, *Britain in Europe* (1970).
50. Initially much of the IRC's work was taken over by the Department of Trade and Industry's Industrial Development Section, later by the National Enterprise Board. In a few cases government aid was offered to merging firms by both bodies.
51. J. D. Gribbin, 'The operation of the mergers panel since 1965', *Trade and Industry* (17 Jan. 1974), pp. 70–3. See also Board of Trade, *Mergers – A Guide to Board of Trade Practice* (1969).
52. *A Review of Monopolies and Mergers Policy* (Cmd. 7198, 1978), p. 24.
53. E.g. G. and P. Polanyi, 'The Fair Trading Bill and monopoly policy', *Three Banks Review* (June 1973); M. A. Crew and C. K. Rowley, 'Antitrust policy: the application of rules', *Moorgate and Wall Street* (Autumn 1971).
54. See e.g. *The Economist* (5 June 1982), pp. 66–8.
55. Only 2 per cent of 'disappearances' by merger in 1919–39 were sales of subsidiaries between companies (calculated from the data in Appendix 1). For postwar data, see B. Chiplin and M. Wright, 'Divestment and structural change in UK industry', *National Westminster Bank Quarterly Review* (Feb. 1980); S. Lye and A. Silberston, 'Merger activity and sales of subsidiaries between company groups', *Oxford Bulletin of Economics and Statistics*, vol. 43 (1981).
56. Lye and Silberston, 'Merger activity'.
57. M. Jarrett and M. Wright, 'New initiatives in the financing of smaller firms', *National Westminster Bank Quarterly Review*

(Aug. 1982). J. Coyne and M. Wright, 'Buy outs and British industry', *Lloyds Bank Review*, no. 146 (Oct. 1982). *Economist* (23 Oct. 1982), pp. 80–2.

58. This may, for example, have happened in the later 1940s and mid-1950s as the protected sellers' market position of the postwar era gave way to a more competitive market environment in Britain.

CHAPTER 11

1. Sir Alfred Mond, *Industry and Politics* (1927), p. 217.
2. F. W. Hirst, *The Stock Exchange* (1932) p. 222.
3. See e.g. J. Child, *The Business Enterprise in Modern Industrial Society* (1969).
4. *Guardian* (5 Oct. 1973), though cf. S. Domberger, 'Price adjustment and market structure', *Economic Journal*, vol. 89 (1979). J. K. Galbraith, *The New Industrial State (1967)*. K. Middlemas, *Politics in Industrial Society* (1979).
5. For typical, if somewhat inflated, examples, see 'The silent social revolution', *The Times* (25 Mar. 1935); R. Samuel, 'Bastard capitalism', in E. P. Thompson (ed.), *Out of Apathy* (1960), pp.19–55.
6. Cf. L. Hannah and J. A. Kay, *Concentration in Modern Industry: Theory, Measurement and the UK Experience* (1977), ch. 3; M. Utton, *The Political Economy of Big Business* (Oxford, 1982).
7. See p. 129 above.
8. S. J. Prais, *The Evolution of Giant Firms in Britain* (Cambridge, 1976); *A Review of Monopolies and Mergers Policy* (Cmd. 7198, 1978); K. Cowling *et al.*, *Mergers and Economic Performance* (Cambridge, 1980).
9. A. Maddison, *Phases of Capitalist Development* (Oxford, 1982).
10. F. Hahn, inaugural lecture, Cambridge. O. E. Williamson, *Markets and Hierarchies* (New York, 1975). P. J. McNulty, 'Economic theory and the meaning of competition', *Quarterly Journal of Economics*, vol. 82 (1968). R. L. Marris, 'Why economics needs a theory of the firm', *Economic Journal*, vol.82 (1972).
11. F. Hahn, 'Reflections on the invisible hand', *Lloyds Bank Review*, no. 144 (Apr. 1982), p. 19.

12. K. Cowling and D. C. Mueller, 'The social costs of monopoly power', *Economic Journal*, vol. 88 (1978). S. Littlechild, 'Misleading calculations of the social costs of monopoly power', *Economic Journal*, vol. 91 (1981). W. S. Comanor and H. Leibenstein, 'Allocative efficiency, X-efficiency, and the measurement of welfare losses', *Economica*, vol. 36 (1969).

13. E.g. there is no sign that the British pharmaceutical industry has been damaged – and it may have been stimulated – by the decision that firms were sufficiently large without further merger to achieve R & D economies (Monopolies and Mergers Commission, *Report on the Proposed Merger between Boots Pure Drug Co. Ltd. and Glaxo Ltd.* (1971)). See also P. Dasgupta and J. Stiglitz, 'Industrial structure and the nature of innovative activity', *Economic Journal*, vol. 90 (1980).

14. The vigorous case to this effect advanced in Industrial Policy Group, *The Growth of Competition* (1970) is marred by their inaccurate evidence on industrial concentration.

15. *Economist* (22 Oct. 1938), pp. 156–7. N. Kaldor and R. Silverman, *A Statistical Analysis of Advertising Expenditure and the Revenue of the Press* (Cambridge 1948). R. Evely and I. M. D. Little, *Concentration in British Industry* (Cambridge, 1960), p. 140. P. Doyle, 'Economic aspects of advertising: a survey', *Economic Journal*, vol. 78 (1968). T. R. Nevett, *Advertising in Britain: A History* (1982).

16. *Economist* (16 May 1981), p. 51. *A Review of Monopolies and Mergers Policy* (Cmd. 7198, 1978), pp. 65–8. There is, however, a danger that if the buying sector is also oligopolistic, then the countervailing power will not be used in the consumer interest, see e.g. W. J. Reader, *Imperial Chemical Industries: A History*, vol. 1 (1970), pp. 372–3.

17. For the significant effect of protectionism on profits see T. Hitiris, 'Effective protection and economic performance in UK manufacturing industry', *Economic Journal*, vol. 88 (1978).

18. R. C. O. Matthews, C. H. Feinstein and J. C. Odling-Smee, *British Economic Growth 1856–1973* (Oxford, 1982), pp. 185–91. Of course, other factors than the degree of competition may have affected the average rate of profit.

19. D. C. Coleman, *Courtaulds, An Economic and Social History*, vol. 3 (Oxford, 1980), part 1. Monopolies Commission, *Report on the Asbestos and Asbestos Cement Industries* (1972). G. C. Allen, 'An

aspect of industrial reorganization', *Economic Journal*, vol. 55 (1945).

20. E. M. H. Lloyd, *Experiments in State Control* (Oxford, 1924), p. 361.

21. A. D. Chandler, *The Visible Hand: The Managerial Revolution in American Business* (Cambridge, Mass., 1977), pp. 320–39. For a dissenting view cf. R. B. Du Boff and E. S. Herman, 'Alfred Chandler's new business history: a review', *Politics and Society*, vol. 10 (1980). Strictly, given incomplete markets and imperfect competition, there is no reason to suppose that the survivors will converge towards a socially optimal pattern.

22. Or, where long-lived, are often so because of consistent excellence rather than unreasonable restrictions on entry. Despite all attempts to break their market power by new entrants such as supermarkets' own brands, Kelloggs Cornflakes have retained a large market share, not fundamentally because of unreasonable advertising expenses or restraint of trade but at least partly because they really are nicest in the view of the consumers.

23. M. Gort and T. F. Hogarty, 'New evidence on mergers', *Journal of Law and Economics*, vol. 13 (1970). Cf. pp. 153–5 above.

24. See p. 74 above.

25. See pp. 125–8 above.

26. See pp. 120–1 above.

27. See pp. 152–3 above.

28. Matthews, Feinstein and Odling-Smee, *British Economic Growth 1856–1973*.

29. ibid., pp. 359–61.

APPENDIX 1

1. H. W. Macrosty, *The Trust Movement in British Industry* (1907).

2. J. M. Rees, *Trusts in British Industry 1914–1921* (1921).

3. P. Fitzgerald, *Industrial Combination in England* (1927). A. F. Lucas, *Industrial Reconstruction and the Control of Competition* (1937).

4. L. Hannah, 'Mergers in British manufacturing industry, 1880–1918', *Oxford Economic Papers*, vol. 26 (1974). L. Hannah, 'The Political Economy of Mergers in Manufacturing Industry in

Britain between the Wars' (unpublished D.Phil thesis, Oxford, 1972).

5. 'Acquisitions and amalgamations of quoted companies 1954–1961', *Economic Trends* (Apr. 1963). 'Acquisitions and mergers of companies', in *Trade and Industry* (published quarterly). Business Statistics Office, *Business Monitor MQ7* (published quarterly). Department of Trade and Industry, *A Survey of Mergers 1958–1968* (1970). I am indebted to Mr J. L. Walker of the Department of Trade and Industry (Economics and Statistics Division) for supplementary advice on the use of the government statistics.

6. (Bolton) Committee of Inquiry into Small Firms, *Report* (Cmd. 4811, 1971), p. 10.

7. Moodies' share price index was used to correct the values for 1919–63 to 1961 share prices. For the period 1880–1918, the London and Cambridge Economic Service share price index, spliced to Moodies at 1919, was used, and for the period 1963–81 the Financial Times Actuaries 500 Industrial Ordinary Share Index, spliced to Moodies at 1963, was used.

8. Gross Domestic Fixed Capital Formation in UK Manufacturing and Building at current prices for 1920–38 and 1949–65, from C. H. Feinstein, *National Income Expenditure and Output of the United Kingdom 1855–1965* (Cambridge, 1972), p. T93; and, for more recent years, from Central Statistical Office, *National Income and Expenditure* (annually).

9. E. T. Penrose, *The Theory of the Growth of the Firm* (Oxford, 1959), pp. 241–2.

10. Hannah 'Political economy of mergers', p. 133.

11. ibid., pp. 136–7, for a justification.

12. National Institute of Economic and Social Research, *Company Income and Finance 1949–53* (1956), p. 23.

13. In comparing merger activity in different decades regard should be paid to the strong *caveats* in the introduction to this appendix.

APPENDIX 2

1. E.g. L. Hannah and J. A. Kay, *Concentration in Modern Industry: Theory Measurement and the UK Experience* (1977); B. Curry and K. D. George, 'Industrial concentration: a survey', *Journal of Industrial Economics*, vol. 31 (1983).

2. Annual data are now published by the Business Statistics Office in *Business Monitor: Report of the Census of Production: Summary Tables*. 1978 was the last date for which this publication was available at the time of going to press.

3. L. Hannah, *The Rise of the Corporate Economy* (1st edn 1976), appendix 2; S. J. Prais, *The Evolution of Giant Firms in Britain: A Study of the Growth of Concentration in Manufacturing Industry in Britain 1909–70* (Cambridge, 1976).

4. C. Shaw, '100 large manufacturing employers of 1907', *Business History*, vol. 25 (1983); L. Johnman, '100 large manufacturing employers of 1935' (unpublished paper, Business History Unit, London School of Economics, 1983). Adjustments were made to allow for omitted firms, as well as to ensure compatibility with later statistics. These estimates are provisional and may be modified by subsequent work.

5. Prais, *Evolution of Giant Firms in Britain*, p. 4 and appendix A, using these alternative methods, derives figures of 24 per cent for 1935 (cf. 23 per cent in Table A.2) and 16 per cent for 1909 (cf. 15 per cent for 1907 in Table A.2). The major explanation of the difference is an adjustment Prais makes to bring the coverage in line with the coverage of the 1958 figure. There may, however, be other changes in coverage of which no account is taken.

6. The method for the first four years is as described in the first edition of this book. For 1948, the 1930–48 changes in the share of the largest 100 firms in market capitalization (Hannah and Kay, *Concentration in Modern Industry*, p. 73) were applied to the 1930 estimates with a 1 percentage point downwards correction for change of coverage. An alternative method of backward extrapolation of profit shares produces a figure of 21 per cent for 1948 (Prais, *Evolution of Giant Firms*, pp. 4, 177–8).

7. Prais, *Evolution of Giant Firms*, pp. 177–8.

8. Currently all the early *Census of Production* returns are still closed to scholars in order to preserve confidentiality. It is, of course, idiotic to suggest that there can be reasonable grounds for maintaining this policy, but the Lord Chancellor had not, at the time of writing, acted on the sensible recommendations of the Wilson Committee (*Modern Public Records: Selection and Access*, Cmd. 8204, 1981).

9. Prais, *Evolution of Giant Firms*, p. 4.

10. The *Economist* (17 July 1982), p. 20, reported that loss-making British Steel had cut its labour force from 226,000 to 103,000 in ten years and was intending to cut it further to 92,400 by March 1983. The *Economist* (24 July 1982), p. 21, suggested that British Shipbuilders had cut its workforce from 86,700 in 1978 to 66,700.

11. P. E. Hart and S. J. Prais, 'The analysis of business concentration: a statistical approach', *Journal of the Royal Statistical Society*, series A, vol. 119 (1956), p. 154. P. E. Hart, 'Concentration in the United Kingdom' in H. Arndt (ed.), *Die Konzentration in der Wirtschaft* (Berlin, 1971), appendix. They also estimated the sizes of firms in 1885 and 1896, but, since the quoted sector was of only minor significance in that period, the results are of little interest for the measurement of overall concentration.

12. Hannah and Kay, *Concentration in Modern Industry*.

13. ibid., for a fuller exposition of the measure.

14. The measure has affinities to other commonly used measures of concentration: $\alpha = 2$ is the familiar Herfindahl index and $\alpha = 1$ (or more strictly, $\alpha \rightarrow 1$) is equivalent to the entropy index of concentration. For $\alpha = 0$, firms acquire importance simply by existing: the index then equals the number of firms.

15. The coverage of the quoted population probably also increases because the constant samples of quoted companies are growing faster than the rest of the manufacturing industry, but it is not possible to correct for this possible source of error, which would tend to understate increases in concentration and exaggerate declines in concentration.

16. Similar trends were originally reported by Hart and Prais ('The analysis of business concentration') so that, in this case at least, the failings of the variance of logarithms as a measure of concentration were not overwhelming.

17. Among the studies of later periods emulating Hart and Prais in using the variance of the logarithms of firms' sizes as a measure of concentration are: M. A. Utton, 'The effects of mergers on concentration: UK manufacturing industry, 1954–1965', *Journal of Industrial Economics*, vol. 20 (1971); J. M. Samuels and A. D. Chesher, 'Growth survival and size of companies 1960–9', in K. Cowling (ed.), *Market Structure and Corporate Behaviour* (1972).

18. Hannah and Kay, *Concentration in Modern Industry*, for the numbers–equivalent measures. The results of this study are reported in five-firm concentration ratio form in the tables in Chapters 7, 9, and 10 above.

APPENDIX 3

1. E.g. National Institute of Economic and Social Research, *Company Income and Finance 1949–53* (privately printed, 1956); *The Times 500* and *The Times 1000* (annually since 1965); G. Whittington, 'Changes in the top 100 quoted companies in the United Kingdom, 1948 to 1968', *Journal of Industrial Economics*, vol. 2 (1972).
2. C. Shaw, 'The large manufacturing employers of 1907', *Business History*, vol. 25 (1983). L. Johnman, '100 large manufacturing employers of 1935' (Business History Unit, LSE, forthcoming).
3. P. L. Payne, 'The emergence of the large-scale company in Great Britain 1870–1914', *Economic History Review*, vol. 20 (1967). S. Yonekawa, 'The strategy and structure of cotton and steel enterprises in Britain, 1900–39', in K. Nakagawa (ed.), *Strategy and Structure of Big Business: Proceedings of the First Fuji Conference* (Tokyo, n.d.).
4. Copies available from the Business History Unit, LSE.
5. See pp. 102–3 above.
6. E.g. Shaw, 'Large manufacturing employers'; L. Hannah and J. A. Kay, *Concentration in Modern Industry* (1977), pp. 93–6.
7. Shaw, 'Large manufacturing employers'.
8. Both lists are drawn from the population of firms described in Hannah and Kay, *Concentration in Modern Industry*. The lists include all large manufacturing companies quoted on the London and provincial stock exchanges and also some private unquoted companies, but not non-corporate manufacturing enterprises or those which are subsidiaries of non-manufacturing entities, e.g. nationalized industries such as the Royal Dockyards, railway workshops, or the Co-operative Wholesale Society – all of which included enterprises which were among the largest manufacturing employers.
9. Five newcomers would then enter the table, making it more comparable with Table A.4: Bolckow Vaughan (£3.7 million),

Swan Hunter, J. Walker & Sons, Ryland, and Wallpaper Manufacturers (each £3.6 million).

10. It is drawn from the population of firms described in Hannah and Kay, *Concentration in Modern Industry*. The enhanced coverage of the sample in 1948 is unlikely to have made a significant difference to the coverage of the top fifty firms.

Index

{ଚ୍ଚଃ}